Database Systems: Design, Implementation and Management

Database Systems: Design, Implementation and Management

Mitchell Penn

WILLFORD PRESS
www.willfordpress.com

Published by Willford Press,
118-35 Queens Blvd., Suite 400,
Forest Hills, NY 11375, USA

ISBN: 978-1-68285-725-0

Cataloging-in-Publication Data

Database systems : design, implementation and management / Mitchell Penn.
p. cm.
Includes bibliographical references and index.
ISBN 978-1-68285-725-0
1. Databases. 2. Database design. 3. Database management. I. Penn, Mitchell.
QA76.9.D32 D38 2019
005.745--dc23

For information on all Willford Press publications
visit our website at www.willfordpress.com

Contents

Preface VII

Chapter 1   **Introduction to Database and its Types** 1

      i.   Animation Database 5

      ii.   Back-end Database 8

      iii. Centralized Database 11

      iv. Cloud Database 13

      v.   Distributed Database 19

      vi. Key-value Database 21

      vii. Navigational Database 26

      viii. Probabilistic Database 28

      ix. Very Large Database 34

      x.   Relational Database 44

      xi. Deductive Database 47

Chapter 2   **Database Models** 57

      i.   Hierarchical Database Model 63

      ii.   Network Model 73

      iii. Entity–attribute–value Model 78

      iv. Associative Model 94

Chapter 3   **Fundamental Concepts of Database Designing** 98

      i.   ACID 98

      ii.   Armstrong's Axioms 100

      iii. Create, Read, Update and Delete 104

      iv. Relation 108

      v.   Database Keys 118

Chapter 4   **Database Designing Languages and Optimization** 124

      i.   Query Language 124

      ii.   Data Control Language 126

      iii. Data Definition Language 128

      iv. Data Manipulation Language 131

v.   Database Administration and Automation 134

vi.   Database Engine 140

vii.   Database Trigger... 144

viii.   Database Tuning... 152

ix.   Database Normalization.. 156

Chapter 5   **Database Management Systems** **165**

i.   Object Oriented Database Management System... 165

ii.   Column Store Database Management System 178

iii.   Federated Database System 183

iv.   In-memory Database... 190

v.   Object-relational Database Management System 194

vi.   Active Database Management System 201

Permissions

Index

Preface

An organized collection of data that is stored and accessed electronically is known as a database. It is designed in a way that it supports easy information retrieval. Database management systems (DBMS) interact with users and applications or with the database itself for the capture and analysis of data. A database is stored in a DBMS-specific format. Different DBMSs share data by using standards like Open Database Connectivity (ODBC) and Structured Query Language (SQL). Databases are classified into in-memory, active, cloud, deductive and distributed databases, among many others. The logical structure of a database and the organization, arrangement and manipulation of data is determined by the database model. Some common models are hierarchical database model, object model, network model, relational model, etc. This book provides comprehensive insights into the field of database systems. Most of the topics introduced in this book cover the diverse aspects of design, implementation and management of database systems. It will serve as a valuable source of reference for those interested in this field.

Given below is the chapter wise description of the book:

Chapter 1- A database is a collection of data that is stored and accessed electronically. This chapter has been carefully written to provide an easy understanding of databases and their different types. It includes vital topics such as animation database, centralized database, cloud database, key-value database, relational database, probabilistic database, etc.

Chapter 2- A database model determines the logical structure of a database and facilitates the easy storage, organization and manipulation of the data. The aim of this chapter is to explore the different kinds of database models, such as hierarchical database model, network model, associative model and entity-attribute-value model among others.

Chapter 3- A database design facilitates the organization of data according to a database model. This chapter aims to provide a comprehensive understanding of the fundamental principles of database designing and presents a detailed discussion on topics such as Atomicity, Consistency, Isolation, Durability (ACID), Armstrong's axioms, database keys, etc.

Chapter 4- A holistic study of database designing requires an understanding of database designing languages and optimization. This chapter discusses in detail the different concepts of query language, data control language, data definition language, data manipulation language, database engine, database tuning and database trigger, among others for an extensive understanding of the subject.

Chapter 5- A database management system is the software that enables the interaction with end users, applications and with the database for capturing and analyzing the data. The topics elaborated in this chapter, such as object oriented database management system, column store database management system, federated database system, in-memory database, etc. will help in providing a better perspective about database management systems.

Indeed, my job was extremely crucial and challenging as I had to ensure that every chapter is informative and structured in a student-friendly manner. I am thankful for the support provided by my family and colleagues during the completion of this book.

Mitchell Penn

Introduction to Database and its Types

A database is a collection of data that is stored and accessed electronically. This chapter has been carefully written to provide an easy understanding of databases and their different types. It includes vital topics such as animation database, centralized database, cloud database, key-value database, relational database, probabilistic database, etc.

Basic Electronic Information Storage Unit

A database is a collection of information organized to provide efficient retrieval. The collected information could be in any number of formats (electronic, printed, graphic, audio, statistical, combinations). There are physical (paper/print) and electronic databases.

A database could be as simple as an alphabetical arrangement of names in an address book or as complex as a database that provides information in a combination of formats.

Examples:

- Phone book
- Address book
- Census Bureau data

Database, also called electronic database, is any collection of data, or information that is specially organized for rapid search and retrieval by a computer. Databases are structured to facilitate the storage, retrieval, modification, and deletion of data in conjunction with various data-processing operations.

A database is stored as a file or a set of files on magnetic disk or tape, optical disk, or some other secondary storage device. The information in these files may be broken down into records, each of which consists of one or more fields. Fields are the basic units of data storage, and each field typically contains information pertaining to one aspect or attribute of the entity described by the database. Records are also organized into tables that include information about relationships between its various fields. Although *database* is applied loosely to any collection of information in computer files, a database in the strict sense provides cross-referencing capabilities. Using keywords and various sorting commands, users can rapidly search, rearrange, group, and select the fields in many records to retrieve or create reports on particular aggregates of data.

Database records and files must be organized to allow retrieval of the information. Queries are the main way users retrieve database information. The power of a DBMS comes from its ability to define new relationships from the basic ones given by the tables and to use them to get responses to queries. Typically, the user provides a string of characters, and the computer searches the database for a corresponding sequence and provides the source materials in which those characters appear; a user can request, for example, all records in which the contents of the field for a person's last name is the word *Smith*.

The many users of a large database must be able to manipulate the information within it quickly at any given time. Moreover, large business and other organizations tend to build up many independent files containing related and even overlapping data, and their data-processing activities often require the linking of data from several files. Several different types of DBMS have been developed to support these requirements.

Common Database Types

Relational Database

A relational database, invented by E.F. Codd at IBM in 1970, is a tabular database in which data is defined so that it can be reorganized and accessed in a number of different ways.

Relational databases are made up of a set of tables with data that fits into a predefined category. Each table has at least one data category in a column, and each row has a certain data instance for the categories which are defined in the columns.

The Structured Query Language (SQL) is the standard user and application program interface for a relational database. Relational databases are easy to extend, and a new data category can be added after the original database creation without requiring that you modify all the existing applications.

Distributed Database

A distributed database is a database in which portions of the database are stored in multiple physical locations, and in which processing is dispersed or replicated among different points in a network.

Distributed databases can be homogeneous or heterogeneous. All the physical locations in a homogeneous distributed database system have the same underlying hardware and run the same operating systems and database applications. The hardware, operating systems or database applications in a heterogeneous distributed database may be different at each of the locations.

Cloud Database

A cloud database is a database that has been optimized or built for a virtualized environment, either in a hybrid cloud, public cloud or private cloud. Cloud databases provide benefits such as the ability to pay for storage capacity and bandwidth on a per-use basis, and they provide scalability on demand, along with high availability.

A cloud database also gives enterprises the opportunity to support business applications in a software-as-a-service deployment.

No-SQL Database

No-SQL databases are useful for large sets of distributed data.

No-SQL databases are effective for big data performance issues that relational databases aren't built to solve. They are most effective when an organization must analyze large chunks of unstructured data or data that's stored across multiple virtual servers in the cloud.

Object-oriented Database

Items created using object-oriented programming languages are often stored in relational databases, but object-oriented databases are well-suited for those items.

An object-oriented database is organized around objects rather than actions, and data rather than logic. For example, a multimedia record in a relational database can be a definable data object, as opposed to an alphanumeric value.

Graph Database

A graph-oriented database, or graph database, is a type of No-SQL database that uses graph theory to store, map and query relationships. Graph databases are basically collections of nodes and edges, where each node represents an entity, and each edge represents a connection between nodes.

Graph databases are growing in popularity for analyzing interconnections. For example, companies might use a graph database to mine data about customers from social media.

Early systems were arranged sequentially (i.e., alphabetically, numerically, or chronologically); the development of direct-access storage devices made possible random access to data via indexes. In flat databases, records are organized according to a simple list of entities; many simple databases for personal computers are flat in structure. The records in hierarchical databases are organized in a treelike structure, with each level of records branching off into a set of smaller categories. Unlike hierarchical databases, which provide single links between sets of records at different levels, network databases create multiple linkages between sets by placing links, or pointers, to one set of records in another; the speed and versatility of network databases have led to their wide use within businesses and in e-commerce. Relational databases are used where associations between files or records cannot be expressed by links; a simple flat list becomes one row of a table, or "relation," and multiple relations can be mathematically associated to yield desired information. Various iterations of SQL (Structured Query Language) are widely employed in DBMS for relational databases. Object-oriented databases store and manipulate more complex data structures, called "objects," which are organized into hierarchical classes that may inherit properties from classes higher in the chain; this database structure is the most flexible and adaptable.

The information in many databases consists of natural-language texts of documents; number-oriented databases primarily contain information such as statistics, tables, financial data, and raw scientific and technical data. Small databases can be maintained on personal-computer systems and may be used by individuals at home. These and larger databases have become increasingly important in business life, in part because they are now commonly designed to be integrated with other office software, including spread sheet programs.

Typical commercial database applications include airline reservations, production management functions, medical records in hospitals, and legal records of insurance companies. The largest databases are usually maintained by governmental agencies, business organizations, and universities. These databases may contain texts of such materials as abstracts, reports, legal statutes, wire services, newspapers and journals, encyclopedias, and catalogs of various kinds. Reference databases contain bibliographies or indexes that serve as guides to the location of information in books, periodicals, and other published literature. Thousands of these publicly accessible databases now exist, covering topics ranging from law, medicine, and engineering to news and current events, games, classified advertisements, and instructional courses.

Increasingly, formerly separate databases are being combined electronically into larger collections known as data warehouses. Businesses and government agencies then employ "data mining" software to analyze multiple aspects of the data for various patterns. For example, a government agency might flag for human investigation a company or individual that purchased a suspicious quantity of certain equipment or materials, even though the purchases were spread around the country or through various subsidiaries.

Animation Database

Animation databases are repositories of animation models and motion sequences.

The techniques for animation databases include partial fuzzy query resolution, animation model/motion comparison, animation sequence segmentation, prediction/resolution of collisions, and handling multiple animation formats. An animation authoring toolkit is being developed with the help of these techniques. The functionality of this toolkit is to aid in generating new animation sequences by reusing existing models and motion sequences.

Animation Database File (ADB)

An Animation Database file is an XML file that contains a set of Fragments and Mannequin Transitions.

You can have as many ADB files as you want in the game to split up your collection of fragments in manageable sets.

ADB files have to refer to the Tag Definition File (xxxTags.xml) and Fragment ID Definition File (xxxActions.xml) used by this ADB. To see Mannequin Files. ADB files can include other ADB files, and those are then called *sub-ADBs*. Sub-ADBs can be used to organize your fragment collections into different files that are used by different users.

Internally the system uses indices to refer to Tags and Fragment IDs. Those indices are local to each Tag or Fragment ID definition file. It is therefore not safe for the client code to assume that the same Fragment ID used in different contexts will have the same value everywhere. As an example, if two different ADBs indirectly refer to the same Fragment ID definition file (through the *Import* element), Fragment IDs defined in this shared file are likely to end up having different values in each context.

Additionally, it is important that all ADBs files used by a controller definition refer to the *same* Fragment ID and Tag definition files. This also means that if you reuse an

ADB with two different controller definitions, you need to use the same Fragment ID and Tag definition files for both.

Creating ADB Files

You can create a new ADB file by hand in the Animations/Mannequin/folder.

You can also create new ADB files automatically by clicking the '+' button while editing context data in the Mannequin Context Editor. The editor will also prompt you to create an ADB file automatically when you refer to a non-existing one in a Preview Setup File (xxxPreview.xml).

To create new sub-ADBs or edit which rules to use to move fragments into sub-ADBs you use the Mannequin Animation DB Editor.

Editing ADB Files

You edit the fragments within ADB files by adding/removing Fragments in the Mannequin Fragment Browser. Which ADB file the fragment is in that you are editing is shown at the top of the fragment browser. This is controlled by which ADB is associated with the context you are currently editing (the drop down box at the top of the fragment browser), as well as the sub-ADB rules you set up in the Mannequin Animation DB Editor for that ADB.

File Format

Here is a simple example of an ADB file:

```
<AnimDB FragDef="Animations/Mannequin/ADB/PlayerActions.xml" TagDef="-
Animations/Mannequin/ADB/PlayerTags.xml">

 <SubADBs>

 <SubADB Tags="rifle" File="Animations/Mannequin/ADB/rifleAnims1P.adb"/>

  <SubADB Tags="pistol" File="Animations/Mannequin/ADB/pistolAnims1P.
adb"/>

   <SubADB File="Animations/Mannequin/ADB/Scripting/Level1/database.
adb">

    <FragmentID Name="script_level1"/>

  </SubADB>

   <SubADB File="Animations/Mannequin/ADB/Scripting/Level2/database.
adb">
```

```
        <FragmentID Name="script_level2"/>
   </SubADB> </SubADBs>
<FragmentList>
 <idlePose>
  <Fragment Tags="nw">
   <AnimLayer>
    <Blend ExitTime="0" StartTime="0" Duration="0"/>
    <Animation name="stand_tac_idlePose_rifle_3p_01" flags="Loop"/>
   </AnimLayer>
   <ProcLayer>
    <Blend ExitTime="0" StartTime="0" Duration="0.41000003"/>
    <Procedural type="PositionAdjust">
     <ProceduralParams />
    </Procedural>
   </ProcLayer>
  </Fragment>
 </idlePose>
</FragmentList>
<FragmentBlendList>
 <Blend from="" to="idlePose">
  <Variant from="" to="">
   <Fragment selectTime="0" enterTime="0">
    <AnimLayer>
     <Blend ExitTime="0" StartTime="0" Duration="0"/>
    </AnimLayer>
   </Fragment>
```

```
        </Variant>

      </Blend>

    </FragmentBlendList>

  </AnimDB>
```

The root element *AnimDB* has to refer to the Fragment ID Definition File (xxxActions. xml) and Tag Definition File (xxxTags.xml) used in this ADB file.

The *SubADBs* section defines the rules used to sort fragments into sub-ADBs. The example shows how fragments with tags «rifle» or «pistol» are stored in separate sub-ADBs. It also shows how fragments with fragment IDs "script_level1" and "script_level2" go in separate sub-ADBs.

The *Fragment List* contains the fragments. Individual fragments are *Fragment* elements inside the element with the name of the Fragment ID. The example shows just one fragment, for the Fragment ID "idle pose". Within the Fragment element is a list of *AnimLayer* and *ProcLayer* elements containing the animation clips and procedural clips respectively. Fragments are sorted according to the priorities of their tags when saving ADB files through the editor.

The *Fragment Blend List* contains the transitions. Each *Fragment* element represents one single transition in the editor. Each *Variant* element maps to the folders in the editor that group similar transitions together with different select times. Each *Blend* element represents the group of transitions between two Fragment IDs (or the fallback <Any>).

Back-end Database

To understand the back end, or the "server side," you also have to know the front end and how the two interact. The front end, also called "client-side" programming, is what happens in the browser—everything the end users see and interact with. The back end, on the other hand, happens on the server (on site, or in the cloud) and databases. It's the machinery that works behind the scenes—everything the end user doesn't see or directly interact with, but that powers what's happening.

It's important to note that this convenient way of divvying up development has changed significantly over the past 10 to 15 years with the explosive growth of JavaScript, which wasn't as ubiquitous on the front end as it is now, or as common on the back end, thanks to Node.js. There's more overlap between the two, especially when it comes to a JavaScript developer's role on a fully JavaScript-powered stack.

Here's a visual to give you an idea of how front-end and back-end development flow.

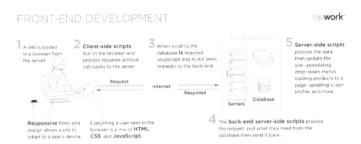

You can see how the server-side (in the green box) manages all those requests that come from users' clicks. Front-end scripts volley those requests over to the server side to be processed, returning the appropriate data to the front end. This often happens in a constant loop of requests and responses to the server.

Now, let's take a look at how back-end architecture works—the software and machinery that take over in step four in the above graphic

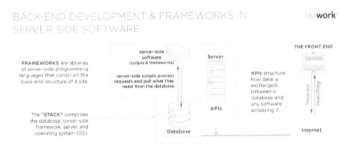

The "traditional" back end is a mix of the server, databases, APIs, and operating systems that power an app's front end.

The back end of applications can look very different from application to application, whether it's the use of cloud-based servers and data warehouses, containerization with a service like Docker, Backend-as-a-Service (BaaS) providers, or APIs to replace more complex processing.

Back-end development can be much more varied than front-end development, which is largely driven by JavaScript, HTML, CSS, and various front-end frameworks using these languages.

To simplify things, we'll break the server side down into four main components of a "software stack": the server, the database, the operating system, and the software.

Databases: The Brains

Databases, in the context of a website, are the brains that make websites dynamic. Any time you request something from a website—whether you're searching for a product in on online store or searching for hotel locations within a specific state—the database is responsible for accepting that query, fetching the data, and returning it to the website.

Databases can also accept new and edited data when users of a website or application interact with them. The client can change information in a database from the browser, whether a user is posting articles to a CMS, uploading photos to a social media profile, or updating their customer information.

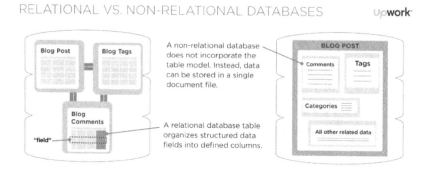

Backend Testing

Backend testing is nothing but server side or Database Testing. The data entered in the front end will be stored in the back-end database. The database may be SQL Server, MySQL, Oracle, DB2, etc. The data will be organized in the tables as record, and it is used to support the content of the page. Database testing mainly includes validating:

- Schema

- Database tables

- Columns

- Keys and Indexes

- Stored procedures

- Triggers

- Database server validations

- Validating data duplication

In back end testing you are not required to use the GUI; you can directly pass the request through some browser with the parameters required for the function and get a response in some default format. e.g. xml or JSON. You also need to connect to database directly and verify the data using SQL queries. Through log files, debugging can be done.

Database or backend testing is important because if it is not done it has some serious complications like deadlock, data corruption, data loss, etc. There are various phases in back-end testing. The first step is to acquire design specification for an SQL server.

The next step is to test specification design, followed by implementing the tests in this design with SQL code.

Types of Database Testing

The types of database testing includes:

- Structural Testing
- Functional Testing
- Non-Functional Testing

Tools used for Database Testing

Some of the useful tools used for database testing includes:

- Data Factory
- Data Generator
- Test Data Generator
- AETG
- TurboData

Advantages for Back End Testing

- Back end testing is not like a Black Box Testing.
- Full control of Test coverage and depth.
- In early development stage, many bugs can be effectively found.

In order to do the back end testing, tester is expected to have strong background in database server and knowledge of structured query language.

Centralized Database

A centralized database consists of a single data server into which all data are stored and from which all data are retrieved. All the data reside at a single location and all applications must retrieve all data from that location.

The centralized approach consists of a central server into which all forecast data are stored. At some predefined time, software on this central server requests data from each of the local data servers scattered throughout the country. These data are received, processed and stored, possibly at lower spatial and temporal resolution than the data from which it was derived.

Application Software

Central data server: Depicts the Centralized Database system

Typical Examples:

- DBMS itself was a centralized DBMS where all the DBMS functionality, application program execution and user interface processing carried out in one machine.

- User management system.

- Central Documents management system.

Advantages

- Decreased Risk: With Centralized data management, all edits and manipulation to core data are housed and stored centrally. This model allows for staunch controls, detailed audit trails, and enables business users to access consistent data.

- Data Consistency: When data feeds are managed in a central repository, an organization can achieve consistent data management and distribution throughout its global offices and internal systems.

- Data Quality: A data-centric approach enables the establishment of a data standard across an enterprise, allowing organizations to make better business assessments.

- Operational Efficiency: When one business unit controls an organization data centrally, the resources previously devoted to data management can be redirected back to core business needs.

- Single Point of Entry: By introducing single point of entry for data, this allows changes from data vendors to be implemented once, rather than in multiple instances.

- Cost Saving: With data management centralized, costs attributed to vendor relationships are better controlled, minimizing any redundancy in market data contracts and their associated costs.

Disadvantages

- Response Time: The size of a centralized database could cause data retrieval delays.

- Equipment Cost: Depend on architecture, probably expensive if main frames are used.

- Incremental Growth: Updating a centralized system is likely to be more difficult and more costly particularly if is it build on main frames. Large systems are typically more problematic to upgrade.

- Single Point of Failure: Entire data is sorted at a single point (central server), if the data failed or corrupted then all the data will be lose.

Factors for Adoption of Centralized Approach

- Data can be organized in single point, by introducing single point of entry for data Database Administrator can implement the data only once instead of in multiple sites.

- Data consistency can achieve by introducing data-centric approach.

- Centralized database approach is suitable for establishment of data standards across an enterprise.

- For batter security purpose Centralized database approach is suitable.

- For quick efficient searching Centralized approach is good one.

- For controlled access to the database repository.

Cloud Database

A cloud database is a collection of content, either structured or unstructured, that resides on a private, public or hybrid cloud computing infrastructure platform.

Two cloud database environment models exist: traditional and database as a service (DBaaS).

In a traditional cloud model, a database runs on an IT department's infrastructure via a virtual machine. Tasks of database oversight and management fall upon IT staffers of the organization.

Database as a Service

By comparison, the DBaaS model is a fee-based subscription service in which the database runs on the service provider's physical infrastructure. Different service levels are usually available. In a classic DBaaS arrangement, the provider maintains the physical infrastructure and database, leaving the customer to manage the database's contents and operation.

Alternatively, a customer can set up a managed hosting arrangement, in which the provider handles database maintenance and management. This latter option may be especially attractive to small businesses that have database needs, but lack the adequate IT expertise.

Cloud Database Benefits

Compared with operating a traditional database on an on-site physical server and storage architecture, a cloud database offers the following distinct advantages:

- Elimination of physical infrastructure: In a cloud database environment, the cloud computing provider of servers, storage and other infrastructure is responsible for maintenance and availability. The organization that owns and operates the database is only responsible for supporting and maintaining the database software and its contents. In a DBaaS environment, the service provider is responsible for maintaining and operating the database software, leaving the DBaaS users responsible only for their own data.

- Cost savings: Through the elimination of a physical infrastructure owned and operated by an IT department, significant savings can be achieved from reduced capital expenditures, less staff, decreased electrical and HVAC operating costs, and a smaller amount of needed physical space.

Dbaas Benefits

In addition to the benefits of employing a cloud database environment model, contracting with a DBaaS provider offers additional benefits:

- Instantaneous scalability: Should added database capacity be necessitated by seasonal business peaks or unexpected spikes in demand, a DBaaS provider can quickly offer additional fee-based capacity, throughput and access bandwidth via its own infrastructure. A database operating in a traditional, on-site infrastructure would likely need to wait weeks or months for the procurement and installation of additional server, storage or communications resources.

- Performance guarantees: Through a service level agreement (SLA), a DBaaS provider may be obligated to provide guarantees that typically quantify minimum uptime availability and transaction response times. An SLA specifies monetary and legal remedies if these performance thresholds are not met.

- Specialized expertise: In a corporate IT environment, except for the largest multinational enterprises, finding world-class database experts may be difficult, and keeping them on staff may be cost prohibitive. In a DBaaS environment, the provider may serve thousands of customers; thus, finding, affording and keeping world-class talent is less of a challenge.

- Latest technology: To remain competitive, DBaaS providers work hard to ensure that all database software, server operating systems and other aspects of the overall infrastructure are kept up to date with security and feature updates regularly issued by software vendors.

- Failover support: For a provider of database services to meet performance and availability guarantees, it is incumbent on that provider to ensure uninterrupted operation should the primary data center fail for any reason. Failover support typically encompasses the operation of multiple mirror image server and data storage facilities. Handled properly, failover to a backup data center should be imperceptible to any customer of that service.

- Declining pricing: With advances in technology and an intensely competitive marketplace among major service providers, pricing for a wide range of cloud-computing services undergoes continual recalibration. Declining prices are a major impetus for migrating on-site databases and other IT infrastructure to the cloud.

Cloud Database Architecture

Cloud databases, like their traditional ancestors, can be divided into two broad categories:

1. Relational.

2. Non-relational.

A relational database, typically written in structured query language (SQL), is composed of a set of interrelated tables that are organized into rows and columns. The relationship among tables and columns (fields) is specified in a schema. SQL databases, by design, rely on data that is highly consistent in its format, such as banking transactions or a telephone directory. Popular choices include MySQL, Oracle, IBM DB2 and Microsoft SQL Server.

Non-relational databases, sometimes called No-SQL, do not employ a table model. Instead, they store content, regardless of its structure, as a single document. This technology is well-suited for unstructured data, such as social media content, photos and videos.

Migrating Legacy Databases to the Cloud

An on-premises database can migrate to a cloud implementation. Numerous reasons exist for doing this, including the following:

- Allows IT to retire on-premises physical server and storage infrastructure;

- Fills the talent gap when IT lacks adequate in-house database expertise;

- Improves processing efficiency, especially when applications and analytics that access the data also reside in the cloud;

- Achieves cost savings through several means, including:

  o Reduction of in-house IT staff;

  o Continually declining cloud service pricing;

  o Paying for only the resources actually consumed, known as pay-as-you-go pricing.

Relocating a database to the cloud can be an effective way to further enable business application performance as part of a wider software-as-a-service deployment. Doing so simplifies the processes required to make information available through internet-based connections. Storage consolidation can also be a benefit of moving a company's databases to the cloud. Databases in multiple departments of a large company, for example, can be combined in the cloud into a single hosted database management system.

Working of Cloud Database

From a structural and design perspective, a cloud database is no different than one that operates on a business's own on-premises servers. The key difference lies in where it resides.

Where an on-premises database is connected to local users through a corporation's internal local area network (LAN), a cloud database resides on servers and storage furnished by a cloud or DBaaS provider, and it is accessed solely via the internet. To a software application, for example, a SQL database residing on-premises or in the cloud should appear identical.

Accessed either through direct queries (such as SQL statements) or via API calls, the database's behavior should be the same. However, it may be possible to discern small differences in response time. An on-premises database, accessed via a LAN, is likely to provide slightly faster response than a cloud-based database, which requires a round trip on the internet for each interaction with the database. In practice, however, the differences are likely to be small.

Advantages of Cloud Databases

Here are the main advantages of cloud databases:

- Getting rid of physical infrastructure—It is the responsibility of the cloud service provider to maintain the database, provide storage and other infrastructure.

- Scalability—Contracting with DBaaS, allows for automatic scalability most of the time, during peak business hours or unexpected spikes during festivals and special days.

- Cost effectiveness—Reduced capital expenditure for enterprises is another advantage, because they no longer have to worry about operational costs or upgrading the infrastructure because all this will be handled by the cloud vendor.

- Latest technology availability—Enterprises no longer have to worry about shelling money on buying new technologies because updated infrastructure is the headache of the cloud vendor.

Cloud Databases Examples

Let's look at some of the best databases that would be best for your business.

Amazon Web Services

Amazon is one of the top ones in the list of cloud database services, and it includes an array of services including No-SQL (offering fast read, write performance, limitless scaling, high availability and schema flexibility), petabyte-scale data-warehouse solution and in-memory caching services.

The key services of AWS are:

- Amazon RDS—for relational databases.

- Amazon Redshift—As quick fully-managed, petabyte-scale data warehouse.

- Amazon DynamoDB—With its managed No-SQL database services.

- Amazon ElastiCache—Providing in-memory caching service.

Additionally, AWS offers Database Migration Services making it easier and inexpensive to migrate to the cloud and with zero downtime. AWS can be quickly managed and installed within minutes.

Microsoft Azure SQL Database

Azure is also pretty much like Amazon and offers both SQL and No-SQL databases. Advantages of having Azure include scalability with absolutely no downtime, built-in security protections, automated tuning, multi-tenancy capabilities and support for development tools.

It makes building and deploying apps easier, enabling developers to monitor them with ease. SQL developers can easily work with QLCMD or the SQL Server Management Studio when working with SQL Azure. And the best part about Azure is that it is a great option for people who hate setting up SQL Server and wants to be free from physical administration.

Microsoft Azure Document DB

As Microsoft Azure supports two different cloud based implementations, it is worth mentioning Microsoft Azure Document DB as well. Launched in 2014, Microsoft Azure Document DB is a No-SQL document database service that supports both JSON and Java script.

Features of Microsoft Azure Document DB include limitless scalability, high level consistency and commendable global replication capabilities. Additionally, it offers 15 millisecond latencies on writes (at least 99% of the time) and 10 millisecond latencies on reads.

Hence, Document DB is a write optimized; latch-free database engine delivering high performance solid-state drives for the cloud. Though Microsoft releases both Mongo DB and Azure Document DB, both the databases share some common ground as well.

Cloud SQL by Google

As it can manage both MySQL and PostgreSQL databases, Cloud SQL with its relational databases and a Big Query analysis tool can easily run queries on cloud-based data for Google Cloud Platform.

It is easy to set up, manage, maintain and administer. Cloud SQL is the answer for developers looking for the best option to save time consuming tasks like applying patches and updates, manage backups and a lot more.

Developers can focus on building great apps and since Cloud SQL uses standard wire protocols, connecting any applications from anywhere becomes easier. The database also supports common features of MySQL or PostgreSQL, with just very few differences.

Oracle Database as a Service

Enterprise developers are also aware of the capabilities of Oracle databases in data centers. Keeping this in mind, Oracle has released its database technology on an SaaS basis. It can support any size workload, right from development to testing, and still provide high-level security encryption spanning multiple layers.

Apart from providing flexibility, management options and various editions, the another noted advantage of Oracle database is that developers can get it up and running within a few minutes. You can add capacity on-demand as well, adding to its scaling. Hence, as your business grows from startup to a large enterprise, Oracle stays with you by scaling OLTP and Data Warehouse workloads as per requirement.

In conclusion, cloud databases are extremely important for removing IT complexities and to drive business goals home.

Apart from handling installation, maintenance and scaling of IT infrastructures, constant upgrades by cloud service providers make it easier for enterprises to cut down operational costs without compromising on security and quality. Flexibility, agility and cost savings are the three main factors why cloud database has become a force to reckon.

Distributed Database

In a distributed database, there are a number of databases that may be geographically distributed all over the world. A distributed DBMS manages the distributed database in a manner so that it appears as one single database to users.

A distributed database is a collection of multiple interconnected databases, which are spread physically across various locations that communicate via a computer network.

Features

- Databases in the collection are logically interrelated with each other. Often they represent a single logical database.

- Data is physically stored across multiple sites. Data in each site can be managed by a DBMS independent of the other sites.

- The processors in the sites are connected via a network. They do not have any multiprocessor configuration.

- A distributed database is not a loosely connected file system.

- A distributed database incorporates transaction processing, but it is not synonymous with a transaction processing system.

Popularity of Distributed Databases

Here are the basic reasons why the centralized model is being left behind by many organizations in favor of database distribution:

1. *Reliability* – Building an infrastructure is similar to investing: diversify to reduce your chances of loss. Specifically, if a failure occurs in one area of the distribution, the entire database does not experience a setback.

2. *Security* – You can give permissions to single sections of the overall database, for better internal and external protection.

3. *Cost-effective* – Bandwidth prices go down because users are accessing remote data less frequently.

4. *Local access* – Similarly to #1 above, if there is a failure in the umbrella network, you can still get access to your portion of the database.

5. *Growth* – If you add a new location to your business, it's simple to create an additional node within the database, making distribution highly scalable.

6. *Speed & resource efficiency* – Most requests and other interactivity with the database are performed at a local level, also decreasing remote traffic.

7. *Responsibility & containment* – Because any glitches or failures occur locally, the issue is contained and can potentially be handled by the IT staff designated to handle that piece of the company.

Uses of Distributed Databases

Often distributed databases are used by organizations that have numerous offices or storefronts in different geographical locations. Typically an individual branch is interacting primarily with the data that pertain to its own operations, with a much less frequent need for general company data. There is an inconsistent need for any central information from the branches in that case. However, the home office of the company still must have a steady influx of information from every location. To solve that issue, a distributed database usually operates by allowing each location of the company to interact directly with its own database during work hours. During non-peak times, each day, the whole database receives a batch of data from each branch.

Types of Distributed Data

Distributed data can be divided into five basic types, as outlined below:

- *Replicated data* – Replication of data is used to create additional instances of data in different parts of the database. Using this tactic, a distributed database can avoid excessive traffic because the identical data can be accessed locally.

  This form of data is subdivided into two different types: read-only and writable data. Read-only versions also allow revisions to the first instance, and then the replications are adjusted accordingly. Writable versions can be adjusted, which then immediately changes the first instance, with various configurations for how and when all replications throughout the system experience the update.

  In this type of distributed data system, updates can be configured based on how crucial it is that the database have the correct specifics moment by moment (or over whatever time period). Note that replication is especially valuable when you do not need any revisions to appear throughout the distributed data system in real time.

This type of data makes it easy to supply data from any section to any other section of the larger database if the latter section's data is compromised by any type of error. Be aware, though, that with replication, *collisions* can occur. Safeguards must be in place to prevent/resolve them.

- *Horizontally fragmented data* – This category of data distribution involves the use of primary keys (each of which refers to one record in the database). Horizontal fragmentation is commonly used for situations in which specific locations of a business usually only need access to the database pertaining to their specific branch.

- *Vertically fragmented data* – With vertical fragmentation, primary keys are again utilized. However, in this case, copies of the primary key are available within each section of the database (accessible to each branch). This type of format works well for situations in which a branch of a business and the central location each interact with the same accounts but perhaps in different manners (such as changes to client contact information vs. changes to financial figures).

- *Reorganized data* – Reorganization means that data has been adjusted in one way or another, as is typical for decision-support databases. In some cases, there are two distinct systems handling transactions and decision-support. While decision-support systems can be trickier to maintain technically, on-line transaction processing (OLTP) often requires reconfiguration to allow for large amounts of requests.

- *Separate-schema data* – This category of data partitions the database and software used to access it to fit different departments and situations – user data vs. product data, for example. Usually, there is overlap between the various databases within this type of distribution.

Key-value Database

A *key-value database* (also known as a key-value store and key-value store database) is a type of No-SQL database that uses a simple key/value method to store data.

The key-value part refers to the fact that the database stores data as a collection of key/value pairs. This is a simple method of storing data, and it is known to scale well.

The key-value pair is a well-established concept in many programming languages. Programming languages typically refer to a key-value as an *associative array* or *data structure*. A key-value is also commonly referred to as a *dictionary* or *hash*.

Examples of Key-value Stores

Below are examples of key-value stores.

These are simple examples, but the aim is to provide an idea of the how a key-value database works.

Phone Directory

Key	Value
Bob	(123) 456-7890
Jane	(234) 567-8901
Tara	(345) 678-9012
Tiara	(456) 789-0123

Artist Info

Key	Value
artist:1:name	AC/DC
artist:1:genre	Hard Rock
artist:2:name	Slim Dusty
artist:2:genre	Country

Stock Trading

This example uses a list as the value.

The list contains the stock ticker, whether it's a "buy" or "sell" order, the number of shares, and the price.

Key	Value
123456789	APPL, Buy, 100, 84.47
234567890	CERN, Sell, 50, 52.78
345678901	JAZZ, Buy, 235, 145.06
456789012	AVGO, Buy, 300, 124.50

IP Forwarding Table

This is an example of an IP forwarding table. It forwards an IP address to a MAC address of a physical computer.

Key	Value
202.45.12.34	01:23:36:0f:a2:33
202.45.123.4	00:25:33:da:4c:01
245.12.33.45	02:03:33:10:e2:b1
101.234.55.1	b8:67:a3:11:23:b1

Types of Data that can be Stored in a Key-value Database

The Key

The key in a key-value pair must (or at least, *should*) be unique. This is the unique identifier that allows you to access the value associated with that key.

In theory, the key could be anything. But this may depend on the DBMS. One DBMS may impose limitations while another may impose none.

In Redis for example, the maximum allowed key size is 512 MB. You can use any binary sequence as a key, from a short string of text, to the contents of an image file. Even the empty string is a valid key.

However, for performance reasons, you should avoid having a key that's too long. But too short can cause readability issues too. In any case, the key should follow an agreed convention in order to keep things consistent.

The Value

The value in a key-value store can be anything, such as text (long or short), a number, markup code such as HTML, programming code such as PHP, an image, etc.

The value could also be a list, or even another key-value pair encapsulated in an object.

Some key-store DBMSs allow you to specify a data type for the value. For example, you could specify that the value should be an integer. Other DBMSs don't provide this functionality and therefore, the value could be of any type.

As an example, the Redis DBMS allows you to specify the following data types:

- Binary-safe strings.

- Lists: collections of string elements sorted according to the order of insertion.

- Sets: collections of unique, unsorted string elements.

- Sorted sets, similar to Sets but where every string element is associated to a floating number value, called *score*. Allows you to do things like, select the top 10, or the bottom 10, etc.

- Hashes, which are maps composed of fields associated with values. Both the field and the value are strings.

- Bit arrays (or simply bitmaps).

- HyperLogLogs: this is a probabilistic data structure which is used in order to estimate the cardinality of a set.

Uses of Key-value Database

Key-value databases can be applied to many scenarios. For example, key-value stores can be useful for storing things such as the following:

1. General Web/Computers

   - User profiles

   - Session information

   - Article/blog comments

   - Emails

   - Status messages

2. E-commerce

   - Shopping cart contents

   - Product categories

   - Product details

   - Product reviews

3. Networking/Data Maintenance

   - Telecom directories

   - Internet Protocol (IP) forwarding tables

   - Data de-duplication

Key-value databases can even store whole webpages, by using the URL as the key and the web page as the value.

Benefits of Key-value Database

Many implementations that are not well-suited to traditional relational databases can benefit from a key-value model, which offers several advantages, including:

- Flexible data modeling: Because a key-value store does not enforce any structure on the data, it offers tremendous flexibility for modeling data to match the requirements of the application.

- High performance: Key-value architecture can be more per formant than relational databases in many scenarios because there is no need to perform lock, join, union, or other operations when working with objects. Unlike traditional relational databases, a key-value store doesn't need to search through columns or tables to find an object. Knowing the key will enable very fast location of an object.

- Massive scalability: Most key-value databases make it easy to scale out on demand using commodity hardware. They can grow to virtually any scale without significant redesign of the database.

- High availability: Key-value databases may make it easier and less complex to provide high availability than can be achieved with relational database. Some key-value databases use a master less, distributed architecture that eliminates single points of failure to maximize resiliency.

- Operational simplicity: Some key-value databases are specifically designed to simplify operations by ensuring that it is as easy as possible to add and remove capacity as needed and that any hardware or network failures within the environment do not create downtime.

Popular Key-value Databases

Amazon Dynamo-DB

Amazon Dynamo-DB is a non-relational database that delivers reliable performance at any scale. It's a fully managed, multi-region, multi-master database that provides consistent single-digit millisecond latency, and offers built-in security, backup and re-store, and in-memory caching. In Dynamo-DB, an Item is composed of a primary or composite key and a flexible number of attributes. There is no explicit limitation on the number of attributes associated with an individual item, but the aggregate size of an item, including all the attribute names and attribute values, cannot exceed 400 KB. A table is a collection of data items, just as a table in a relational database is a collection of rows. Each table can have an infinite number of data items.

Apache Cassandra

Apache Cassandra is a commonly used, high-performance non-relational database. AWS customers who currently maintain Cassandra on-premises may want to take advantage of the scalability, reliability, security, and economic benefits of running Cassandra on Amazon EC2.

EC2 and Amazon Elastic Block Store (Amazon EBS) provide secure, resizable compute capacity and storage in the AWS Cloud. When combined, you can deploy Cassandra and scale capacity according to your requirements. Given the number of possible deployment topologies, it's not always trivial to select the most appropriate strategy suitable for your use case.

DataStax Enterprise (DSE) is the always-on data platform for cloud applications powered by Apache Cassandra. DSE is designed to handle big data workloads across multiple nodes with no single point of failure. DSE addresses the problem of failures by employing a peer-to-peer distributed system across homogeneous nodes where data is distributed among all nodes in the cluster. DSE offers advanced functionality designed to accelerate your ability to create intelligent and compelling cloud applications. Integrated within each node of DSE are powerful indexing, search, analytics, and graph functionalities that are provided by combining Cassandra with Apache Solr, Apache Spark, and DSE Graph. You can write data once and access it using a variety of workloads or access patterns, all from a single cohesive solution.

Navigational Database

A navigational database is the combination of both the hierarchical and network model of database interfaces. Navigational techniques utilize "pointers" and "paths" to navigate among data records. The opposing model is the relational, which uses "declarative" techniques in which you ask the system for what you want instead of how to navigate to it. Traditionally navigational interfaces are procedural, though one could characterize some modern systems like X-Path as being simultaneously navigational and declarative.

The Hierarchical model is considered navigational because it is necessary to navigate up and down to "parents" and "children". In addition to that, file/folder paths are considered "paths" in the navigational model that are followed to the proper location. For instance, with the navigational model, one may ask for the location of a "record" down the hall, 3 doors to the left, in the back of the room, on top of the filing cabinet. This is opposed to the relational that may ask for all records in a filing cabinet. In general, navigational systems will use combinations of paths and prepositions such as "next", "previous", "first", "last", "up", "down", etc.

Navigational models are allegedly derived from a speech by Charles Bachman in which he describes the "programmer as navigator" while accessing his favored type of database.

Some criticism of navigational techniques includes the comparison to the "Go to" of pre-structured programming and the undisciplined method of the model. The downfall of this "Go to" methodology is that it is very unorganized. In this sense, the relational model is a much more efficient one to use in large scale operations. But, in practice relational has yet to successfully scale down to smaller-use data. Whether this is an in-born fault of relational or just lack of implementation improvement research is difficult to say at this point. Some fault the SQL language rather than relational theory in general. That being said, navigational techniques are still the preferred way to handle smaller-scale structures.

"Paths" are often formed by concatenation of node names or node addresses. Example:

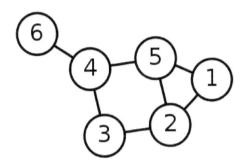

Sample database nodes: A labeled graph on 6 vertices and 7 edges. (Numbers are used for illustration purposes only. In practice more meaningful names are often used. Other potential attributes are not shown).

> Node6.Node4.Node5.Node1

Or

> Node6/Node4/Node5/Node1

If there is no link between given nodes, then an error condition is usually triggered with a message such as "Invalid Path". The path "Node6.Node2.Node1" would be invalid in most systems because there is no direct link between Node 6 and Node 2.

It has been suggested that navigational database engines are easier to build and take up less memory (RAM) than relational equivalents. However, the existence of relational or relational-based products of the late 1980s that possessed small engines (by today's standards) because they didn't use SQL suggests this is not necessarily the case.

A current example of navigational structuring can be found in the Document Object Model (DOM) often used in web browsers and closely associated with JavaScript. The DOM "engine" is essentially a light-weight navigational database. The World Wide Web itself and Wikipedia could potentially be considered forms of navigational databases, though they focus on human-readable text rather than data (on a large scale, the Web is a network model and on smaller or local scales, such as domain and URL partitioning, it uses hierarchies). In contrast, the Linked Data facet of the Semantic is specifically concerned with network-scale machine-readable data, and follows precisely the 'follow your nose' paradigm implied by the navigational idea.

Probabilistic Database

A probabilistic database is a database in which every tuple t belongs to the database with some probability $P(t)$; when $P(t) = 1$ then the tuple is certain to belong to the database; when $0 < P(t) < 1$ then it belongs to the database only with some probability; when $P(t) = 0$ then the tuple is certain not to belong to the database, and it is not necessary to bother representing it. A traditional (deterministic) database corresponds to the case when $P(t) = 1$ for all tuples t. Tuples with $P(t) > 0$ are called *possible tuples*. In addition to indicating the probabilities for all tuples, a probabilistic database must also indicate somehow how the tuples are correlated. In the simplest cases the tuples are declared to be either independent (when $P(t_{1t2}) = P(t_{1t2})$), or exclusive (or disjoint, when $P(t_{1t2}) = 0$).

Probabilities and their Meaning in Databases

Where do the probabilities in a probabilistic database come from? And what exactly do they mean? The answer to these questions may differ from application to application, but it is rarely satisfactory. Information extraction systems are based on probabilistic models, so the data they extract is probabilistic RFID readings are cleaned using particle filters that also produce probability distributions data analytics in financial prediction rely on statistical models that often generate probabilistic data. In some cases, the probability values have a precise semantics, but that semantics is often associated with the way the data is derived and not necessarily with how the data will be used. In other cases we have no probabilistic semantics at all but only a subjective confidence level that needs to be converted into a probability: for example, Google Squared does not even associate numerical scores, but defines a fixed number of confidence levels (high, low, etc.), which need to be converted into a probabilistic score in order to be merged with other data and queried. Another example is Bio Rank , which uses as input subjective and relative weights of evidence and converts those into probabilistic weights in order to compute relevance scores to rank most likely functions for proteins.

No matter how they were derived, we always map a confidence score to the interval and interpret it as a probability value. The important invariant is that a larger value always represents a higher degree of confidence, and this carries over to the query output: answers with a higher (computed) probability are more credible than answers with a lower probability. Typically, a probabilistic database ranks the answers to a query by their probabilities: the ranking is often more informative than the absolute values of their probabilities.

Possible Worlds Semantics

The meaning of a probabilistic database is surprisingly simple: it means that the database instance can be in one of several states, and each state has a probability. That is, we are not given a single database instance but several possible instances, and each has some probability.

Each subset of tuples is called a *possible world* and has a probability: the sum of probabilities of all possible worlds is 1.0. Similarly, for a database where the uncertainty is at the attribute level, a possible world is obtained by choosing a possible value for each uncertain attribute, in each tuple.

Thus, a probabilistic database is simply a probability distribution over a set of possible worlds. While the number of possible worlds is astronomical, e.g., 2^{537000} possible worlds for NELL, this is only the semantics: in practice we use much more compact ways to represent the probabilistic database

Types of Uncertainty

Two types of uncertainty are used in probabilistic databases: tuple-level uncertainty and attribute-level uncertainty.

In *tuple-level uncertainty*, a tuple is a random variable; we do not know whether the tuple belongs to the database instance or not. The random variable associated to the tuple has a Boolean domain: it is *true* when the tuple is present and *false* if it is absent. Such a tuple is also called a *maybe tuple*. In *attribute-level uncertainty*, the value of an attribute A is uncertain: for each tuple, the attribute A represents a random variable, and its domain is the set of values that the attribute may take for that tuple.

We will find it convenient to convert attribute-level uncertainty into tuple-level uncertainty and consider only tuple-level uncertainty during query processing. This translation is done as follows. For every tuple t, where the attribute A takes possible values $a1$, $a2, a3,...$, we create several clone tuples $t1, t2, t3,...$ that are identical to t except for the attribute A, whose values are $t1.A = a1, t2.A = a2$, etc. Now each tuple ti is uncertain and described by a random variable, and the tuples $t1, t2,...$ are mutually exclusive. A block of exclusive tuples is also called an *X-tuple*.

Types

The simplest probabilistic database is a *tuple-independent* database, where the tuples are independent probabilistic events. Another popular kind is the *block independent-disjoint* probabilistic database, or BID, where the tuples are partitioned into blocks, such that all tuples within a block are disjoint (i.e., mutually exclusive) events, and all tuples from different blocks are independent events. Attribute level uncertainty can be naturally represented as a BID table. While sometimes one needs to represent more complex correlations between the tuples in a database, this is usually achieved by decomposing the database into independent and disjoint components, in a process much like traditional database normalization. Another classification of probabilistic databases is into *discrete* and *continuous*. In the former, attributes are discrete random variables; in the latter, they are continuous random variables.

Probabilistic Databases vs. Graphical Models

A graphical model (GM) is a concise way to represent a joint probability distribution over a large set of random variables $X_1, X_2,..., X_n$. The "graph" has one node for each random variable X_i and an edge (X_i, X_j) between all pairs of variables that are correlated in the probability space obtained by fixing the values of all the other variables. GMs have been extensively studied in knowledge representation and machine learning since they offer concise ways to represent complex probability distributions.

Any probabilistic database is a particular type of a GM, where each random variable is associated to a tuple (or to an attribute value, depending on whether we model tuple-level or attribute-level uncertainty). Query answers can also be represented as a GM, by creating new random variables corresponding to the tuples of all intermediate results, including one variable for every answer to the query. Thus, GMs can be used both to represent probabilistic databases that have non-trivial correlations between their tuples and to compute the probabilities of all query answers. However, there are some significant distinctions between the assumptions made in GMs and in probabilistic databases, which are summarized in, and are discussed:

- First, the probabilistic model in probabilistic databases is simple and usually (but not always) consists of a collection of independent, or disjoint-independent tuples; this simple model can be used as a building block for more complex probabilistic models. In contrast, the probabilistic model in GMs is complex: they were designed explicitly to represent complex correlations between the random variables. Thus, the probabilistic model in databases is simple in the sense that there are no correlations at all or only disjoint events.

- Second, the notion of a query is quite different. In GMs, the query is simple: it asks for the probability of some output variables given some evidence; a typical query is $P(X_1X_3|X_2X_5X_7)$, which asks for the probability of (certain values of) the random variables X_1, X_3, given the evidence (values for) X_2, X_5, X_7. In probabilistic databases, the query is complex: it is an expression in the Relational Calculus, or in SQL, as we have illustrated over the NELL database.

- Third, the network in GMs depends only on the data and is independent on the query, while in probabilistic databases the network depends on both the data and the query. Thus, the network in GMs is static while in probabilistic databases it is dynamic. The network in probabilistic databases is the query's lineage, obtained from both the databases instance and the query and may be both large (because the database is large) and complex (because the query is complex). The distinction between a static network in GM and a dynamic network in probabilistic databases affects dramatically our approach to probabilistic inference.

The complexity of the probabilistic inference problem is measured in terms of the size of the network (for GMs) and in the size of the database (for probabilistic databases). In this respect, the network in GMs is analogous to the database instance in databases. However, the key parameter influencing the complexity is different. In GM, the main complexity parameter is the network's tree width; all probabilistic inference algorithms for GM run in time that is exponential in the tree width of the network. In probabilistic databases, the main complexity parameter is the query: we fix the query then ask for the complexity of probabilistic inference in terms of the size of the database instance. This is called *data complexity* by Vardi (1982). We will show that, depending on the query, the data complexity can range from polynomial time to #P-hard.

- Finally, probabilistic databases are an evolution of standard, relational database. In particular, they must use techniques that integrate smoothly with existing query processing techniques, such as indexes, cost-based query optimizations, the use of database statistics, and parallelization. This requires both a conceptual approach to probabilistic inference that is consistent with standard query evaluation and a significant engineering effort to integrate this probabilistic inference with a relational database system. In contrast, probabilistic inference algorithms for GM are stand-alone, and they are currently not integrated with relational query processing systems.

Applications of Probabilistic Databases

In recent years, there has been an increased interest in probabilistic databases. The main reason for this has been the realization that many diverse applications need a generic platform for managing probabilistic data.

Information extraction (IE), already mentioned in this chapter, is a very natural application for probabilistic databases because some important IE techniques already generate probabilistic data. For example, Conditional Random Fields (CRFs) define a probability space over the possible ways to parse a text. Typically, IE systems retain the most probable extraction, but show that by storing multiple (or even all) alternative extractions of a CRF in a probabilistic database, one can increase significantly the overall recall of the system, thus justifying the need for a probabilistic database and describe a system, Bayes Store, which stores the CRF in a relational database system and pushes the probabilistic inference inside the engine, describe an application of probabilistic databases to the Named Entity Recognition (NER) problem. In NER, each token in a text document must be labeled with an entity, such as PER (person entity such as Bill), ORG (organization such as IBM), LOC (location such as New York City), MISC (miscellaneous entity-none of the above), and O (not a named entity). By combining Markov Chain Monte Carlo with incremental view update techniques, they show considerable speedups on a corpus of 1788 New York Times articles from the year 2004. Fink et al. describe a system that can answer relational queries on probabilistic tables constructed by aggregating Web data using Google Squared and on other online data that can be brought in tabular form.

A related application is *wrapper induction*. Dalvi et al. describe an approach for robust wrapper induction that uses a probabilistic change model for the data. The goal of the wrapper is to remain robust under likely changes to the data sources.

RFID data management extracts and queries complex events over streams of readings of RFID tags. Due to the noisy nature of the RFID tag readings these are usually converted into probabilistic data, using techniques such particle filters, then are stored in a probabilistic database.

Probabilistic data is also used in *data cleaning*. Andritsos et al. show how to use a simple BID data model to capture key violations in databases, which occur often when integrating data from multiple sources. Antova et al. and Antova et al. study data cleaning in a general-purpose uncertain resp. probabilistic database system, by iterative removal of possible worlds from a representation of a large set of possible worlds. Given that a limited amount of resources is available to clean the database, Cheng et al. describe a technique for choosing the set of uncertain objects to be cleaned, in order to achieve the best improvement in the quality of query answers. They develop a quality metric for a probabilistic database, and they investigate how such a metric can be used for data cleaning purposes.

In *entity resolution*, entities from two different databases need to be matched, and the challenge is that the same object may be represented differently in the two databases. In *de-duplication,* we need to eliminate duplicates from a collection of objects, while facing the same challenge as before, namely that an object may occur repeatedly, using different representations. Probabilistic databases have been proposed to deal with this problem too. Hassanzadeh and Miller keep duplicates when the correct cleaning strategy is not certain and utilize an efficient probabilistic query-answering technique to return query results along with probabilities of each answer being correct. Sismanis et al. [2009] propose an approach that maintains the data in an unresolved state and dynamically deals with entity uncertainty at query time. Beskales et al. describe Prob-Clean, a duplicate elimination system that encodes compactly the space of possible repairs.

Arumugam et al. and Jampani et al. Xu et al. describe applications of probabilistic databases to *business intelligence* and *financial risk assessment,* consider applications of probabilistic data to *business processes.*

Scientific data management is a major application domain for probabilistic databases. One of the early works recognizing this potential is by Nierman and Jagadish. They describe a system, Pro TDB (Probabilistic Tree Data Base) based on a probabilistic XML data model and they apply it to protein chemistry data from the bioinformatics domain. Detwiler et al. [2009] describe Bio Rank, a mediator-based data integration systems for exploratory queries that keeps track of the uncertainties introduced by joining data elements across sources and the inherent uncertainty in scientific data. The system uses the uncertainty for ranking uncertain query results, in particular for predicting protein functions. They use the uncertainty in scientific data integration for ranking uncertain query results, and they apply this to protein function prediction. They show that the use of probabilities increases the system's ability to predict less-known or previously unknown functions but is not more effective for predicting well-known functions than deterministic methods. Potamias et al. [2010] describe an application of probabilistic databases for the study of protein-protein interaction. They consider the protein-protein interaction network (PPI) created by Krogan et al. where two proteins are linked if it is likely that they interact and model it as a probabilistic graph. Another application of probabilistic graph databases to protein prediction is described by Zou et al. Verona diagrams on uncertain data are considered by Cheng et al.

Dong et al. consider uncertainty in *data integration*; they introduce the concept of probabilistic schema mappings and analyze their formal foundations. They consider two possible semantics, by-table and by-tuple. Gal et al. study how to answer aggregate queries with COUNT, AVG, SUM, MIN, and MAX over such mappings, by considering both by-table and by- tuple semantics. Cheng et al. [2010a] study the problem of managing possible mappings between two heterogeneous XML schemas, and they propose a data structure for representing these mappings that takes advantage of their high degree of overlap. van Keulen and de Keijzer consider user feedback in probabilistic data integration. Fagin et al. [2010] consider probabilistic data exchange and establish a foundational framework for this problem.

Several researchers have recognized the need to redesign major components of data management systems in order to cope with uncertain data. Cormode et al. and Cormode and Garofalakis redesign the histogram synopses, both for internal DBMS decisions (such as indexing and query planning) and for approximate query processing. Their histograms retain the possible-worlds semantics of probabilistic data, allowing for more accurate, yet concise, representation of the uncertainty characteristics of data and query results. Zhang et al. describe a data mining algorithm on probabilistic data. They consider a collection of X-tuples and search for approximately likely frequent items, with guaranteed high probability and accuracy. Rastogi et al. describe how to redesign access control to data when the database is probabilistic. They observe that access is often controlled by data, for example, a physician may access a patient's data only if the database has a record that the physician treats that patient; but in probabilistic databases the grant/deny decision is uncertain. The authors described a new access control method that adds a degree of noise to the data that is proportional to the degree of uncertainty of the access condition. Atallah and Qi [2009] describe how to extend skyline computation to probabilistic databases, with-out using "thresholding", while Zhang et al. [2009] describe continuous skyline queries over sliding windows on uncertain data elements regarding given probability thresholds. Jestes et al. ex- tend the string similarity problem, which is used in many database queries, to probabilistic strings; they consider both the "string level model", consisting of a complete distribution on the possible strings, and the "character level model", where characters are independent events, and derive solutions for the Expected Edit Distance (EED). Xu et al. generalize the simple selection problem to probabilistic databases: the attribute in the data is uncertain and given by a probabilistic histogram, and the value being searched is also uncertain. They use the Earth Mover's Distance to define the similarity between the two uncertain values and describe techniques for computing it.

A class of applications of probabilistic databases is in *inferring missing attribute values* in a deterministic database by mining portions of the data where those values are present. The result is a probabilistic database since the missing values cannot be inferred exactly, but one can derive a probability distribution on their possible values. Wolf et al. develop methods for mining attribute correlations (in terms of Approximate Functional Dependencies), value distributions (in the form of Naïve Bayes Classifiers), and selectivity estimates for that purpose. Stoyanovich et al. use *ensembles* and develop an elegant and effective theory for inferring missing values from various subsets of the defined attributes. Dasgupta et al. describe an interesting application of probabilistic data for acquiring unbiased samples from online hidden database, which offer query interfaces that return restricted answers (e.g., only top-k of the selected tuples), accompanied by a total count of the total number of tuples.

Finally, we mention an important subarea of probabilistic databases that we do not cover in this book: ranking the query answers by using both a user defined scoring criterion *and* the tuple probability, e.g., It is often the case that the user can specify a particular ranking criteria, for example, rank products by prices or rank locations by some distance, which has a well-defined semantics even on a deterministic database. If the database is probabilistic, then ranking becomes quite challenging because the system needs to account both for the user defined criterion and for the output probability.

Very Large Database

A very large database (VLDB) is a type of database that consists of a very high number of database records, rows and entries, which are spanned across a wide file system. VLDB is similar to a standard database but contains a very large amount of data. As such, it requires special management, maintenance and technologies to operate.

VLDB is primarily an enterprise class database. Although there is no specific limitation of a VLDB, it can consist of billions of records and have a cumulative size in thousands of gigabytes, or even some hundred terabytes. A VLDB is generally a repository for big data, a transactional processing system or a combination of the two. A VLDB is maintained through standard relational database management system (RDBMS) software and requires capable hardware computing and storage resources. Moreover, a VLDB also requires the underlying system to be capable enough to scale up to address its ever-increasing size.

The database or data warehouse will grow in the specific areas consisting of transactional information. The information describing the transaction itself is usually not as frequently changing and is capable of being termed: Meta Data – or data about data. Most of the transactions around the world consist of: date and time (when did the transaction occur?), who (the individual conducting, initiating, or entering the transaction), and what (the content of the transaction itself). Beyond these three components, the transactions typically include many descriptive elements and relationships between information – all of which must be recognized, but should be stored in a minimalist fashion in the database. Therefore, compression ratio's, growth ratio's, and metrics ranging from implementation time, to overall sizing should be computable attributes following a mostly accurate profiling activity.

The keys are: how many *types* of transactions, and how many total transactions are being entered in to the system?

The theory goes on to say: the relationship between hardware, software, speed, and RDBMS, and data set growth appears to be closely related – as well as consistent in nature. Therefore most common techniques included in mathematical algorithms should hold true for splitting data in to chunks while holding other elements constant. As a result, speed should only change if one of the other variables change.

The suggested very broad formula for this theory might be: speed = [(hardware)*(software)] bytes per second / (size of data in bytes).

 With this formula, if the size of the data increases, while the hardware and software stay constant, the speed decreases. Or vise-versa if the hardware increases and the size of the data stay the same the speed should increase. Of course the dependency is on the bottleneck of the system. A delicate balance is achieved in keeping these three "points" moving in ever larger directions in equal portions. Think of three sides of a triangle:

The pressure is in the middle of the triangle, pushing outward. Speed is the size of the arrow set inside the triangle. Increasing one, doesn't necessarily increase speed. A number of factors must be addressed. If you picture a pyramid, the 3d dimension might be the number of parallel processes capable of executing the requests. Consider the volume of a pyramid as the resulting speed, the more volume, potentially the more speed for more data. For this example, the items considered for each piece are discussed below:

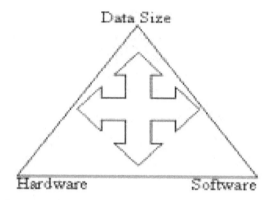

- Hardware = Size + Speed;

  o Size = Amount of RAM, # of parallel CPU's, # of controllers, # of disks;

  o Speed = RAM speed, Disk Speed, Bus Speed, Network Speed (bandwidth), and removing the # of idle cycles per second per CPU, as well as the # of blocked I/O processes per second per CPU.

- Software = # of parallel processes + # of partitions + operating speed of software (throughput).

If the formula holds true, then there are a number of things that can be done to achieve better performance.

We are seeing rapid change in both technology and the requirements for analysis of massive sets of information. More and more businesses are looking at the related issues and recognizing that patterns, trends, and analysis of these items is becoming critical to the success of the business. Ok – enough business talk. What about the technical end of it? Because of the business, the IT specialists left to implement these complex problems are beginning to deal with physical problems they've never had to think about before. OLTP simply "deleted" or rolled off the unused portion of the data, Data Warehouses physically were unable (until recently) to hold such massive sets of information. The focus has simply changed, the name of the game for IT is to get the most accurate answer from a compilation of as much information as possible – and do it as quickly as possible, providing that much desired competitive edge in business.

In recognizing speed as a foremost goal, we begin to realize that one of IT's responsibilities is integrating, understanding, and tuning all of these different components. Not to mention the mountains of data exist within an enterprise. Technically, having a VLDB situation without the expertise to predict it, manage it, grow it, or architect it – is like having the information aboard the best aircraft carrier in the world without having the aircraft. What's the point? More simply put – it's like a rowboat without the oars.

More and more IT personnel need to understand the varying levels in order to tune the correct component. This is analogous to improving a car with the best carburetor money can buy, but then putting the same old fuel in to the engine, maybe the engine is too small? Maybe the fuel is bad? Maybe there isn't enough horsepower to take advantage of the best carburetor? Anyhow, by understanding only a single component of this particular triangle, only certain levels of performance and management of VLDB can be achieved. Provided the amount of money it costs a business to house, build and deploy VLDB this would be a grave mistake on the business's part to not properly train IT employees.

Who interacts from a business perspective is interested in VLDB even if they don't know it. They need to understand that the questions they are beginning to ask about the content (specifically the historical patterns of the content) require more and more analysis. Which in turn, most statisticians will tell you that to predict for 6 months (most accurately), should have at least 12 months behind it. In other words: twice as much data for half the amount of prediction over time. All of these statistics prove true when coming to most accurate conclusions in VLDB. Sure sample sets can be implemented, but what if that key factor is missed?

From an IT perspective, everybody that touches, maintains, architects/designs, or builds a data warehouse is interested (or should be) in VLDB. The list of roles include: systems architect, systems administrator, enterprise architect, database administrator, ETL operator, dss/olap (Business Intelligence individual), operations for backup/restore and disaster recovery.

VLDB / VLDW Concepts

1. Architecture Overview

Architecture plays a much larger role in VLDB than most care to think about. In order to understand VLDB/VLDW we must consider the architecture and the concepts behind what makes it all work. The architecture is like the set of blueprints for a house, without the overview of what to put where, and the guidelines or steps to build it. It becomes difficult to create correctly. All too often most projects begin with the right intentions, but forget to include the architecture components. This leaves the foundations of VLDB extremely weak, and many problems begin to crop up as data set size grows rapidly.

An example paradigm might be as follows:

Suppose you had a lumber yard, and in that yard you had 1 stack of 500 foot boards, 8 feet high, and 6 feet deep. These boards are stacked neatly on one side of the lumber-yard. Your objective is to move the boards across to the other side of the yard. Do you simply start by grabbing a board, and attempting to move it by hand, one by one across to the other side? Most often all the options of how the board(s) can be moved are considered. In doing so, you find out that there's a forklift of standard size is available. Does this mean you can move all the boards now? Not necessarily. The boards are too long, and too heavy for a single forklift, so additional options must be considered.

In this paradigm, if the boards represent data, the forklift represents the database/query or software, and possibly a CPU (the engine of the forklift). If the boundaries of the lumberyard aren't considered, there could be trouble. Again, the architecture or the entire process (all the options) must be considered before the best option for the situation at hand is chosen. If the worst option is chosen (because the entire architecture was not considered), then the boards may break – or it may take a very long time to move the boards, or halfway through, no more boards could be moved. Maybe some of the other boards have now been placed in the way of completing the task.

Four other co-workers join you, each with their own forklift, and your boss has just told you these boards need to be moved within the next 2 hours. This further complicates the problem. Now there are five people, five forklifts, and still 500 ft long boards. After discussing it, everyone agrees that there are two options: cut the boards in to 5 portions of 100 feet each and each move the stacks independently, or put all five forklifts at the same time under the boards and try to move the entire stack all at once. Of course this would require great synchronization so as not to disturb the stack or have it fall over.

After further consideration the option for cutting the boards is chosen, the stacks are moved efficiently across the yard, and the job is done in 1 hour and 45 minutes. Just in time for the boss to come out, and start congratulating you – explaining how he can't move the boards in trucks anyway if they were still longer than 100 ft. Or maybe he begins to yell, for the lack of asking about the fact that these 500 ft boards were specifically ordered at that length, and you and your co-workers should have asked first. What happened here? You solved the problem with two possible outcomes (probably more outcomes available). But, was the architecture right to solve the problem? The problem itself was solved, but can be considered a success only if the requirements were discovered before delving in to the actual application of solving the problem. Let's examine one more possibility.

You and your co-workers go back, ask the boss hey, do you want these in 500 ft lengths, or do you mind if we cut them? If we cut them we can move them with our 5 forklifts, if you want them in one length, we need to use the crane to haul the whole stack across the yard. The boss thinks for a minute and responds, the crane is more expensive, but the customer wants the boards in 500ft lengths. Go ahead and use the crane to move the boards. Successfully, the boards are moved across the yard in 45 minutes, in a single stack – uncut.

Interesting, now there's another solution to the same problem: an introduction of a high-priced item, but one that can accomplish the task successfully according to the requirements. The items in this real-world case should be thought of as follows: the boards are data in a table. Cutting the boards is like partitioning them. The forklifts are like CPU's with RAM for a carrying capacity, and they have a certain speed. The more forklifts, the faster the stacks can be moved, at a maximum of 5 stacks – other forklifts would simply sit idle. Each forklift operating independently is like a parallel process, capable of accessing a partition. If the boards are in a single stack – the forklifts must operate together at the same time (as if they were one large forklift).

The crane is a high-priced item that can meet the requirements, but it can do it faster. It's like having more CPU's, more RAM, faster machines, faster bus speeds, faster disks, more controllers, etc. Higher cost gets the job done faster than lower cost, but it's over-kill unless this kind of operation will take place regularly. If the data set grows (more boards, more stacks), then it would make sense to invest in a crane, but only after the forklifts are overwhelmed or the time frame is squeezed to tightly.

Ok, enough of the theory. Let's get down to brass tacks. The bottom line is: architecture, engineering, and requirements are extremely important in considering VLDB. As this series will now delve in to the technical sides of all of this.

2. Thread

A thread is typically defined as an independent process which can execute asynchronous to other processes. Usually a thread is capable of operating independently of other threads, or processes. When a thread has to wait on the results of another thread, it will sit in "idle mode" until a token is passed (semaphore/mutex). Ok, in English – a thread can be likened to a car. Put four cars coming to a stop at a 4 way stop sign, each car is running independently of the other cars. They all arrive at the stop at different times. Then each car proceeds to go in turn and continue on their way. Think of each car being a thread, the stop sign being a semaphore or shared lock, by which all cars must stop first before proceeding, and each car can only proceed when the intersection is cleared.

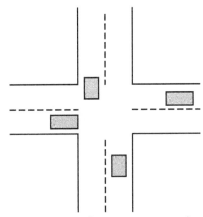

Figure: Four way stop intersection each car represents a thread. All cars must stop before proceeding, but all cars are in motion independent of one another

Threads can also be thought of in terms of different users connecting to the database. Each has their own connection, and each can execute different queries at the same time, or they can execute the same query at the same time. The threads allow for multiple processes to occur at the same time. This concept is very important in understanding how multi-threaded architectures work. A multi-threaded architecture provides the system with the ability to run multiple threads or processes at the same time. The system performs management of the 4 way stop (with stop lights), so that accidents and traffic jams are avoided as best as possible.

Why is this important? It is important to recognize threads as a basis of architecture for systems with VLDB, so that larger tasks or requests (such as massive inserts, selects, deletes or updates) can be split in to smaller multiple tasks that can run at the same time – thus shortening the overall time frame necessary to complete the task. Going back to the analogy used earlier, it's similar to having N# forklifts. Each thread is a forklift, the operators (people) are like the system that communicates and manages what each thread is doing. It can take lots of little threads working together to complete what otherwise is a huge task, in a short period of time. However, without the Operating System providing parallel processing capabilities, threads still execute in order (serially). It would be like having five forklifts, but only one key that fits all, you can only operate one forklift at a time.

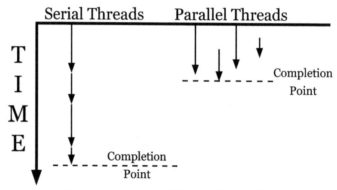

Figure: Serial vs parallel thread execution

The time line increases, for serial execution are multiples longer than that of parallel execution. The parallel threads all execute together at the same time, while the serial threads execute one after the other.

3. Parallel Processing

Parallel Processing is the ability of the system to run, manage, and maintain multiple threads at the same time (synchronously). It's the five keys and five operators needed to run each forklift independently. Degree of parallelism is a measure which indicates how many parallel processes can run at once before the system is overloaded or maximized. For instance, if you have five stacks of lumber, and seven forklifts, you can still only operate five forklifts at a time, indicating a degree of parallelism of five. This is a very simplistic explanation of the parallel processing theories. There are many books in the marketplace that describe in great detail how parallel processing and degree of parallelism is reached. It is not the scope of this series to discuss each in extreme detail, only to introduce the concepts as they relate to VLDB.

Parallel processing enables speed, and division of tasks across CPU's. This is also where the concept of load balancing comes in to play. Load balancing is the process by which the operating system decides where to run the threads, how many threads to run, and which ones need to sit idle. It attempts to maximize the overall usage of the hardware resources available. Load balancing in the lumberyard would consist of deciding which forklifts are out of gas and need to sit idle. Maybe one of the forklifts can carry a larger capacity load than the other, so it may be used to carry a slightly larger pile in a shorter time frame. Maybe it carries two smaller piles more quickly to the other side of the yard. Load balancing is dynamic in nature. Threads are swapped to and from different CPU's unless they are "CPU BOUND" during execution. CPU Bound means that the threads have been tied to run on a specific CPU, and only that CPU. According to the load balancer, cannot be moved to run on another CPU. Very few programs allow this level of control by the designer or operator. This is a double-edged sword, and can be tremendously beneficial, or extremely dangerous depending on how it's set up.

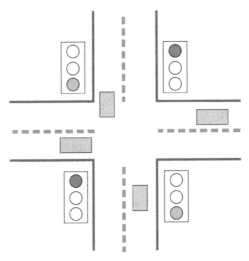

Figure: Four-way intersection

In this case, the stoplights represent the Operating System, and the capacities for executing or managing parallel processes. The threads (cars) are the processes.

Why is parallel processing important to VLDB? It allows multiple processes (SQL queries for instance) to execute at the exact same time frame, and with the same priority. It also provides the vehicle for very large tasks to be split in to multiple smaller tasks for the purposes of faster execution times. Without parallel processing, it becomes difficult if not impossible to handle systems of scale. Parallel processing also plays a huge role in the success of partitioning the data, which in the example provided here – are the stacks of lumber being cut in to shorter stacks.

Ok, so now that threads exist, and parallel processes exist to manage threads, how does the system decide who takes priority and when? The answer is through a technique called pre-emptive multi-tasking.

4. Pre-emptive Multi-tasking

Pre-emptive multi-tasking is the ability to handle parallel processes, but to grant priorities to certain processes so they may interrupt other processes at specific points in time, or in reaction to specific events. In the case of the Four-way intersection with stoplights, a pre-emptive task would be an ambulance, which changes all the lights to red, but is still (in most cases) able to go through the intersection. It's a random occurrence that's unpredictable, but when it happens, it takes priority over the cars on the road. The multi-tasking part is parallel processing, it allows multiple tasks to interrupt other tasks at the same time – for instance, three ambulances at three different intersections, all have the same effect and the same priority on the road. Hopefully not all the ambulances head towards the same intersection at the same time – this would cause collision, and the ambulances would have to slow down, stop and wait until each one makes it through the intersection. This concept is called Blocked-I/O or blocked processing.

Why is pre-emptive multi-tasking important? What does it mean to the VLDB world, and how does it play in the operating system? It's important because it allows the operating system to manage execution priorities. For instance, if you type a key on your keyboard the system must respond immediately, regardless of what it's doing. This is an example of a hardware interrupt, one of the highest priority tasks that can occur on a system. It allows the system to react to a series of unpredictable events at the time they happen. The system considers it less important to update the screen than to respond to a keyboard event. These priorities also run through different software in the operating system. In fact, in near real time systems or true pre-emptive multi-tasking systems such as Unix, these priorities can even be assigned. Unix term for this is "niceness". Setting the "nice" for software sets the priority of its interrupt levels.

For instance, you can tell the system what's an ambulance, versus a fire-truck versus a car, etc.. This is important, to be able to set the priority in VLDB means that the database software can take precedence over other software running on the same system. Once priority is decided, the software makes the request to the operating system that enters a queue. When the system has time or needs to execute the request it pulls it from the queue, assigns it to a processor, then it begins executing.

Unfortunately there are still systems out there that claim to be multi-threaded. This may be true, but when it comes down to brass tacks they are not true pre-emptive multi-tasking. These systems block processes from executing on an order of magnitude more frequently than those systems with true pre-emptive multi-tasking. It's one of the primary differences between Unix and Microsoft's Windows platforms.

5. A Blocked Process

A blocked process is a thread that is sitting in idle mode, waiting for another of its requests to complete. It can be likened to going to a gas station, finding out they are filling the gas tanks below the surface – so you have to wait maybe five minutes before you can fill up your car (when they turn the pumps back on). But, before you can get gas, these events such as turning the pumps back on must happen first. This sequencing of events causes you to wait. This is equivalent to "idle state" for the thread that was executing.

The thread sitting in idle, waiting for something else to happen or complete is called a blocked process or blocked thread. Blocked I/O simply means that the thread is waiting for a disk operation to complete which is the most common event to block threads. There are many different methods for threads or processes to become blocked, if you want to find out more about these things you can find books on multi-threaded processing which walk through all the details.

Are blocked processes bad? Not necessarily, unless there are too many processes waiting in the wings to execute. Sometimes multiple threads are waiting on each other this could be equated to deadlock situation in a database. Deadlocks cause machines to freeze up – frequently requiring cold boots. Blocked processes are a problem for the resource monitors, because the CPU utilization rates drop during processing while the CPU suspends the thread in "idle" or wait state until the blocked lock releases and continues to execute. The problem is, the actual utilization of the CPU may drop, but 100% of all available resources are taken, causing CPU load to be significantly higher than utilization rates.

The less blocking that the processes or threads do the faster the execution of the overall processing. The problem is, no matter what's done, there will always be interrupting threads with higher priorities, some of which require one or more lower priority processes to become blocked. Why is this important to VLDB? When dealing with massive sets of information, it is most optimal to have the process broken up in to smaller more manageable processes, but also to have them be able to be independently executed. When the dependencies from the separate threads have been removed they can execute in parallel and have less "blocked" action. As long as each thread is going after independent data sets on disk, again this leads to partitioning the large data set in the database. If you have four threads going after the same data, then you'll end up with dueling threads. It would be similar to having four forklifts trying to lift the same stack of lumber at the same time. It makes no sense.

6. Pipes

Pipes are conceptual term used for throughput – at least in this document. The pipes are the ability of the system to perform movement of X amount of information in Y time frame through a series of circuits or connectivity. Ok – what was that again? Basically with the lumber yard, it may be the number of stacks or total amount of lumber that a delivery truck can carry over the course of a single tank of gas. It's the transport mechanism for the information inside the system. Without proper sizing of the transport mechanism the job takes too long, costs too much, or produces too much waste or excess. In technical terms, that relates to over-utilization of available resources, under-utilization of available resources, or too tight a time frame in which to move too much information.

Just like everything else, pipes come in all shapes, sizes, and colors. Virtual pipes can have any attribute you wish to assign to it. Anyhow the throughput of these pipes is what matters most. How fast can a pre-determined amount of information travel from point a to point b? It may be a network connection, or disk connection, or disk controller, bus speed on the CPU board. It could even represent the speed of the CPU – yes it's all about speed and performance. As mentioned earlier, throughput is a critical success factor to VLDB. Especially since users are less and less willing to wait for responses from the systems they access, they need/want immediate answers from mountains of data.

The pipes come in to play, with how many pipes are available, their bandwidth (diameter & volume). These are frequently the most expensive components to "get right" in the complex world of servers and connectivity, but in most cases, they are the most beneficial to increasing throughput. Going back to the triangle of power introduced in the first series, the connectivity between the points is the pipe system.

Relational Database

A relational database (RDB) is a collective set of multiple data sets organized by tables, records and columns. RDBs establish a well-defined relationship between database tables. Tables communicate and share information, which facilitates data search-ability, organization and reporting.

RDBs use Structured Query Language (SQL), which is a standard user application that provides an easy programming interface for database interaction.

RDB is derived from the mathematical function concept of mapping data sets and was developed by Edgar F. Codd.

Most programmers deal with the nuts and bolts of saving and retrieving data files, details that can be complex and cumbersome. Although any good software developer might be able to create data-management code from scratch, reinventing the wheel isn't necessary, particularly when working with a program that is designed to work with a database. The database handles all the low-level details of data management, retrieving data efficiently and reliably. Databases also have robust, sophisticated security features, allowing appropriate levels of access for administrators, customers, and many other kinds of users.

Data Items

A relational database stores data in basic elements called fields or data items. A data item is a specific piece of information, such as a zip code, a phone number, a credit card number, or a ship date. Each item is defined in terms of the type of information stored in it, such as numbers, dates, or text. A warehouse record, for example, might include an item cost, which is a numeric data type. The distinction between types is important because the warehouse owner might want to find a total cost by adding individual costs together. A database can't add text character fields, but it can add numeric fields.

Data Tables

A data *table* is a useful grouping of data elements. A customer table, for example, consists of elements such as a customer ID, name, phone number, and address; each record in the table has data representing one customer. Most databases have several tables organized by a common purpose; for example, an engineering database might have tables for parts, drawings, materials, and suppliers.

Indexes and Keys

A database administrator can designate some of a table's fields for high-speed lookups; these fields are called *keys* or *indexes*. If a table has no indexes, the database must read every record, one after the other, to find a particular one. For larger databases with millions of records, this process can be prohibitively slow. Setting aside a customer number as an index, for example, tells the database to permit fast lookups by customer number, cutting search times to a fraction of a second.

Common Elements and Linking Tables

The "relational" part of a database is its ability to relate, or join, information from multiple tables. In most databases, some tables have one or more elements in common, such as a customer number that is found in both the customer table and an order table. Although a customer has only one record in the customer table, that customer may have dozens of records in the order table—one for each purchase. Linking tables together with common elements creates a temporary "virtual table" that contains useful combinations of information. For example, a manager wants a list of customers and the last date they bought something. The name is in the customer table, but the date is in the order table. By temporarily joining the customer and order tables, the manager can obtain both pieces of information.

Types of Databases

There are a number of database categories, from basic flat files that aren't relational to No-SQL to newer graph databases that are considered even more relational than standard relational databases.

A flat file database consists of a single table of data that has no interrelation -- typically text files. This type of file enables users to specify data attributes, such as columns and data types.

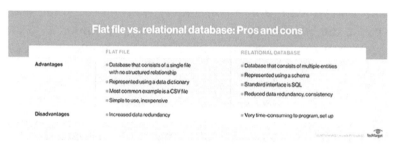

Standard relational databases enable users to manage predefined data relationships across multiple databases. Popular relational databases include Microsoft SQL Server, Oracle Database, MySQL and IBM DB2. Cloud-based relational databases, or database as a service (DBaaS), are also widely used because they enable companies to outsource database maintenance, patching and infrastructure support requirements. Cloud relational databases include Amazon Relational Database Service (RDS), Google Cloud SQL, IBM DB2 on Cloud, Microsoft Azure SQL Database and Oracle Database Cloud Service.

A No-SQL database is an alternative to relational databases that's especially useful for working with large sets of distributed data. These databases can support a variety of data models, including key-value, document, columnar and graph formats.

A graph database expands beyond traditional column- and row-based relational data models; this No-SQL database uses nodes and edges that represent connections between data relationships and can discover new relationships between the data. Graph databases are more sophisticated than relational databases, and thus, their uses include fraud detection or web recommendation engines.

Advantages of Relational Databases

The main advantages of relational databases are that they enable users to easily categorize and store data that can later be queried and filtered to extract specific information for reports. Relational databases are also easy to extend and aren't reliant on physical organization. After the original database creation, a new data category can be added without all existing applications being modified.

Other relational database advantages include:

- Accurate: Data is stored just once, which eliminates data deduplication.

- Flexible: Complex queries are easy for users to carry out.

- Collaborative: Multiple users can access the same database.

- Trusted: Relational database models are mature and well-understood.

- Secure: Data in tables within relational database management systems (RDBMSes) can be limited to allow access by only particular users.

Deductive Database

A *deductive database* is a finite collection of facts and rules. By applying the rules of a deductive database to the facts in the database, it is possible to infer additional facts, i.e. facts that are implicitly true but are not explicitly represented in the database.

When we think about the world, we usually think in terms of objects and relationships among these objects. Objects include things like people and offices and buildings. Relationships include things like the parenthood, ancestry, office assignments, office locations, and so forth.

In sentential databases, we encode each instance of a relationship in the form of a *sentence* consisting of a *relation constant* representing the relationship and some *terms* representing the objects involved in the instance.

The *vocabulary* of a database is a collection of object constants, function constants, and relation constants. Each function constant and relation constant has an associated arty, i.e. the number of objects involved in any instance of the corresponding function or relation.

A *term* is either a symbol or a functional term. A *functional term* is an expression consisting of an n-ary function constant and n terms. In what follows, we write functional terms in traditional mathematical notation - the function followed by its *arguments* enclosed in parentheses and separated by commas. For example, if f is a binary function constant and if a and b are object constants, then f(a,a) and f(a,b) and f(b,a) and f(b,b) are all functional terms. Functional terms can be nested within other functional terms. For example, if f(a,b) is a functional term, then so is f(f(a,b),b).

A *datum* is an expression formed from an n-ary relation constant and n terms. We write data in mathematical notation. For example, we might write parent(art,bob) to express the fact that Art is the parent of Bob.

A *dataset* is any set of data that can be formed from the vocabulary of a database. Intuitively, we can think of the data in a dataset as the facts that we believe to be true in the world; data that are not in the dataset are assumed to be false.

As an example of these concepts, consider a small interpersonal database. The objects in this case are people. The relationships specify properties of these people and their interrelationships.

In our example, we use the binary relation constant parent to specify that one person is a parent of another. The sentences below constitute a database describing six instances of the parent relation. The person named art is a parent of the person named bob; art is also a parent of bea, and so forth.

parent(art,bob)

parent(art,bea)

parent(bob,carl)

parent(bea,coe)

parent(carl,daisy)

parent(carl,daniel)

The adult relation is unary relation, i.e. a simple property of a person, not a relationship other people. Everyone in our database is an adult except for daisy and daniel.

adult(art)

adult(bob)

adult(bea)

adult(carl)

adult(coe)

We can express gender with two unary relation constants male and female. The following data expresses the genders of all of the people in our database. Note that, in principle, we need only one relation here, since one gender is the complement of the other. However, representing both allows us to enumerate instances of both gender equally efficiently, which can be useful in certain applications.

male(art)	female(bea)
male(bob)	female(coe)
male(cal)	female(daisy)
male(daniel)	

As an example of a ternary relation, consider the data shown below. Here, we use prefers to represent the fact that the first person likes the second person more than the third person. For example, the first sentence says that Art prefers bea to bob; the second sentence says that carl prefers daisy to daniel.

prefers(art,bea,bob)

prefers(carl,daisy,daniel)

Note that the order of arguments in such sentences is arbitrary. Given the meaning of the prefers relation in our example, the first argument denotes the subject, the second argument is the person who is preferred, and the third argument denotes the person who is less preferred. We could equally well have interpreted the arguments in other orders. The important thing is consistency - once we choose to interpret the arguments in one way, we must stick to that interpretation everywhere.

Logic Programs

The rules in a deductive database are often called a logic program. The language of logic programs includes the language of databases but provides additional expressive features.

One key difference is the inclusion of a new type of symbol, called a *variable*. Variables allow us to state relationships among objects without explicitly naming those objects. In what follows, we use individual capital letters as variables, e.g. X, Y, Z.

In the context of logic programs, a *term* is defined as an object constant, a variable, or a functional term, i.e. an expression consisting of an *n*-ary function constant and *n* simpler terms.

An *atom* in a logic program is analogous to a datum in a database except that the constituent terms may include variables.

A *literal* is either an atom or a negation of an atom (i.e. an expression stating that the atom is false). A simple atom is called a *positive* literal, The negation of an atom is called a *negative* literal. In what follows, we write negative literals using the negation sign ~. For example, if p(a,b)is an atom, then ~p(a,b) denotes the negation of this atom.

A *rule* is an expression consisting of a distinguished atom, called the *head* and a conjunction of zero or more literals, called the *body*. The literals in the body are called *sub goals*. In what follows, we write rules as in the example shown below. Here, r(X,Y) is the head, p(X,Y) & ~q(Y) is the body; and p(X,Y) and ~q(Y) are sub goals.

$$r(X,Y) :- p(X,Y) \& \sim q(Y)$$

Semantically, a rule is something like a reverse implication. It is a statement that the conclusion of the rule is true whenever the conditions are true. For example, the rule above states that r is true of any object X and any object Y *if* p is true of X and Y and q is not true of Y. For example, if we know p(a,b) and we know that q(b) is false, then, using this rule, we can conclude that r(a,b) must be true.

A *logic program* is a finite set of atoms and rules as just defined. In order to simplify our definitions and analysis, we occasionally talk about infinite sets of rules. While these sets are useful, they are not themselves logic programs.

Unfortunately, the language of rules, as defined so far, allows for logic programs with some unpleasant properties. To avoid programs of this sort, it is common in deductive databases to add a couple of restrictions that together eliminate these problems.

The first restriction is *safety*: A rule in a logic program is *safe* if and only if every variable that appears in the head or in any negative literal in the body also appears in at least one positive literal in the body. A logic program is safe if and only if every rule in the program is safe.

All of the examples above are safe. By contrast, the two rules shown below are not safe. The first rule is not safe because the variable Z appears in the head but does not appear in any positive sub goal. The second rule is not safe because the variable Z appears in a negative sub goal but not in any positive sub goal.

```
s(X,Y,Z)  :- p(X,Y)
t(X,Y) :- p(X,Y) & ~q(Y,Z)
```

To see why safety is matters in the case of the first rule, suppose we had a database in which p(a,b) is true. Then, the body of the first rule is satisfied if we let X be a and Y be b. In this case, we can conclude that every corresponding instance of the head is true. But what should we substitute for Z? Intuitively, we could put anything there; but there could be infinitely many possibilities. For example, we could write any number there. While this is conceptually okay, it is practically problematic.

To see why safety matters in the second rule, suppose we had a database with just two facts, viz. p(a,b) and q(b,c). In this case, if we let X be a and Y be b and Z be anything other than c, then both sub goals true, and we can conclude t(a,b). The main problem with this is that many people incorrectly interpret that negation as meaning there is no Z for which q(Y,Z) is true, whereas the correct reading is that q(Y,Z) needs to be false for just one binding of Z. As we will see in the examples below, there is a simple way of expressing this other meaning without writing unsafe rules.

In logic programming, these problems are avoided by requiring all rules to be safe. While this does restrict what one can say, the good news is that it is usually possible to ensure safety by adding additional sub goals to rules to ensure that the restrictions are satisfied.

The second restriction is called *stratified negation*: It is essential in order to avoid ambiguities. Unfortunately, it is a little more difficult to understand than safety.

The *dependency graph* for a logic program is a directed graph with two type of arcs, *positive* and *negative*. The nodes in the dependency graph for a program represent the relations in the program. There is a positive arc in the graph from one node to another if and only if the former node appears in a positive sub goal of a rule in which the latter node appears in the head. There is a negative arc from one node to another if and only if the former node appears in a negative sub goal of a rule in which the latter node appears in the head.

As an example, consider the following logic program. r(X,Y) is true if p(X,Y) and q(Y) are true. s(X,Y) is true if r(X,Y) is true and s(Y,X) is false.

```
r(X,Y)  :-  p(X,Y) & q(Y)
s(X,Y)  :-  r(X,Y) & ~s(Y,X)
```

The dependency graph for this program contains nodes for p, q, r, and s. Due to the first rule, there is a positive arc from p to r and a positive arc from q to r. Due to the second rule, there is a positive arc from r to s and a negative arc from s to itself.

A negation in a logic program is said to be *stratified with respect to negation* if and only if there is no negative arc in any cycle in the dependency graph. The logic program just shown is *not* stratified with respect to negation because there is a cycle involving a negative arc.

The problem with un-stratified logic programs is that there is a potential ambiguity. As an example, consider the program above and assume we had a database containing p(a,b), p(b,a), q(a), and q(b). From these facts we can conclude r(a,b) and r(b,a) are both true, So far so good. But what can we say about s? If we take s(a,b) to be true and s(b,a) to be false, then the second rule is satisfied. If we take s(a,b) to be false and s(b,a) to be true, then the second rule is again satisfied. We can also take them both to be true. The upshot is that there is ambiguity about s. By concentrating exclusively on programs that are stratified with respect to negation, we avoid such ambiguities.

It is common in logic programming to require that all logic programs be both safe and stratified with respect to negation. The restrictions are easy to satisfy in most applications; and, by obeying these restrictions, we ensure that our logic programs produce finite, unambiguous answers for all questions.

- The principle use of rules is to define new relations in terms of existing relations. The new relations defined in this way are often called *view relations* (or simply views) to distinguish them from *base relations*, which are defined by explicit enumeration of instances.

To illustrate the use of rules in defining views, consider once again the world of interpersonal relations. Starting with the base relations, we can define various interesting view relations.

As an example, consider the sentences shown below:

a) The first sentence defines the father relation in terms of parent and male.

b) The second sentence defines mother in terms of parent and female.

$$father(X,Y) :- parent(X,Y) \& male(X)$$
$$mother(X,Y) :- parent(X,Y) \& female(X)$$

The rule below defines the grandparent relation in terms of the parent relation. A person X is the grandparent of a person Z if X is the parent of a person Y and Y is the parent of Z. The variable Y here is a *thread variable* that connects the first sub goal to the second but does not itself appear in the head of the rule.

grandparent(X,Z) :- parent(X,Y) & parent(Y,Z)

Note that the same relation can appear in the head of more than one rule. For example, the person relation is true of a person Y if there is an X such that X is the parent of Y *or* if Y is the parent of some person Z. Note that in this case the conditions are disjunctive (at least one must be true), whereas the conditions in the grandfather case are conjunctive (both must be true).

person(X) :- parent(X,Y)

person(Y) :- parent(X,Y)

A person X is an ancestor of a person Z if X is the parent of Z or if there is a person Y such that X is an ancestor of and Y is an ancestor of Z. This example shows that is possible for a relation to appear in its own definition. (But recall our discussion of stratification for a restriction on this capability.):

ancestor(X,Y) :- parent(X,Y)

ancestor(X,Z) :- ancestor(X,Y) & ancestor(Y,Z)

A childless person is one who has no children. We can define the property of being childless with the rules shown below. The first rule states that a person X is childless if X is a person and it is not the case that X is a parent. The second rule says that is parent is true of X if X is the parent of some person Y.

childless(X) :- person(X) & ~isparent(X,Y)

isparent(X) :- parent(X,Y)

Note the use of the helper relation is parent here. It is tempting to write the childless rule as childless(X):- person(X) & ~parent(X,Y). However, this would be wrong. This would define X to be childless if X is a person and there is *some* Y such that X is ~parent(X,Y) is true. But we really want to say that ~parent(X,Y) holds for *all* Y. Defining isparent and using its negation in the definition of childless allows us to express this *universal quantification*.

Errors and Warnings

In our development thus far, we have assumed that the extension of an n-ary relation may be any set of n-tuples from the domain. This is rarely the case. Often, there are constraints that limit the set of possibilities. For example, a person cannot be his own parent. In some cases, constraints involve multiple relations. For example, all parents are adults; in other words, if an entity appears in the first column of the parent relation, it must also appear as an entry in the adult relation.

In many database texts, constraints are written in direct form - by writing rules that say, in effect, that if certain things are true in an extension, then other things must also be true. The *inclusion dependency* mentioned above is an example - if an entity appears in the first column of the parent relation, it must also appear as an entry in the adult relation.

In what follows, we use a slightly less direct approach - we encode limitations by writing rules that say when a database is *not* well-formed. We simply invent a new 0-ary relation, here called illegal, and define it to be true in any extension that does not satisfy our constraints.

This approach works particularly well for consistency constraints like the one stating that a person cannot be his own parent.

illegal :- parent(X,X)

It also works well for *mutual exclusion* constraints like the one below, which states that a person cannot be in both the male and the female relations.

illegal :- male(X) & female(X)

Using this technique, we can also write the *inclusion dependency* mentioned earlier. There is an error if an entity is in the first column of the parent relation and it does not occur in the adult relation.

illegal :- parent(X,Y) & ~adult(X)

Database management systems can use such constraints in a variety of ways. They can be used to optimize the processing of queries. They can also be used to check that updates do not lead to unacceptable extensions.

- Updates: In updating a database, a user specifies a sentence to add to a database or a sentences to delete. In some cases, the user can group several changes of this sort in a single, so-called, atomic transaction. If the result of executing the transaction satisfies the constraints, the update is performed; otherwise it is rejected.

Unfortunately, if a user forgets to include an addition or deletion required by the constraints, this can lead to errors. In order to simplify the update process for the user, some database systems provide the administrator the ability to write update rules, i.e. rules that are executed by the system to augment a specified transaction with the additions and deletions necessary to avoid errors. In what follows, we show one way that this can be done.

Our update language includes four special operators - pluses, minus, pos, and neg. pluss takes a sentence as argument and is true if and only if the *user* specifies that sentence as an addition in a transaction. minus takes a sentence as argument and is true if and only if the *user* specifies that sentence as an addition in a transaction. Pose takes a sentence as argument and is true if and only if the *system* concludes that the specified sentence should be added to the database. neg takes a sentence as argument and is true if and only if the *system* concludes that the specified sentence should be added to the database. Update rules are rules that define pos and neg in terms of pulses and minus and the current state of the database.

As an example of this mechanism in action, consider the rules shown below. The first dictates that the system remove a sentence of the form male(X) whenever the user adds a sentence of the form female(X). The second rule is analogous to the first with male and female reversed. Together, these two rules enforce the mutual exclusion on male and female.

$$neg(male(X)) :- pluss(female(X))$$
$$neg(female(X)) :- pluss(male(X))$$

Similarly, we can enforce the inclusion dependency on parent and adult by writing the following rule. If the user adds a sentence of the form parent(X,Y), then the system also adds a sentence of the form adult(X).

$$pos(adult(X)) :- pluss(parent(X,Y))$$

Another use of this update mechanism is to maintain materialized views. (A *materialized view* is a defined relation that is stored explicitly in the database, usually to save re computation.)

Suppose, for example, we were to materialize the father relation defined earlier. Then we could write the update rules to maintain this materialized view. According to the first rule, the system should add a sentence of the form father(X,Y) whenever the user adds parent(X,Y) and male(X) is known to be true and the user does not delete that fact. The other rules cover the other cases.

$$pos(father(X,Y)) :- pluss(parent(X,Y)) \& male(X) \& \sim minus(male(X))$$
$$pos(father(X,Y)) :- parent(X,Y) \& pluss(male(X)) \& \sim minus(parent(X,Y))$$
$$pos(father(X,Y)) :- pluss(parent(X,Y)) \& pluss(male(X))$$

$$neg(father(X,Y)) :- minus(parent(X,Y))$$
$$neg(father(X,Y)) :- minus(male(X))$$

Note that not all constraints can be enforced using update rules. For example, if a user suggests adding the sentence parent(art,art) to the database in our interpersonal relations example, there is nothing the system can do to repair this error except to reject the transaction. In some cases, there is no way to make a repair unambiguously; more information is needed from the user. For example, we might have a constraint that every person is in either the male or the female relation. If the user specifies a parent fact involving a new person but does not specify the gender of that person, there is no way for the system to decide that gender for itself.

Special Relations

In practical logic programming languages, it is common to "build in" commonly used concepts. These typically include arithmetic functions (such as +, *, `max`, `min`), string functions (such as concatenation), comparison operators (such as < and >), and equality (=). It is also common to include aggregate operators, such as `countofall`, `avgofall sumofall`, and so forth.

In many practical logic programming languages, mathematical functions are represented as relations. For example, the the binary addition operator + is often represented by the the the ternary relation constant plus. For example, the following rule defines the combined age of two people. The combined age of X and Y is S if the age of X is M and the age of Y is N and S is the result of adding M and N.

combinedage(X,Y,S) :- age(X,M) & age(Y,N) & plus(M,N,S)

Similarly, aggregate operators are typically represented as relations. For example the following rule defines the number of a person's grandchildren using the countofall relation in this way. N is the number of grandchildren of X if N is the count of all Z such that X is the grandparent of Z.

grandchildren(X,N) :- person(X) & countofall(Z,grandparent(X,Z),N)

In logic programming languages that provide such built-in concepts, there are usually syntactic restrictions on their use. For example, if a rule contains a sub goal with a comparison relation, then every variable that occurs in that sub goal must occur in at least one positive literal in the body and that occurrence must precede the sub goal with the comparison relation. If a rule mentions an arithmetic function, then any variable that occurs in all but the last position of that sub goal must occur in at least one positive literal in the body and that occurrence must precede the sub goal with the arithmetic relation.

References

- Ainmation-database, multimedialab: cs.utdallas.edu, Retrieved 12 May 2018
- A-beginners-guide-to-back-end-development: upwork.com, Retrieved 19 March 2018
- What-is-backend-testing: guru99.com, Retrieved 10 March 2018
- A-centralized-database-approach, information-technology: ukessays.com, Retrieved 30 June 2018

- Cloud-database: searchcloudapplications.techtarget.com, Retrieved 22 April 2018

- Distributed-dbms-databases, distributed-dbms: tutorialspoint.com, Retrieved 29 April 2018

- About-distributed-databases-and-distributed-data-systems, cloud-hosting: atlantic.net, Retrieved 30 May 2018

- What-is-a-key-value-database: database.guide, Retrieved 19 June 2018

- Key-value-databases, resources: basho.com, Retrieved 31 March 2018

Database Models

A database model determines the logical structure of a database and facilitates the easy storage, organization and manipulation of the data. The aim of this chapter is to explore the different kinds of database models, such as hierarchical database model, network model, associative model and entity-attribute-value model among others.

A database model shows the logical structure of a database, including the relationships and constraints that determine how data can be stored and accessed. Individual database models are designed based on the rules and concepts of whichever broader data model the designers adopt. Most data models can be represented by an accompanying database diagram.

Types

There are many kinds of data models. Some of the most common ones include:

- Hierarchical database model

- Relational model

- Network model

- Object-oriented database model

- Entity-relationship model

- Document model

- Entity-attribute-value model

- Star schema

- The object-relational model, which combines the two that make up its name.

You may choose to describe a database with any one of these depending on several factors. The biggest factor is whether the database management system you are using supports a particular model. Most database management systems are built with a particular data model in mind and require their users to adopt that model, although some do support multiple models.

In addition, different models apply to different stages of the database design process. High-level conceptual data models are best for mapping out relationships between data in ways that people perceive that data. Record-based logical models, on the other hand, more closely reflect ways that the data is stored on the server.

Selecting a data model is also a matter of aligning your priorities for the database with the strengths of a particular model, whether those priorities include speed, cost reduction, usability, or something else.

Relational Model

The most common model, the relational model sorts data into tables, also known as relations, each of which consists of columns and rows. Each column lists an attribute of the entity in question, such as price, zip code, or birth date. Together, the attributes in a relation are called a domain. A particular attribute or combination of attributes is chosen as a primary key that can be referred to in other tables, when it's called a foreign key.

Each row, also called a tuple, includes data about a specific instance of the entity in question, such as a particular employee.

The model also accounts for the types of relationships between those tables, including one-to-one, one-to-many, and many-to-many relationships. Here's an example:

Student ID	First name	Last name
52-743965	Charles	Peters
48-209689	Anthony	Sondrup
14-204968	Rebecca	Phillips

ProviderID	Provider name
156-983	UnitedHealth
146-823	Blue Shield
447-784	Carefirst Inc.

Student ID	ProviderID	Type of plan	Start date
52-743965	156-983	HSA	04/01/2016
48-209689	146-823	HMO	12/01/2015
14-204968	447-784	HSA	03/14/2016

Within the database, tables can be normalized, or brought to comply with normalization rules that make the database flexible, adaptable, and scalable. When normalized, each piece of data is atomic, or broken into the smallest useful pieces.

Relational databases are typically written in Structured Query Language (SQL).

Hierarchical Model

The hierarchical model organizes data into a tree-like structure, where each record has a single parent or root. Sibling records are sorted in a particular order. That order is used as the physical order for storing the database. This model is good for describing many real-world relationships.

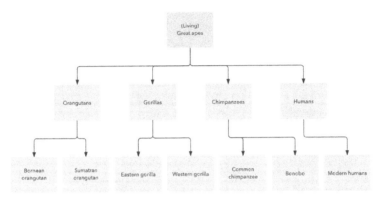

This model was primarily used by IBM's Information Management Systems in the 60s and 70s, but they are rarely seen today due to certain operational inefficiencies.

Network Model

The network model builds on the hierarchical model by allowing many-to-many relationships between linked records, implying multiple parent records. Based on mathematical set theory, the model is constructed with sets of related records. Each set consists of one owner or parent record and one or more member or child records. A record can be a member or child in multiple sets, allowing this model to convey complex relationships.

It was most popular in the 70s after it was formally defined by the Conference on Data Systems Languages (CODASYL).

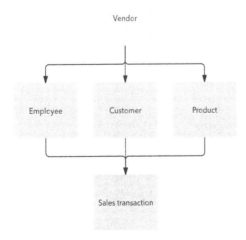

Object-oriented Database Model

This model defines a database as a collection of objects, or reusable software elements, with associated features and methods. There are several kinds of object-oriented databases:

- A multimedia database incorporates media, such as images, that could not be stored in a relational database.

- A hypertext database allows any object to link to any other object. It's useful for organizing lots of disparate data, but it's not ideal for numerical analysis.

- The object-oriented database model is the best known post-relational database model, since it incorporates tables, but isn't limited to tables. Such models are also known as hybrid database models.

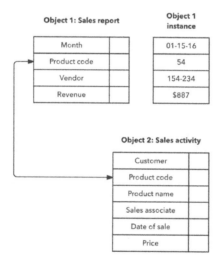

Object-relational Model

This hybrid database model combines the simplicity of the relational model with some of the advanced functionality of the object-oriented database model. In essence, it allows designers to incorporate objects into the familiar table structure.

Languages and call interfaces include SQL3, vendor languages, ODBC, JDBC, and proprietary call interfaces that are extensions of the languages and interfaces used by the relational model.

Entity-relationship Model

This model captures the relationships between real-world entities much like the network model, but it isn't as directly tied to the physical structure of the database. Instead, it's often used for designing a database conceptually.

Here, the people, places, and things about which data points are stored are referred to as entities, each of which has certain attributes that together make up their domain. The cardinality, or relationships between entities are mapped as well.

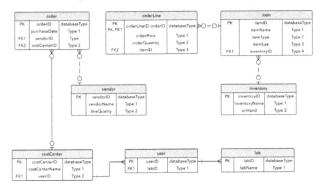

A common form of the ER diagram is the star schema, in which a central fact table connects to multiple dimensional tables.

Other Database Models

A variety of other database models have been or are still used today.

Inverted File Model

A database built with the inverted file structure is designed to facilitate fast full text searches. In this model, data content is indexed as a series of keys in a lookup table, with the values pointing to the location of the associated files. This structure can provide nearly instantaneous reporting in big data and analytics, for instance.

This model has been used by the ADABAS database management system of Software AG since 1970, and it is still supported today.

Flat Model

The flat model is the earliest, simplest data model. It simply lists all the data in a single table, consisting of columns and rows. In order to access or manipulate the data, the computer has to read the entire flat file into memory, which makes this model inefficient for all but the smallest data sets.

Multidimensional Model

This is a variation of the relational model designed to facilitate improved analytical processing. While the relational model is optimized for online transaction processing (OLTP), this model is designed for online analytical processing (OLAP).

Each cell in a dimensional database contains data about the dimensions tracked by the database. Visually, it's like a collection of cubes, rather than two-dimensional tables.

Semi Structured Model

In this model, the structural data usually contained in the database schema is embedded with the data itself. Here the distinction between data and schema is vague at best. This model is useful for describing systems, such as certain Web-based data sources, which we treat as databases but cannot constrain with a schema. It's also useful for describing interactions between databases that don't adhere to the same schema.

Context Model

This model can incorporate elements from other database models as needed. It cobbles together elements from object-oriented, semi structured, and network models.

Associative Model

This model divides all the data points based on whether they describe an entity or an association. In this model, an entity is anything that exists independently, whereas an association is something that only exists in relation to something else.

The associative model structures the data into two sets:

- A set of items, each with a unique identifier, a name and a type;

- A set of links, each with a unique identifier and the unique identifiers of a source, verb, and target. The stored fact has to do with the source, and each of the three identifiers may refer either to a link or an item.

Other, less common database models include:

- Semantic model, which includes information about how the stored data relates to the real world;

- XML database, which allows data to be specified and even stored in XML format;

- Named graph;

- Triple-store.

No-SQL Database Models

In addition to the object database model, other non-SQL models have emerged in contrast to the relational model:

- The graph database model, which is even more flexible than a network model, allowing any node to connect with any other.

- The multi value model, which breaks from the relational model by allowing attributes to contain a list of data rather than a single data point.

- The document model, which is designed for storing and managing documents or semi-structured data, rather than atomic data.

Databases on the Web

Most websites rely on some kind of database to organize and present data to users. Whenever someone uses the search functions on these sites, their search terms are converted into queries for a database server to process. Typically, middleware connects the web server with the database.

The broad presence of databases allows them to be used in almost any field, from online shopping to micro-targeting a voter segment as part of a political campaign. Various industries have developed their own norms for database design, from air transport to vehicle manufacturing.

Hierarchical Database Model

A hierarchical database consists of a collection of records that are connected to each other through links. A record is similar to a record in the network model. Each record is a collection of fields (attributes), each of which contains only one data value. A link is an association between precisely two records. Thus, a link here is similar to a link in the network model.

Consider a database that represents a customer-account relationship in a banking system. There are two record types: customer and account. It consists of three fields: customer name, customer street and customer city. Similarly, the account record consists of two fields: account number and balance.

A sample database appears in figure. It shows that customer Hayes has account A-102, customer Johnson has accounts A-101 and A-201, and customer Turner has account A-305.

Note that the set of all customer and account records is organized in the form of a rooted tree, where the root of the tree is a dummy node. As we shall see, a hierarchical database is a collection of such rooted trees, and hence forms a forest. We shall refer to each such rooted tree as a database tree.

The content of a particular record may have to be replicated in several different locations. For example, in our customer-account banking system, an account may belong to several customers. The information pertaining to that account, or the information pertaining to the various customers to which that account may belong, will have to be replicated. This replication may occur either in the same database tree or in several different trees. Record replication has two major drawbacks:

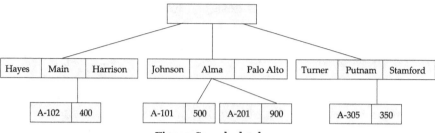

Figure: Sample database

1. Data inconsistency may result when updating takes place.

2. Waste of space is unavoidable.

Tree-structure Diagrams

A tree-structure diagram is the schema for a hierarchical database. Such a diagram consists of two basic components:

1. Boxes, which correspond to record types.

2. Lines, which correspond to links.

A tree-structure diagram serves the same purpose as an entity–relationship (E-R) diagram; namely, it specifies the overall logical structure of the database. A tree structure diagram is similar to a data-structure diagram in the network model. The main difference is that, in the latter, record types are organized in the form of an arbitrary graph, whereas in the former, record types are organized in the form of a rooted tree.

We have to be more precise about what a rooted tree is. First, there can be no cycles in the underlying graph. Second, there is a record type that is designated as the root of the tree. The relationships formed in the tree-structure diagram must be such that only one-to-many or one-to-one relationships exist between a parent and a child. The general form of a tree-structure diagram appears in Figure below Note that the arrows are pointing from children to parents. A parent may have an arrow pointing to a child, but a child must have an arrow pointing to its parent.

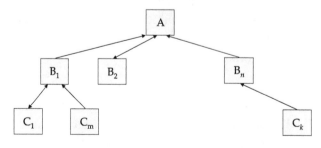

Figure: General structure of a tree-structure diagram

The database schema is represented as a collection of tree-structure diagrams. For each such diagram, there exists one single instance of a database tree. The root of this tree is a dummy node. The children of the dummy node are instances of the root record type in the tree-structure diagram. Each record instance may, in turn, have several children, which are instances of various record types, as specified in the corresponding tree-structure diagram.

Single Relationships

Consider the E-R diagram of figure (a); it consists of the two entity sets customer and account related through a binary, one-to-many relationship depositor, with no descriptive attributes. This diagram specifies that a customer can have several accounts, but an account can belong to only one customer. The corresponding tree structure diagram appears in figure below. The record type customer corresponds to the entity set customer.

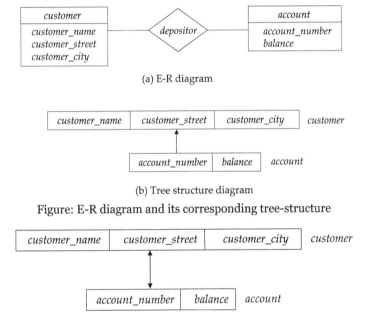

(a) E-R diagram

(b) Tree structure diagram

Figure: E-R diagram and its corresponding tree-structure

Figure: Tree-structure diagram with one-to-one relationship

It includes three fields: customer name, customer street, and customer city. Similarly, account is the record type corresponding to the entity set account. It includes two fields: account number and balance. Finally, the relationship depositor has been replaced with the link depositor, with an arrow pointing to customer record type.

An instance of a database corresponding to the described schema may thus contain a number of customer records linked to a number of account records, as in Figure below Since the relationship is one to many from customer to account, a customer can have more than one account, as does Johnson, who has both accounts A-101 and A-201. An account, however, cannot belong to more than one customer; none do in the sample database.

If the relationship depositor is one to one, then the link depositor has two arrows: one pointing to account record type, and one pointing to customer record type. A sample database corresponding to this schema appears in figure below Since the relationship is one to one, an account can be owned by precisely one customer, and a customer can have only one account, as is indeed the case in the sample database.

If the relationship depositor is many to many then the trans- formation from an E-R diagram to a tree-structure diagram is more complicated. Only one-to-many and one-to-one relationships can be directly represented in the hierarchical model.

There are many different ways to transform this E-R diagram to a tree-structure diagram. All these diagrams, however, share the property that the underlying database tree (or trees) will have replicated records.

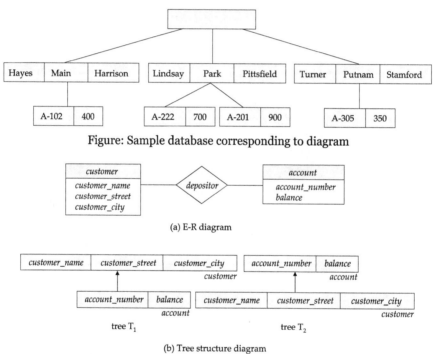

Figure: Sample database corresponding to diagram

(a) E-R diagram

(b) Tree structure diagram

Figure: E-R diagram and its corresponding tree-structure diagrams

The decision regarding which transformation should be used depends on many factors, including:

- The type of queries expected on the database;

- The degree to which the overall database schema being modeled fits the given;

- E-R diagram.

We shall present a transformation that is as general as possible. That is, all other possible transformations are a special case of this one transformation.

To transform the E-R diagram of Figure E.6a into a tree-structure diagram, we take these steps:

- Create two separate tree-structure diagrams, T1 and T2, each of which has the customer and account record types. In tree T1, customer is the root; in tree T2, account is the root.

- Create the following two links:

  - Depositor, a many-to-one link from account record type to customer record type, in T1.

  - Account customer, a many-to-one link from customer record type to account record type, in T2.

The resulting tree-structure diagrams appear in Figure above The presence of two diagrams permits customers who do not participate in the depositor relation- ship as well as accounts that do not participate in the depositor relationship and permits efficient access to account information for a given customer as well as customer information for a given account.

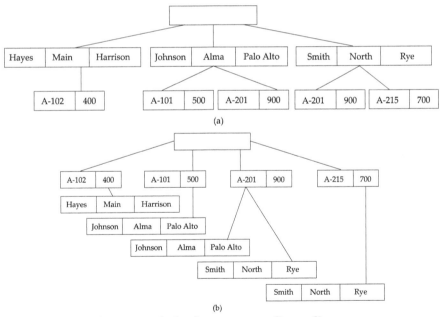

Figure: Sample database corresponding to diagram

A sample database corresponding to the tree-structure diagram of figure (b) appears in figure. There are two database trees. The first tree corresponds to the tree-structure diagram T1; the second tree corresponds to the tree-structure diagram T2. As we can see, all customer and account records are replicated in both database trees. In addition, account record A-201 appears twice in the first tree, whereas customer records Johnson and Smith appear twice in the second tree.

If a relationship also includes a descriptive attribute, the transformation from an E-R diagram to a tree-structure diagram is more complicated. A link cannot contain any data value. In this case, a new record type needs to be created, and the appropriate links need to be established. The manner in which links are formed depends on the way the relationship depositor is defined.

Consider the above E-R diagram suppose that we add the attribute access date to the relationship depositor, to denote the most recent date on which a customer accessed the account. This newly derived E-R diagram appears in figure (a). To transform this diagram into a tree-structure diagram, we must;

- Create a new record type access date with a single field.

- Create the following two links:

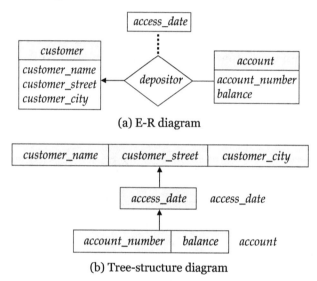

(a) E-R diagram

(b) Tree-structure diagram

Figure: E-R diagram and its corresponding tree-structure diagram

- ○ Customer date, a many-to-one link from access date record type to customer

- Record type;

- ○ Date account, a many-to-one link from account record type to access date-record type.

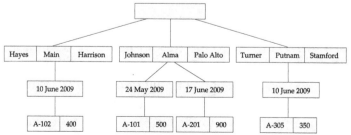

Figure: Sample database corresponding to diagram

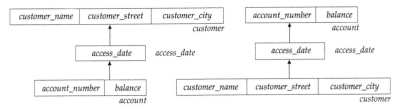

Figure: Tree-structure diagram with many-to-many relationships

The resulting tree-structure diagram is illustrated in figure (b).

An instance corresponding to the described schema appears in figure. It shows that:

- Hayes has account A-102, which was last accessed on 10 June 2009.

- Johnson has two accounts: A-101, which was last accessed on 24 May 2009, and A-201, which was last accessed on 17 June 2009.

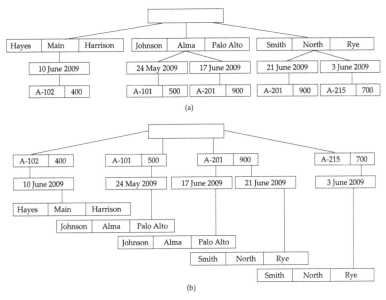

Figure: Sample database corresponding to diagram of Figure just above.

Turner has account A-305, which was last accessed on 10 June 2009.

Note that two different accounts can be accessed on the same date, as were accounts A-102 and A-305. These accounts belong to two different customers, so the access date record must be replicated to preserve the hierarchy.

If the relationship depositor were one to one with the attribute date, then the transformation algorithm would be similar to the one described. The only difference would be that the two links customer date and date account would be one-to-one links.

Assume that the relationship depositor is many to many with the attribute access date; here again, we can choose among a number of alternative transformations.

We shall use the most general transformation; it is similar to the one applied to the case where the relationship depositor has no descriptive attribute. The record type customer, account, and access date need to be replicated, and two separate tree-structure diagrams must be created, as in sample database corresponding to this schema is in Figure above.

Until now, we have considered only binary relationships. We shift our attention here to general relationships. The transformation of E-R diagrams corresponding to general relationships into tree-structure diagrams is complicated.

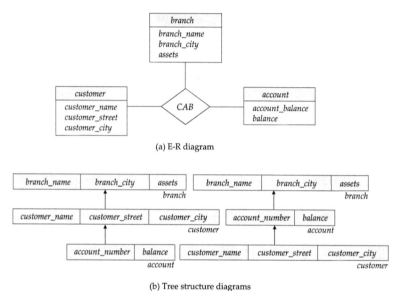

(a) E-R diagram

(b) Tree structure diagrams

Figure: E-R diagram and its corresponding tree-structure diagrams

Rather than present a general transformation algorithm, we present a single ex- ample to illustrate the overall strategy that you can apply to deal with such a transformation.

Consider the E-R diagram of Figure above, which consists of the three entity sets customer, account, and branch, related through the general relationship set CAB with no descriptive attribute.

There are many different ways to transform this E-R diagram into a tree- structure diagram. Again, all share the property that the underlying database tree (or trees) will have replicated records. The most straightforward transformation is to create two tree-structure diagrams, as shown in figure above.

An instance of the database corresponding to this schema is illustrated in figure below. It shows that Hayes has account A-102 in the Perry ridge branch; Johnson has accounts A-101 and A-201 in the Downtown and Perry ridge branches, respectively; and Smith has accounts A-201 and A-215 in the Perry ridge and Mianus branches, respectively.

We can extend the preceding transformation algorithm in a straightforward manner to deal with relationships that span more than three entity sets. We simply replicate the various record types, and generate as many tree-structure diagram as necessary.

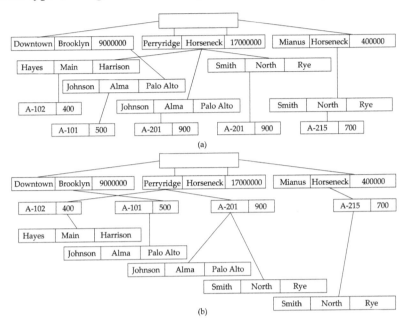

Figure: Sample database corresponding to diagram

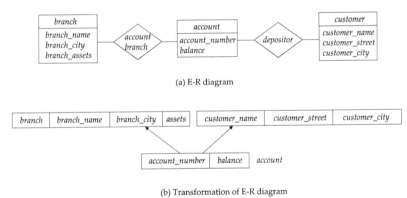

(a) E-R diagram

(b) Transformation of E-R diagram

Figure: E-R diagram and its transformation

We can extend this approach, in turn, to deal with a general relationship that has descriptive attributes. We need only to create a new record type with one field for each descriptive attribute, and then to insert that record type in the appropriate location in the tree-structure diagram.

Characteristics of a Hierarchical Data Model

Structure

The main characteristic of a hierarchical data model is the treelike structure. For example, a company database might organize using one branch for Staff, followed by Departments, Teams and then Team Members. This parent-child structure is consistent throughout the database, and each child segment can only have one parent segment. Each segment, or record, can have any number of field elements giving information on that record. For example, the team member record would have details like name, supervisor and contact details.

One-to-many and Redundancy

Because hierarchical models do not allow for composite records -- that is, for an entry to have more than one parent - the database has a one-to-many structure; one company can have many departments, and one department can have many team leaders. This can lead to redundancy in the model. For example, a branch below Team Members might be called Ongoing Projects. Since multiple staff members may work on one project, the project information must be duplicated, possibly leading to consistency issues.

Navigation

The hierarchical data model is a navigational data model; the access paths in the model are limited by predetermined structures. To obtain a specific file record, the query moves from the root segment in the database down through the branches. This is fine if you already know the location of the records you seek, but if you are making exploratory queries, this is slow, as the database must read all the records on a given level before moving to the next one.

Logical Parent Pointers

The limitations of the hierarchical structure are assuaged somewhat by using logical parent pointers. Developed by IBM in their Information Management System data model, this involves setting up a new database for entries that have many-to-many relationships and linking the two. For example, the Ongoing Projects branch would have pointers that link the user to a separate Projects database where project information is contained. This is similar to how the XML Extensible Markup Language IDREF function works.

Advantages

The model allows easy addition and deletion of new information. Data at the top of the Hierarchy is very fast to access. It was very easy to work with the model because it worked well with linear type data storage such as tapes. The model relates very well to natural hierarchies such as assembly plants and employee organization in corporations. It relates well to anything that works through a one to many relationship. For example; there is a president with many managers below them, and those managers have many employees below them, but each employee has only one manager.

Disadvantages

This model has many issues that hold it back now that we require more sophisticated relationships. It requires data to be repetitively stored in many different entities. The database can be very slow when searching for information on the lower entities. We no longer use linear data storage mediums such as tapes so that advantage is null. Searching for data requires the DBMS to run through the entire model from top to bottom until the required information is found, making queries very slow. Can only model one to many relationships, many to many relationships are not supported.

Network Model

A network model is a database model that is designed as a flexible approach to representing objects and their relationships. A unique feature of the network model is its schema, which is viewed as a graph where relationship types are arcs and object types are nodes.

The network model replaces the hierarchical tree with a graph thus allowing more general connections among the nodes. The main difference of the network model from the hierarchical model, is its ability to handle many to many (N:N) relations. In other words, it allows a record to have more than one parent. Suppose an employee works for two departments. The strict hierarchical arrangement is not possible here and the tree becomes a more generalized graph - a network. The network model was evolved to specifically handle non-hierarchical relationships. As shown below data can belong to more than one parent. Note that there are lateral connections as well as top-down connections. A network structure thus allows 1:1 (one: one), l: M (one: many), M: M (many: many) relationships among entities.

In network database terminology, a relationship is a set. Each set is made up of at least two types of records: an owner record (equivalent to parent in the hierarchical model) and a member record (similar to the child record in the hierarchical model).

The database of Customer-loan, is now represented for network model as shown in figure.

In can easily depict that now the information about the joint loan L1 appears single time, but in case of hierarchical model it appears for two times. Thus, it reduces the redundancy and is better as compared to hierarchical model.

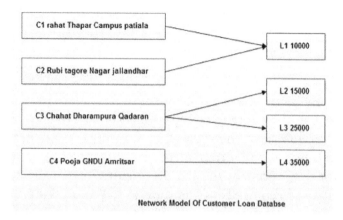

Network Model Of Customer Loan Databse

Network View of Sample Database

Considering again the sample supplier-part database, its network view is shown. In addition to the part and supplier record types, a third record type is introduced which we will call as the connector. A connector occurrence specifies the association (shipment) between one supplier and one part. It contains data (quantity of the parts supplied) describing the association between supplier and part records.

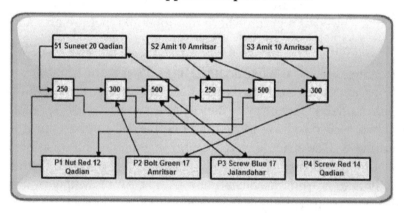

All connector occurrences for given supplier are placed on a chain .The chain starts from a supplier and finally returns to the supplier. Similarly, all connector occurrences for a given part are placed on a chain starting from the part and finally returning to the same part.

Operations on Network Model

Detailed description of all basic operations in network model is as under:

- Insert Operation: To insert a new record containing the details of a new supplier, we simply create a new record occurrence. Initially, there will be no connector. The new supplier's chain will simply consist of a single pointer starting from the supplier to itself.

For example, supplier S4 can be inserted in network model that does not supply any part as a new record occurrence with a single pointer from S4 to itself. This is not possible in case of hierarchical model. Similarly a new part can be inserted who does not supplied by any supplier.

Consider another case if supplier S1 now starts supplying P3 part with quantity 100, then a new connector containing the 100 as supplied quantity is added in to the model and the pointer of S1 and P3 are modified as shown in the below.

We can summarize that there is no insert anomalies in network model as in hierarchical model.

- Update Operation: Unlike hierarchical model, where updation was carried out by search and had many inconsistency problems, in a network model updating a record is a much easier process. We can change the city of SI from Qadian to Jalandhar without search or inconsistency problems because the city for S1 appears at just one place in the network model. Similarly, same operation is performed to change the any attribute of part.

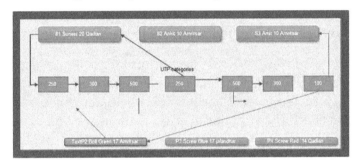

- Delete Operation: If we wish to delete the information of any part say PI, then that record occurrence can be deleted by removing the corresponding pointers and connectors, without affecting the supplier who supplies that part i.e. P1, the model is modified as shown. Similarly, same operation is performed to delete the information of supplier.

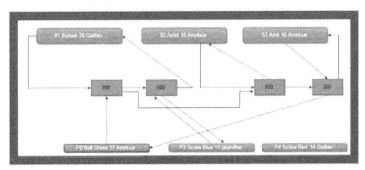

In order to delete the shipment information, the connector for that shipment and its corresponding pointers are removed without affecting supplier and part information.

For example, if supplier SI stops the supply of part PI with 250 quantity the model is modified as shown below without affecting P1 and S1 information.

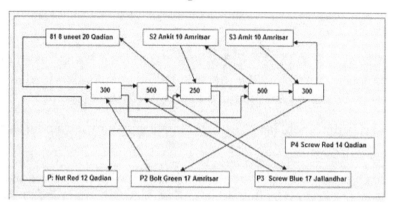

Retrieval Operation

Record retrieval methods for network model are symmetric but complex. In order to understand this considers the following example queries.

- Query 1: Find Supplier Number for Suppliers who Supply Part P2.

Solution: In order to retrieve the required information, first we search for the required part i.e. P2 we will get only one occurrence of P2 from the entire database, Then a loop is constructed to visit each connector under this part i.e. P2. Then for each connector we check the supplier over that connector and supplier number for the concerned supplier record occurrence is printed as shown in below algorithm.

Algorithm:

get [next] part where PNO=P2;

do until no more connectors under this part;

get next connector under this part;

get supplier over this connector;

print SNO;

- Query 2: Find Part Number for Parts Supplied by Supplier S2.

Solution: In order to retrieve the required information, same procedure is adopted. First we search for the required supplier i.e. S2 and we will get only one occurrence of S2 from the entire database. Then a loop is constructed to visit each connector under this supplier i.e. S2. Then for each connector we check the part over that connector and part number for the concerned part record occurrence is printed as shown in below algorithm.

Algorithm:

get [next] supplier where SNO=S2;

do until no more connectors under this supplier;

get next connector under this supplier;

get part over this connector;

print PNO;

end;

From both the above algorithms, we can conclude that retrieval algorithms are symmetric, but they are complex because they involved lot of pointers.

As explained earlier, we can conclude that network model does not suffers from the Insert anomalies, Update anomalies and Deletion anomalies, also the retrieve operation is symmetric, as compared to hierarchical model, but the main disadvantage is the complexity of the model. Since, each above operation involves the modification of pointers, which makes whole model complicated and complex.

Advantages of Network Model

The Network model retains almost all the advantages of the hierarchical model while eliminating some of its shortcomings.

The main advantages of the network model are:

- Conceptual simplicity: Just like the hierarchical model, the network model IS also conceptually simple and easy to design.

- Capability to handle more relationship types: The network model can handle the one to- many (l:N) and many to many (N:N) relationships, which is a real help in modeling the real life situations.

- Ease of data access: The data access is easier and flexible than the hierarchical model.

- Data Integrity: The network model does not allow a member to exist without an owner. Thus, a user must first define the owner record and then the member record. This ensures the data integrity.

- Data independence: The network model is better than the hierarchical model in isolating the programs from the complex physical storage details.

- Database Standards: One of the major drawbacks of the hierarchical model was the non-availability of universal standards for database design and modeling. The network model is based on the standards formulated by the DBTG and augmented by ANSI/SP ARC (American National Standards Institute/Standards Planning and Requirements Committee) in the 1970s. All the network database management systems conformed to these standards. These standards included a Data Definition Language (DDL) and the Data Manipulation Language (DML), thus greatly enhancing database administration and portability.

Disadvantages of Network Model

Even though the network database model was significantly better than the hierarchical database model, it also had many drawbacks. Some of them are:

- System complexity: All the records are maintained using pointers and hence the whole database structure becomes very complex.

- Operational Anomalies: As discussed earlier, network model's insertion, deletion and updating operations of any record require large number of pointer adjustments, which makes its implementation very complex and complicated.

- Absence of structural independence: Since the data access method in the network database model is a navigational system, making structural changes to the database is very difficult in most cases and impossible in some cases. If changes are made to the database structure then all the application programs need to be modified before they can access data. Thus, even though the network database model succeeds in achieving data independence, it still fails to achieve structural independence.

Because of the disadvantages mentioned and the implementation and administration complexities, the relational database model replaced both the hierarchical and network database models in the 1980s. The evolution of the relational database model is considered as one of the greatest events-a major breakthrough in the history of database management.

Entity–attribute–value Model

One problem many developers encounter while defining and analyzing data requirements is the situation where a number of different attributes can be used to describe an object, but only few attributes actually apply to each one. One option is to create a table with a column representing each attribute; this is suitable for objects with a fixed number of attributes, where all or most attributes have values for a most objects. However, in our case we would end up with records where majority of columns would be empty, because attributes may be unknown or inapplicable. To solve the above problem you can apply the EAV (Entity, Attribute, Value) model. This pattern is also known under several alternative names including "object-at-tribute-value" model and "open schema". In the EAV data model only non-empty values are stored in database, where each attribute-value (or key-value) pair describes one attribute of a given entity. EAV tables are often characterized as "long and skinny"; "long" refers to multiple rows describing entity, and "skinny" to the small number of columns used.

The entity-attribute-value model is useful for situations where attributes are dynamically added to or removed from an entity. It is normally composed of three tables.

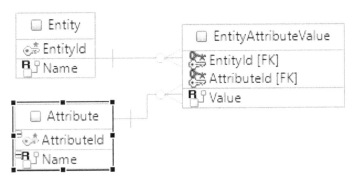

Here's an example of data in the model

EntityId	Name
1	45 Shepherd
2	Laser Pistol
3	Apoca-Fist
4	D4TH Blossom
5	Rapid-Fire SMG
6	Black Hole Launcher
7	Dubstep Gun
8	Sniper Rifle
9	Genki Manapult

EntityId	AttributeId	Value
1	2	100
1	3	300
1	4	YES
2	1	40
2	2	100
2	3	90
2	5	YES
3	2	2
3	3	2000
6	7	It really, really sucks.
7	8	A Bass Renaissance

AttributeId	Name
1	Magazine Size
2	Range
3	Power
4	Dual Wieldable
5	Is DLC
6	Fire Mode
7	Slogan
8	Song

You'll notice in this example that each entity does not have all the attributes, or the same attributes as some other entities, or even any attributes at all. These are dynamic relationships, created on the fly by users in the front-end application. This is the scenario that the Entity-attribute-value model is meant for.

In the example above the primary key of Entity Attribute Value is {Entity Id, Entity Attribute Id}, which means that each entity can have a particular attribute 0 or 1 times. This may be undesirable for your business case, for example if your entities were people they could legitimately have 0 or 1 or many phone numbers. If this is the case, you can assign a surrogate key to Entity Attribute Value.

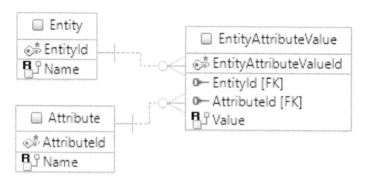

This will support a zero-to-many relationship for entities to attributes.

Because the attributes are dynamic, their value types are dynamic also. In this example Value column is set to varchar (128) so that a wide variety of values can be placed into in. Users can and will store text and numeric data in the Value column.

This can sometimes be a stumbling block if you have an application that needs to use values from the Entity Attribute Value table. There might be a "freight rate" attribute, for example, that your application needs to include in a calculation. But because it is a varchar field it could contain non-numeric data.

In this case you can create multiple value columns with different specific types. This way the attribute's value type can be specified as 'numeric', and your application will only check the appropriate value column.

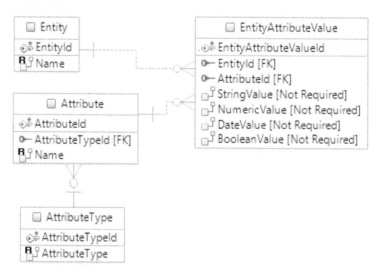

There is some criticism for this model. It can sometimes be tempting to run wild with it, thinking that this is generic enough that anything can fit, so why create a bunch of unnecessary tables. And so it sometimes becomes a one-size-fits-all model, ripe for the inner-platform effect.

EAV Databases

The term "EAV database" refers to a database design where a significant proportion of the data is modeled as EAV. However, even in a database described as "EAV-based", some tables in the system are traditional relational tables.

- EAV modeling makes sense for categories of data, such as clinical findings, where attributes are numerous and sparse. Where these conditions do not hold, standard relational modeling (i.e., one column per attribute) is preferable; using EAV does not mean abandoning common sense or principles of good relational design. In clinical record systems, the subschemas dealing with patient demographics and billing are typically modeled conventionally. (While most vendor database schemas are proprietary, VistA, the system used throughout the United States Department of Veterans Affairs (VA) medical system, known as the Veterans Health Administration (VHA), is open-source and its schema is readily inspectable, though it uses a MUMPS database engine rather than a relational database.).

- EAV database is essentially unmaintainable without numerous supporting tables that contain supporting metadata. The metadata tables, which typically outnumber the EAV tables by a factor of at least three or more, are typically standard relational tables. An example of a metadata table is the Attribute Definitions table mentioned above.

EAV versus Row Modeling

The EAV data described above is comparable to the contents of a supermarket sales receipt (which would be reflected in a Sales Line Items table in a database). The receipt lists only details of the items actually purchased, instead of listing every product in the shop that the customer might have purchased but didn't. Like the clinical findings for a given patient, the sales receipt is sparse:

- The "entity" is the sale/transaction id — a foreign key into a sales transactions table. This is used to tag each line item internally, though on the receipt the information about the Sale appears at the top (shop location, sale date/time) and at the bottom (total value of sale).

- The "attribute" is a foreign key into a products table, from where one looks up description, unit price, discounts and promotions, etc. (Products are just as volatile as clinical findings, possibly even more so: new products are introduced every month, while others are taken off the market if consumer acceptance is poor. No competent database designer would hard-code individual products such as Doritos or Diet Coke as columns in a table.).

- The "values" are the quantity purchased and total line item price.

Row modeling, where facts about something (in this case, a sales transaction) are recorded as multiple rows rather than multiple columns, is a standard data modeling technique. The differences between row modeling and EAV (which may be considered a generalization of row-modeling) are:

- A row-modeled table is homogeneous in the facts that it describes: a Line Items table describes only products sold. By contrast, an EAV table contains almost any type of fact.

- The data type of the value column/s in a row-modeled table is pre-determined by the nature of the facts it records. By contrast, in an EAV table, the conceptual data type of a value in a particular row depends on the attribute in that row. It follows that in production systems, allowing direct data entry into an EAV table would be a recipe for disaster, because the database engine itself would not be able to perform robust input validation.

In a clinical data repository, row modeling also finds numerous uses; the laboratory test subschema is typically modeled this way, because lab test results are typically numeric, or can be encoded numerically.

The circumstances where you would need to go beyond standard row-modeling to EAV are listed below:

- The data type of individual attributes varies (as seen with clinical findings).

- The categories of data are numerous, growing or fluctuating, but the number of instances (records/rows) within each category is very small. Here, with conventional modeling, the database's entity–relationship diagram might have hundreds of tables: the tables that contain thousands/ millions of rows/instances are emphasized visually to the same extent as those with very few rows. The latter are candidates for conversion to an EAV representation.

This situation arises in ontology-modeling environments, where categories ("classes") must often be created on the fly, and some classes are often eliminated in subsequent cycles of prototyping.

- Certain ("hybrid") classes have some attributes that are non-sparse (present in all or most instances), while other attributes are highly variable and sparse. The latter are suitable for EAV modeling. For example, descriptions of products made by a conglomerate corporation depend on the product category, e.g., the attributes necessary to describe a brand of light bulb are quite different from those required to describe a medical imaging device, but both have common attributes such as packaging unit and per-item cost.

Entity

In clinical data, the entity is typically a clinical event, as described above. In more general-purpose settings, the entity is a foreign key into an "objects" table that records common information about every "object" (thing) in the database – at the minimum, a preferred name and brief description, as well as the category/class of entity to which it belongs. Every record (object) in this table is assigned a machine-generated object ID.

The "objects table" approach was pioneered by Tom Slezak and colleagues at Lawrence Livermore Laboratories for the Chromosome 19 database, and is now standard in most large bioinformatics databases. The use of an objects table does not mandate the concurrent use of an EAV design: conventional tables can be used to store the category-specific details of each object.

The major benefit to a central objects table is that, by having a supporting table of object synonyms and keywords, one can provide a standard Google-like search mechanism across the entire system where the user can find information about any object of interest without having to first specify the category that it belongs to. (This is important in bioscience systems where a keyword like "acetylcholine" could refer either to the molecule itself, which is a neurotransmitter, or the biological receptor to which it binds.)

Attribute

In the EAV table itself, this is just an attribute ID, a foreign key into an Attribute Definitions table, as stated above. However, there are usually multiple metadata tables that contain attribute-related information, and these are discussed shortly.

Value

Coercing all values into strings, as in the EAV data example above, results in a simple, but non-scalable, structure: constant data type inter-conversions are required if one wants to do anything with the values, and an index on the value column of an EAV table is essentially useless. Also, it is not convenient to store large binary data, such as images, in Base64 encoded form in the same table as small integers or strings. Therefore, larger systems use separate EAV tables for each data type (including binary large objects, "BLOBS"), with the metadata for a given attribute identifying the EAV table in which its data will be stored. This approach is actually quite efficient because the modest amount of attribute metadata for a given class or form that a user chooses to work with can be cached readily in memory. However, it requires moving of data from one table to another if an attribute's data type is changed. (This does not happen often, but mistakes can be made in metadata definition just as in database schema design.).

Representing Substructure: EAV with Classes and Relationships (EAV/CR)

In a simple EAV design, the values of an attribute are simple or primitive data types as far as the database engine is concerned. However, in EAV systems used for representation of highly diverse data, it is possible that a given object (class instance) may have substructure: that is, some of its attributes may represent other kinds of objects, which in turn may have substructure, to an arbitrary level of complexity. A car, for example, has an engine, a transmission, etc., and the engine has components such as cylinders. (The permissible substructure for a given class is defined within the system's attribute metadata. Thus, for example, the attribute "random-access-memory" could apply to the class "computer" but not to the class "engine").

To represent substructure, one incorporates a special EAV table where the value column contains references to other entities in the system (i.e., foreign key values into the objects table). To get all the information on a given object requires a recursive traversal of the metadata, followed by a recursive traversal of the data that stops when every attribute retrieved is simple (atomic). Recursive traversal is necessary whether details of an individual class are represented in conventional or EAV form; such traversal is performed in standard object–relational systems, for example. In practice, the number of levels of recursion tends to be relatively modest for most classes, so the performance penalties due to recursion are modest, especially with indexing of object IDs.

EAV/CR (EAV with Classes and Relationships) refers to a framework that supports complex substructure. Its name is somewhat of a misnomer: while it was an outshoot of work on EAV systems, in practice, many or even most of the classes in such a system may be represented in standard relational form, based on whether the attributes are sparse or dense. EAV/CR is really characterized by its very detailed metadata, which is rich enough to support the automatic generation of browsing interfaces to individual classes without having to write class-by-class user-interface code. The basis of such browser interfaces is that it is possible to generate a batch of dynamic SQL queries that is independent of the class of the object, by first consulting its metadata and using metadata information to generate a sequence of queries against the data tables, and some of these queries may be arbitrarily recursive. This approach works well for object-at-a-time queries, as in Web-based browsing interfaces where clicking on the name of an object brings up all details of the object in a separate page: the metadata associated with that object's class also facilitates presentation of the object's details, because it includes captions of individual attributes, the order in which they are to be presented as well as how they are to be grouped.

One approach to EAV/CR is to allow columns to hold JSON structures, which thus provide the needed class structure. For example, PostgreSQL, as of version 9.4, offers JSON binary column (JSONB) support, allowing JSON attributes to be queried, indexed and joined.

Critical Role of Metadata in EAV Systems

In the words of Prof. Dr. Daniel Masys (formerly Chair of Vanderbilt University's Medical Informatics Department), the challenges of working with EAV stem from the fact that in an EAV database, the "physical schema" (the way data are stored) is radically different from the "logical schema" – the way users, and many software applications such as statistics packages, regard it, i.e., as conventional rows and columns for individual classes. (Because an EAV table conceptually mixes apples, oranges, grapefruit and chop suey, if you want to do any analysis of the data using standard off-the-shelf software, in most cases you have to convert subsets of it into columnar form. The process of doing this, called pivoting, is important enough to be discussed separately.)

Metadata helps perform the sleight of hand that lets users interact with the system in terms of the logical schema rather than the physical: the software continually consults the metadata for various operations such as data presentation, interactive validation, bulk data extraction and ad hoc query. The metadata can actually be used to customize the behavior of the system.

EAV systems trade off simplicity in the physical and logical structure of the data for complexity in their metadata, which, among other things, plays the role that database constraints and referential integrity do in standard database designs. Such a tradeoff is generally worthwhile, because in the typical mixed schema of production systems, the data in conventional relational tables can also benefit from functionality such as automatic interface generation. The structure of the metadata is complex enough that it comprises its own subschema within the database: various foreign keys in the data tables refer to tables within this subschema. This subschema is standard-relational, with features such as constraints and referential integrity being used to the hilt.

The correctness of the metadata contents, in terms of the intended system behavior, is critical and the task of ensuring correctness means that, when creating an EAV system, considerable design efforts must go into building user interfaces for metadata editing that can be used by people on the team who know the problem domain (e.g., clinical medicine) but are not necessarily programmers. (Historically, one of the main reasons why the pre-relational TMR system failed to be adopted at sites other than its home institution was that all metadata was stored in a single file with a non-intuitive structure. Customizing system behavior by altering the contents of this file, without causing the system to break, was such a delicate task that the system's authors only trusted themselves to do it.).

Where an EAV system is implemented through RDF, the RDF Schema language may conveniently be used to express such metadata. This Schema information may then be used by the EAV database engine to dynamically re-organize its internal table structure for best efficiency.

Some Final Caveats Regarding Metadata

- Because the business logic is in the metadata rather than explicit in the database schema (i.e., one level removed, compared with traditionally designed systems), it is less apparent to one who is unfamiliar with the system. Metadata-browsing and metadata-reporting tools are therefore important in ensuring the maintainability of an EAV system. In the common scenario where metadata is implemented as a relational sub-schema, these tools are nothing more than applications built using off-the-shelf reporting or querying tools that operate on the metadata tables.

- It is easy for an insufficiently knowledgeable user to corrupt (i.e., introduce inconsistencies and errors in) metadata. Therefore, access to metadata must be restricted, and an audit trail of accesses and changes put into place to deal with situations where multiple individuals have metadata access. Using an RDBMS for metadata will simplify the process of maintaining consistency during metadata creation and editing, by leveraging RDBMS features such as support for transactions. Also, if the metadata is part of the same database as the data itself, this ensures that it will be backed up at least as frequently as the data itself, so that it can be recovered to a point in time.

- The quality of the annotation and documentation within the metadata (i.e., the narrative/explanatory text in the descriptive columns of the metadata sub-schema) must be much higher, in order to facilitate understanding by various members of the development team. Ensuring metadata quality (and keeping it current as the system evolves) takes very high priority in the long-term management and maintenance of any design that uses an EAV component. Poorly-documented or out-of-date metadata can compromise the system's long-term viability.

Information Captured in Metadata

Attribute Metadata

- Validation metadata: include data type, range of permissible values or membership in a set of values, regular expression match, default value, and whether the value is permitted to be null. In EAV systems representing classes with substructure, the validation metadata will also record what class, if any, a given attribute belongs to.

- Presentation metadata: how the attribute is to be displayed to the user (e.g., as a text box or image of specified dimensions, a pull-down list or a set of radio buttons). When a compound object is composed of multiple attributes, as in the EAV/CR design, there is additional metadata on the order in which the attributes should be presented, and how these attributes should optionally be grouped (under descriptive headings).

- For attributes which happen to be laboratory parameters, ranges of normal values, which may vary by age, sex, physiological state and assay method, are recorded.

- Grouping metadata: Attributes are typically presented as part of a higher-order group, e.g., a specialty-specific form. Grouping metadata includes information such as the order in which attributes are presented. Certain presentation metadata, such as fonts/colors and the number of attributes displayed per row, apply to the group as a whole.

Advanced Validation Metadata

- Dependency metadata: in many user interfaces, entry of specific values into certain fields/attributes is required to either disable/hide certain other fields or enable/show other fields. (For example, if a user chooses the response "No" to a Boolean question "Does the patient have diabetes?", then subsequent questions about the duration of diabetes, medications for diabetes, etc. must be disabled.) To effect this in a generic framework involves storing of dependencies between the controlling attributes and the controlled attributes.

- Computations and complex validation: As in a spreadsheet, the value of certain attributes can be computed, and displayed, based on values entered into fields that are presented earlier in sequence. (For example, body surface area is a function of height and width). Similarly, there may be "constraints" that must be true for the data to be valid: for example, in a differential white cell count, the sum of the counts of the individual white cell types must always equal 100, because the individual counts represent percentages. Computed formulas and complex validation are generally effected by storing expressions in the metadata that are macro-substituted with the values that the user enters and can be evaluated. In Web browsers, both JavaScript and VBScript have an Eval() function that can be leveraged for this purpose.

Validation, presentation and grouping metadata make possible the creation of code frameworks that support automatic user interface generation for both data browsing as well as interactive editing. In a production system that is delivered over the Web, the task of validation of EAV data is essentially moved from the back-end/database tier (which is powerless with respect to this task) to the middle /Web server tier. While back-end validation is always ideal, because it is impossible to subvert by attempting direct data entry into a table, middle tier validation through a generic framework is quite workable, though a significant amount of software design effort must go into building the framework first. The availability of open-source frameworks that can be studied and modified for individual needs can go a long way in avoiding wheel reinvention.

Scenarios that are Appropriate for EAV Modeling

EAV modeling, under the alternative terms "generic data modeling" or "open schema", has long been a standard tool for advanced data modelers. Like any advanced technique, it can be double-edged, and should be used judiciously.

Also, the employment of EAV does not preclude the employment of traditional relational database modeling approaches within the same database schema. In EMRs that rely on an RDBMS, such as Cerner, which use an EAV approach for their clinical-data subschema, the vast majority of tables in the schema are in fact traditionally modeled, with attributes represented as individual columns rather than as rows.

The modeling of the metadata subschema of an EAV system, in fact, is a very good fit for traditional modeling, because of the inter-relationships between the various components of the metadata. In the Trial DB system, for example, the number of metadata tables in the schema outnumber the data tables by about ten to one. Because the correctness and consistency of metadata is critical to the correct operation of an EAV system, the system designer wants to take full advantages of all of the features that RDBMSs provide, such as referential integrity and programmable constraints, rather than having to reinvent the RDBMS-engine wheel. Consequently, the numerous metadata tables that support EAV designs are typically in third-normal relational form.

Commercial electronic health record Systems (EHRs) use row-modeling for classes of data such as diagnoses, surgical procedures performed on and laboratory test results, which are segregated into separate tables. In each table, the "entity" is a composite of the patient ID and the date/time the diagnosis was made (or the surgery or lab test performed); the attribute is a foreign key into a specially designated lookup table that contains a controlled vocabulary - e.g., ICD-10 for diagnoses, Current Procedural Terminology for surgical procedures, with a set of value attributes. (E.g., for laboratory-test results, one may record the value measured, whether it is in the normal, low or high range, the ID of the person responsible for performing the test, the date/time the test was performed, and so on. As stated earlier, this is not a full-fledged EAV approach because the domain of attributes for a given table is restricted, just as the domain of product IDs in a supermarket's Sales table would be restricted to the domain of Products in a Products table.

However, to capture data on parameters that are not always defined in standard vocabularies, EHRs also provide a "pure" EAV mechanism, where specially designated power-users can define new attributes, their data type, maximum and minimal permissible values (or permissible set of values/codes), and then allow others to capture data based on these attributes. In the Epic (TM) EHR, this mechanism is termed "Flow sheets", and is commonly used to capture inpatient nursing observation data.

Modeling Sparse Attributes

The typical case for using the EAV model is for highly sparse, heterogeneous attributes, such as clinical parameters in the electronic medical record (EMRs). Even here, however, it is accurate to state that the EAV modeling principle is applied to a sub-schema of the database rather than for all of its contents. (Patient demographics, for example, are most naturally modeled in one-column-per-attribute, traditional relational structure.)

Consequently, the arguments about EAV vs. "relational" design reflect incomplete understanding of the problem: An EAV design should be employed only for that sub-schema of a database where sparse attributes need to be modeled: even here, they need to be supported by third normal form metadata tables. There are relatively few database-design problems where sparse attributes are encountered: this is why the circumstances where EAV design is applicable are relatively rare. Even where they are encountered, a set of EAV tables is not the only way to address sparse data: an XML-based solution is applicable when the maximum number of attributes per entity is relatively modest, and the total volume of sparse data is also similarly modest. An example of this situation is the problems of capturing variable attributes for different product types.

Sparse attributes may also occur in E-commerce situations where an organization is purchasing or selling a vast and highly diverse set of commodities, with the details of individual categories of commodities being highly variable. The Magento E-commerce software employs an EAV approach to address this issue.

Modeling Numerous Classes with very few instances Per Class: Highly Dynamic Schemas

Another application of EAV is in modeling classes and attributes that, while not sparse, are dynamic, but where the number of data rows per class will be relatively modest – a couple of hundred rows at most, but typically a few dozen – and the system developer is also required to provide a Web-based end-user interface within a very short turn-around time. "Dynamic" means that new classes and attributes need to be continually defined and altered to represent an evolving data model. This scenario can occur in rapidly evolving scientific fields as well as in ontology development, especially during the prototyping and iterative refinement phases.

While creation of new tables and columns to represent a new category of data is not especially labor-intensive, the programming of Web-based interfaces that support browsing or basic editing with type- and range-based validation is. In such a case, a more maintainable long-term solution is to create a framework where the class and attribute definitions are stored in metadata, and the software generates a basic user interface from this metadata dynamically.

The EAV/CR framework, mentioned earlier, was created to address this very situation. Note that an EAV data model is not essential here, but the system designer may consider it an acceptable alternative to creating, say, sixty or more tables containing a total of not more than two thousand rows. Here, because the number of rows per class is so few, efficiency considerations are less important; with the standard indexing by class ID/attribute ID, DBMS optimizers can easily cache the data for a small class in memory when running a query involving that class or attribute.

In the dynamic-attribute scenario, it is worth noting that Resource Description

Framework (RDF) is being employed as the underpinning of Semantic-Web-related ontology work. RDF, intended to be a general method of representing information, is a form of EAV: an RDF triple comprises an object, a property, and a value.

At the end of Jon Bentley's book "Writing Efficient Programs", the author warns that making code more efficient generally also makes it harder to understand and maintain, and so one does not rush in and tweak code unless one has first determined that there is a performance problem, and measures such as code profiling have pinpointed the exact location of the bottleneck. Once you have done so, you modify only the specific code that needs to run faster. Similar considerations apply to EAV modeling: you apply it only to the sub-system where traditional relational modeling is known a priori to be unwieldy (as in the clinical data domain), or is discovered, during system evolution, to pose significant maintenance challenges. Database Guru (and currently a vice-president of Core Technologies at Oracle Corporation) Tom Kyte, for example, correctly points out drawbacks of employing EAV in traditional business scenarios, and makes the point that mere "flexibility" is not a sufficient criterion for employing EAV. (However, he makes the sweeping claim that EAV should be avoided in all circumstances, even though Oracle's Health Sciences division itself employs EAV to model clinical-data attributes in its commercial systems ClinTrial and Oracle Clinical.).

Working with EAV Data

The Achilles heel of EAV is the difficulty of working with large volumes of EAV data. It is often necessary to transiently or permanently inter-convert between columnar and row-or EAV-modeled representations of the same data; this can be both error-prone if done manually as well as CPU-intensive. Generic frameworks that utilize attribute and attribute-grouping metadata address the former but not the latter limitation; their use is more or less mandated in the case of mixed schemas that contain a mixture of conventional-relational and EAV data, where the error quotient can be very significant.

The conversion operation is called pivoting. Pivoting is not required only for EAV data but also for any form or row-modeled data. (For example, implementations of the Apriori algorithm for Association Analysis, widely used to process supermarket sales data to identify other products that purchasers of a given product are also likely to buy, pivot row-modeled data as a first step.) Many database engines have proprietary SQL extensions to facilitate pivoting, and packages such as Microsoft Excel also support it. The circumstances where pivoting is necessary are considered below:

- Browsing: of modest amounts of data for an individual entity, optionally followed by data editing based on inter-attribute dependencies. This operation is facilitated by caching the modest amounts of the requisite supporting metadata.

Some programs, such as Trial DB, access the metadata to generate semi-static Web pages that contain embedded programming code as well as data structures holding metadata.

- Bulk extraction: transforms large (but predictable) amounts of data (e.g., a clinical study's complete data) into a set of relational tables. While CPU-intensive, this task is infrequent and does not need to be done in real-time; i.e., the user can wait for a batched process to complete. The importance of bulk extraction cannot be overestimated, especially when the data is to be processed or analyzed with standard third-party tools that are completely unaware of EAV structure. Here, it is not advisable to try to reinvent entire sets of wheels through a generic framework, and it is best just to bulk-extract EAV data into relational tables and then work with it using standard tools.

- Ad hoc query: interfaces to row- or EAV-modeled data, when queried from the perspective of individual attributes, (e.g., "retrieve all patients with the presence of liver disease, with signs of liver failure and no history of alcohol abuse") must typically show the results of the query with individual attributes as separate columns. For most EAV database scenarios ad hoc query performance must be tolerable, but sub-second responses are not necessary, since the queries tend to be exploratory in nature.

Relational Division

However, the structure of EAV data model is a perfect candidate for Relational Division. With a good indexing strategy it's possible to get a response time in less than a few hundred milliseconds on a billion row EAV table. Microsoft SQL Server MVP Peter Larsson has proved this on a laptop and made the solution general available.

Optimizing Pivoting Performance

- One possible optimization is the use of a separate "warehouse" or query able schema whose contents are refreshed in batch mode from the production (transaction) schema. The tables in the warehouse are heavily indexed and optimized using de normalization, which combines multiple tables into one to minimize performance penalty due to table joins. This is the approach that Kalido uses to convert highly normalized EAV tables to standard reporting schemas.

- Certain EAV data in a warehouse may be converted into standard tables using "materialized views", but this is generally a last resort that must be used carefully, because the number of views of this kind tends to grow non-linearly with the number of attributes in a system.

- In-memory data structures one can use hash tables and two-dimensional arrays in memory in conjunction with attribute-grouping metadata to pivot data, one group at a time. This data is written to disk as a flat delimited file, with the internal names for each attribute in the first row: this format can be readily bulk-imported into a relational table. This "in-memory" technique significantly outperforms alternative approaches by keeping the queries on EAV tables as simple as possible and minimizing the number of I/O operations. Each statement retrieves a large amount of data, and the hash tables help carry out the pivoting operation, which involves placing a value for a given attribute instance into the appropriate row and column. Random Access Memory (RAM) is sufficiently abundant and affordable in modern hardware that the complete data set for a single attribute group in even large data sets will usually fit completely into memory, though the algorithm can be made smarter by working on slices of the data if this turns out not to be the case.

Obviously, no matter what approaches you take, querying EAV will not be as fast as querying standard column-modeled relational data for certain types of query, in much the same way that access of elements in sparse matrices are not as fast as those on non-sparse matrices if the latter fit entirely into main memory. (Sparse matrices, represented using structures such as linked lists, require list traversal to access an element at a given X-Y position, while access to elements in matrices represented as 2-D arrays can be performed using fast CPU register operations.) If, however, you chose the EAV approach correctly for the problem that you were trying to solve, this is the price that you pay; in this respect, EAV modeling is an example of a space (and schema maintenance) versus CPU-time tradeoff.

EAV vs. the Universal Data Model

Originally postulated by Maier, Ullman and Vardi, the "Universal Data Model" (UDM) seeks to simplify the query of a complex relational schema by naive users, by creating the illusion that everything is stored in a single giant "universal table". It does this by utilizing inter-table relationships, so that the user does not need to be concerned about what table contains what attribute. C.J. Date, however, pointed out that in circumstances where a table is multiply related to another (as in genealogy databases, where an individual's father and mother are also individuals, or in some business databases where all addresses are stored centrally, and an organization can have different office addresses and shipping addresses), there is insufficient metadata within the database schema to specify unambiguous joins. When UDM has been commercialized, as in SAP Business Objects, this limitation is worked around through the creation of "Universes", which are relational views with pre-defined joins between sets of tables: the "Universe" developer disambiguates ambiguous joins by including the multiply-related table in a view multiple times using different aliases.

Apart from the way in which data is explicitly modeled (UDM simply uses relational views to intercede between the user and the database schema), EAV differs from Universal Data Models in that it also applies to transactional systems, not only query oriented (read-only) systems as in UDM. Also, when used as the basis for clinical-data query systems, EAV implementations do not necessarily shield the user from having to specify the class of an object of interest. In the EAV-based i2b2 clinical data mart, for example, when the user searches for a term, she has the option of specifying the category of data that the user is interested in. For example, the phrase "lithium" can refer either to the medication (which is used to treat bipolar disorder), or a laboratory assay for lithium level in the patient's blood. (The blood level of lithium must be monitored carefully: too much of the drug causes severe side effects, while too little is ineffective).

Graph Databases

An alternative approach to managing the various problems encountered with EAV-structured data is to employ a graph database. These represent entities as the nodes of a graph or hyper graph, and attributes as links or edges of that graph. The issue of table joins are addressed by providing graph-specific query languages, such as Apache Tinker Pop, or the Open Cog atom space pattern matcher.

EAV and Cloud Computing

Many cloud computing vendors offer data stores based on the EAV model, where an arbitrary number of attributes can be associated with a given entity. Roger Jennings provides an in-depth comparison of these. In Amazon's offering, Simple DB, the data type is limited to strings, and data that is intrinsically non-string must be coerced to string (e.g., numbers must be padded with leading zeros) if you wish to perform operations such as sorting. Microsoft's offering, Windows Azure Table Storage, offers a limited set of data types: byte, bool, Date, time, double, Guid, int, long and string. The Google App Engine offers the greatest variety of data types: in addition to dividing numeric data into int, long, float. it also defines custom data types such as phone number, E-mail address, geocode and hyperlink. Google, but not Amazon or Microsoft, lets you define metadata that would prevent invalid attributes from being associated with a particular class of entity, by letting you create a metadata model.

Google lets you operate on the data using a subset of SQL; Microsoft offer a URL-based querying syntax that is abstracted via a LINQ provider; Amazon offer a more limited syntax. Of concern, built-in support for combining different entities through joins is currently (April 10) non-existent with all three engines. Such operations have to be performed by application code. This may not be a concern if the application servers are co-located with the data servers at the vendor's data center, but a lot of network traffic would be generated if the two were geographically separated.

An EAV approach is justified only when the attributes that are being modeled are numerous and sparse: if the data being captured does not meet this requirement, the cloud vendors' default EAV approach is often a mismatch for applications that require a true back-end database (as opposed to merely a means of persistent data storage). Retrofitting the vast majority of existing database applications, which use a traditional data-modeling approach, to an EAV-type cloud architecture, would require major surgery. Microsoft discovered, for example, that its database-application-developer base was largely reluctant to invest such effort. More recently, therefore, Microsoft has provided a premium offering – a cloud-accessible full-fledged relational engine, SQL Server Azure, which allows porting of existing database applications with modest changes.

One limitation of SQL Azure is that physical databases are limited to 500GB in size as of January 2015. Microsoft recommends that data sets larger than this be split into multiple physical databases and accessed with parallel queries.

Tree Structures and Relational Databases

There exist several other approaches for the representation of tree-structured data, be it XML, JSON or other formats, such as the nested set model, in a relational database. On the other hand, database vendors have begun to include JSON and XML support into their data structures and query features, like in IBM DB2, where XML data is stored as XML separate from the tables, using X-path queries as part of SQL statements, or in PostgreSQL, with a JSON data type that can be indexed and queried. These developments accomplish, improve or substitute the EAV model approach.

It should be noted, however, that the uses of JSON and XML are not necessarily the same as the use of an EAV model, though they can overlap. XML is preferable to EAV for arbitrarily hierarchical data that is relatively modest in volume for a single entity: it is not intended to scale up to the multi-gigabyte level with respect to data-manipulation performance. XML is not concerned per-se with the sparse-attribute problem, and when the data model underlying the information to be represented can be decomposed straightforwardly into a relational structure, XML is better suited as a means of data interchange than as a primary storage mechanism. EAV, as stated earlier, is specifically (and only) applicable to the sparse-attribute scenario. When such a scenario holds, the use of data type-specific attribute-value tables than can be indexed by entity, by attribute, and by value and manipulated through simple SQL statements is vastly more scalable than the use of an XML tree structure. The Google App Engine, mentioned above, uses strongly-typed-value tables for a good reason.

Associative Model

The associative data model is a model for databases. Unlike the relational model, which is record based and deals with entities and attributes, this model works with entities that have a discreet independent existence, and their relationships are modeled as associations.

The associative model was bases on a subject-verb-object syntax with bold parallels in sentences built from English and other languages. Some examples of phrases that are suitable for the Associative model could include:

- Cyan **is** a color;

- Marc **is** a musician;

- Musicians **play** instruments;

- Swings **are in** a park;

- A park **is in** a city (the bold text indicates the verbs).

By studying the example above it is easy to see that the verb is actually a way of association. The association's sole purpose is to identify the relationship between the subject and the object.

The associative database had two structures, there are a set of items and a set of links that are used to connected them together. With the item structure the entries must contain a unique indication, a type, and a name. Entries in the links structure must also have a unique indicator along with indicators for the related source, subject, object, and verb.

Associative Data Model is Different

The associative model structure is efficient with the storage room fore there is no need to put aside existing space for the data that is not yet available. This differs from the relational model structure. With the relational model the minimum of a single null byte is stored for missing data in any given row. Also some relational databases set aside the maximum room for a specified column in each row.

The associative database creates storage of custom data for each user, or other needs clear cut and economical when considering maintenance or network resources. When different data needs to be stored the Associative model is able to manage the task more effectively then the relational model.

With the associative model there are entities and associations. The entity is identified as discrete and has an independent existence, where-as the association depends on other things. Let's try to simplify this a little before moving on.

Let's say the entity is an organization, the associations would be the customer and the employees. It is possible for the entity to have many business roles at the same time, each role would be recorded as an association. When the circumstances change, one or more of the associations may no longer apply, but the entity will continue to endure.

The associative model is designed to store metadata in the same structures where the data itself is stored. This metadata describes the structure of the database and the how different kinds of data can interconnect. Simple data structures need more to transport a database competent of storing the varying of data that a modernized business requires along with the protection and managements that is important for internet implementation.

The associative model is built from chapters and the user's view the content of the database is controlled by their profile. The profile is a list of chapters. When some links between items in the chapters inside as well as outside of a specific profile exist, those links will not be visible to the user.

There is a combination of chapters and profiled that can simplify the making of the database to specific users or ever subject groups. The data that is related to one of the user groups would remain unseen to another, and would be replaced by a different data set.

Disadvantages of Associative Data Model

With the associative model there is not record. When assembling all of the current information on a complex order the data storage needs to be re-visited multiple times. This could pose as a disadvantage. Some calculations seem to suggest that Associative database would need as many as four times the data reads as the relational database.

All of the changes and deletions to the associative model are directly affected by adding links to the database. However we must not that a deleted association is not actually deleted itself. Rather it is linked to an assertion that has been deleted. Also when an entity is re-named it is not actually re-named but rather linked to its new name.

In order to reduce the complexity that is a direct result from the parameterization required by heftier software packages we can rely on the chapters, profiles and the continuation of database engines that expect data stored to be different between the individual entities or associations. To set or hold back program functions in a database the use of "Flags" has begun to be practiced.

The packages that are based on an associative model would use the structure of the database along with the metadata to control this process. This can ultimately lead to the generalization of what are often lengthy and costly implementation processes.

A generalization such as this would produce considerable cost reductions for users purchasing or implementing bigger software packages, this could reduce risks related with the changes of post implementation as well.

Associative Model does Suit the Demands of Data

Some ask if there is still an ongoing demand for a better database. Honestly, there will always be that demand. The weaker points of the current relational model are now apparent, due to the character of the data we still need to store changing. Binary structures that are supportive to multimedia have posed real challenged for relational databases in the same way that the object-oriented programming methods did.

When we look back on the object databases we can see that they have no conquered the market, and have their cousins the hybrid relational products with their object extensions. So will the Associative model solve some of the issues surrounding the relational model? The answer is not entirely clear, though it may resolve some issues it is not completely clear how efficiently the model will manage when set against the bigger binary blocks of data.

The security of data is crucial, as is the speed of transaction. User interfaces and database management facilities should but up to pace. When a database is designed to aid in the use of internet applications it should allow backups without needing to take the data off-line as well.

Programming interfaces need to be hearty and readily available to a range of development languages, the Associative database will need to show that it is good practice to store data using the subject-verb-object method in every case as well. There will always be questions about maintaining performance as the database grows, this should be expected.

In conclusion, areas of the associative database design do seem simpler then the relational models, still as we have pointed out there are also areas that call for careful attention. There are issues related to the creation of chapters that remain daunting at best.

Even so, if the concept of the associative model proves itself to be a genuinely feasible and is able to bring out a new and efficient database, then others could bring to life products that are built upon the base ideas that exist with this model.

There is definitely an undeniable demand for a faster operating database model that will scale up to bigger servers and down to the smaller devices.

References

- Nadkarni, Prakash (2011), Metadata-driven Software Systems in Biomedicine, Springer, ISBN 978-0-85729-509-5

- Characteristics-of-a-hierarchical-data-model: techwalla.com, Retrieved 11 May 2018

- The-entity-attribute-value-model: sqlspellbook.com, Retrieved 11 June 2018

- c Dinu, Valentin; Nadkarni, Prakash; Brandt, Cynthia (2006), "Pivoting approaches for bulk extraction of Entity–Attribute–Value data", Computer Methods and Programs in Biomedicine, 82 (1): 38–43, doi:10.1016/j.cmpb.2006.02.001, PMID 16556470

- Network-model-databases-30613: techopedia.com, Retrieved 31 March 2018

- The-associative-model, data-modeling: learn.geekinterview.com, Retrieved 25 May 2018

- Dinu, Valentin; Nadkarni, Prakash (2007), "Guidelines for the effective use of entity-attribute-value modeling for biomedical databases", International journal of medical informatics, 76 (11–12): 769–79, doi:10.1016/j.ijmedinf.2006.09.023, PMC 2110957, PMID 17098467

- Network-model, what-is-a-database, fundamental: ecomputernotes.com, Retrieved 17 April 2018

Fundamental Concepts of Database Designing

A database design facilitates the organization of data according to a database model. This chapter aims to provide a comprehensive understanding of the fundamental principles of database designing and presents a detailed discussion on topics such as Atomicity, Consistency, Isolation, Durability (ACID), Armstrong's axioms, database keys, etc.

ACID

Atomicity Consistency Isolation Durability (ACID) is a concept referring to a database system's four transaction properties: atomicity, consistency, isolation and durability.

Atomicity

By this, we mean that either the entire transaction takes place at once or doesn't happen at all. There is no midway i.e. transactions do not occur partially. Each transaction is considered as one unit and either runs to completion or is not executed at all. It involves following two operations:

- Abort: If a transaction aborts, changes made to database are not visible.

- Commit: If a transaction commits, changes made are visible. Atomicity is also known as the 'All or nothing rule'. Consider the following transaction T consisting of T1 and T2: Transfer of 100 from account X to account Y.

Before: X : 500	**Y: 200**
Transaction T	
T1	T2
Read (X)	Read (Y)
X: = X – 100	Y: = Y + 100
Write (X)	Write (Y)
After: X : 400	**Y : 300**

If the transaction fails after completion of T1 but before completion of T2 (say, after write (X) but before write (Y)), then amount has been deducted from X but not added to Y. This results in an inconsistent database state. Therefore, the transaction must be executed in entirety in order to ensure correctness of database state.

Consistency

This means that integrity constraints must be maintained so that the database is consistent before and after the transaction. It refers to correctness of a database. Referring to the example above,

The total amount before and after the transaction must be maintained.

Total before T occurs = 500 + 200 = 700.

Total after T occurs = 400 + 300 = 700.

Therefore, database is consistent. Inconsistency occurs in case T1 completes but T2 fails. As a result T is incomplete.

Isolation

This property ensures that multiple transactions can occur concurrently without leading to inconsistency of database state. Transactions occur independently without interference. Changes occurring in a particular transaction will not be visible to any other transaction until that particular change in that transaction is written to memory or has been committed. This property ensures that the execution of transactions concurrently will result in a state that is equivalent to a state achieved these were executed serially in some order. Let X= 500, Y = 500.

Consider two transactions T and T".

T	T"
Read (X)	Read (X)
X: = X*100	Read (Y)
Write (X)	Z: = X + Y
Read (Y)	Write (Z)
Y: = Y – 50	
Write	

Suppose T has been executed till Read (Y) and then T" starts. As a result , interleaving of operations takes place due to which T" reads correct value of X but incorrect value of Y and sum computed by:

T": (X+Y = 50, 000+500=50, 500).

Is thus not consistent with the sum at end of transaction:

T: (X+Y = 50, 000 + 450 = 50, 450).

This results in database inconsistency, due to a loss of 50 units. Hence, transactions must take place in isolation and changes should be visible only after a they have been made to the main memory.

Durability

This property ensures that once the transaction has completed execution, the updates and modifications to the database are stored in and written to disk and they persist even is system failure occurs. These updates now become permanent and are stored in a non-volatile memory. The effects of the transaction, thus, are never lost.

The ACID properties, in totality, provide a mechanism to ensure correctness and consistency of a database in a way such that each transaction is a group of operations that acts a single unit, produces consistent results, acts in isolation from other operations and updates that it makes are durably stored.

Armstrong's Axioms

A *functional dependency* (FD) is a relationship between two attributes, typically between the PK and other non-key attributes within a table. For any relation R, attribute Y is functionally dependent on attribute X (usually the PK), if for every valid instance of X, that value of X uniquely determines the value of Y. This relationship is indicated by the representation below:

$$X ----> Y$$

The left side of the above FD diagram is called the *determinant*, and the right side is the *dependent*. Here are a few examples.

In the first example, below, SIN determines Name, Address and Birthdate. Given SIN, we can determine any of the other attributes within the table.

$$SIN ----> Name, Address, Birthdate$$

For the second example, SIN and Course determine the date completed (Date Completed). This must also work for a composite PK.

$$SIN, Course ----> DateCompleted$$

The third example indicates that ISBN determines Title.

$$ISBN ----> Title$$

Rules of Functional Dependencies

Consider the following table of data r(R) of the relation schema R(ABCDE) shown in table below.

A	B	C	D	E
a1	b1	c1	d1	e1
a2	b1	C2	d2	e1
a3	b2	C1	d1	e1
a4	b2	C2	d2	e1
a5	b3	C3	d1	e1

Table R

Table: Functional dependency example

As you look at this table, ask yourself: *What kind of dependencies can we observe among the attributes in Table R?* Since the values of A are unique (a1, a2, a3, etc.), it follows from the FD definition that:

$$A \rightarrow B, \quad A \rightarrow C, \quad A \rightarrow D, \quad A \rightarrow E$$

- It also follows that $A \rightarrow BC$ (or any other subset of ABCDE).

- This can be summarized as $A \rightarrow BCDE$.

- From our understanding of primary keys, A is a primary key.

Since the values of E are always the same (all e1), it follows that:

$$A \rightarrow E, \quad B \rightarrow E, \quad C \rightarrow E, \quad D \rightarrow E$$

However, we cannot generally summarize the above with $ABCD \rightarrow E$ because, in general, $A \rightarrow E$, $B \rightarrow E$, $AB \rightarrow E$.

Other observations:

1. Combinations of BC are unique, therefore $BC \rightarrow ADE$.

2. Combinations of BD are unique, therefore $BD \rightarrow ACE$.

3. If C values match, so do D values.

    a. Therefore, $C \rightarrow D$

    b. However, D values don't determine C values

    c. So C does not determine D, and D does not determine C.

Looking at actual data can help clarify which attributes are dependent and which are determinants.

Inference Rules

Armstrong's axioms are a set of inference rules used to infer all the functional dependencies on a relational database. They were developed by William W. Armstrong. The following describes what will be used, in terms of notation, to explain these axioms.

Let R(U) be a relation scheme over the set of attributes U. We will use the letters X, Y, Z to represent any subset of and, for short, the union of two sets of attributes, instead of the usual X U Y.

Axiom of Reflexivity

This axiom says, if Y is a subset of X, then X determines Y:

$$\text{If } Y \subseteq X, \text{ then } X \to Y$$

Figure above Equation for axiom of reflexivity.

For example, PartNo —> NT123

Where, X (PartNo) is composed of more than one piece of information; i.e., Y (NT) and partID.

Axiom of Augmentation

The axiom of augmentation, also known as a partial dependency, says if X determines Y, then XZ determines YZ for any Z.

$$\text{If } X \to Y, \text{ then } XZ \to Y\,Z \text{ for any } Z$$

The axiom of augmentation says that every non-key attribute must be fully dependent on the PK. In the example shown below, StudentName, Address, City, Prov, and PC (postal code) are only dependent on the StudentNo, not on the StudentNo and Grade.

StudentNo, Course —> StudentName, Address, City, Prov, PC, Grade, DateCompleted

This situation is not desirable because every non-key attribute has to be fully dependent on the PK. In this situation, student information is only partially dependent on the PK (StudentNo).

To fix this problem, we need to break the original table down into two as follows:

- Table above: Student No, Course, Grade, Date Completed;
- Table above: Student No, Student Name, Address, City, Prov, PC.

Axiom of Transitivity

The axiom of transitivity says if X determines Y, and Y determines Z, then X must also determine Z.

$$\text{If } X \rightarrow Y \text{ and } Y \rightarrow Z, \text{then } X \rightarrow Z$$

The table below has information not directly related to the student; for instance, ProgramID and ProgramName should have a table of its own. ProgramName is not dependent on StudentNo; it's dependent on ProgramID.

StudentNo —> StudentName, Address, City, Prov, PC, ProgramID, ProgramName

This situation is not desirable because a non-key attribute (ProgramName) depends on another non-key attribute (ProgramID).

To fix this problem, we need to break this table into two: one to hold information about the student and the other to hold information about the program.

- Table above: StudentNo —> StudentName, Address, City, Prov, PC, ProgramID;

- Table above: ProgramID —> ProgramName.

However we still need to leave an FK in the student table so that we can identify which program the student is enrolled in.

Union

This rule suggests that if two tables are separate, and the PK is the same, you may want to consider putting them together. It states that if X determines Y and X determines Z then X must also determine Y and Z.

$$\text{If } X \rightarrow Y \text{ and } X \rightarrow Z \text{ then } X \rightarrow YZ$$

For example, if:

- SIN —> EmpName

- SIN —> SpouseName

You may want to join these two tables into one as follows:

$$\text{SIN} \rightarrow \text{EmpName, SpouseName}$$

Some database administrators (*DBA*) might choose to keep these tables separated for a couple of reasons. One, each table describes a different entity so the entities should be kept apart. Two, if SpouseName is to be left NULL most of the time, there is no need to include it in the same table as EmpName.

Decomposition

Decomposition is the reverse of the Union rule. If you have a table that appears to contain two entities that are determined by the same PK, consider breaking them up into two tables. This rule states that if X determines Y and Z, then X determines Y and X determines Z separately.

$$\text{If } X \rightarrow Y\,Z \text{ then } X \rightarrow Y \text{ and } X \rightarrow Z$$

Dependency Diagram

A dependency diagram, shown figure below, illustrates the various dependencies that might exist in a *non-normalized table*. A non-normalized table is one that has data redundancy in it.

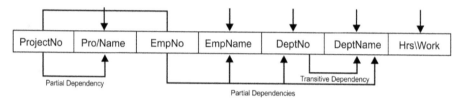

Figure: Dependency diagram

The following dependencies are identified in this table:

- ProjectNo and EmpNo, combined, are the PK.
- Partial Dependencies:
    - ProjectNo —> ProjName
    - EmpNo —> EmpName, DeptNo,
    - ProjectNo, EmpNo —> HrsWork
- Transitive Dependency:
    - DeptNo —> DeptName

Create, Read, Update and Delete

Within computer programming, the acronym CRUD stands for create, read, update and delete. These are the four basic functions of persistent storage. Also, each letter in the acronym can refer to all functions executed in relational database applications and mapped to a standard HTTP method, SQL statement or DDS operation.

It can also describe user-interface conventions that allow viewing, searching and modifying information through computer-based forms and reports. In essence, entities are read, created, updated and deleted. Those same entities can be modified by taking the data from a service and changing the setting properties before sending the data back to the service for an update. Plus, CRUD is data-oriented and the standardized use of HTTP action verbs.

Standard CRUD Operations

This table lists the standard create, read, update, and delete (CRUD) operations for a business object service.

Operation	Method Name	Description
create Operation	createServiceDataObjectName	Creates a service data object and its descendants.
delete Operation	deleteServiceDataObjectName	Deletes a business object.
get Operation	getServiceDataObjectName	Retrieves a single business object by the primary key.
find Operation	findServiceDataObjectName	Finds and returns a list of business objects that meet the specified search criteria.
find by additional predefined search criteria Operation	findServiceDataObjectNameSearchCriteriaName	Finds and returns a list of business objects that meet the specified search criteria and the additional predefined search criteria.
update Operation	updateServiceDataObjectName	Updates a business object.
merge Operation	mergeServiceDataObjectName	Updates a business object, if it exists. Otherwise creates a new business object.
process Operation	processServiceDataObjectName	Performs create, update, delete, or merge operation on a list of business objects. The specified operation is applied to all the objects in a given list.
process change summary Operation	processCSServiceDataObjectName	Performs create, update, or delete operations on a list of business objects. Allows you to specify different operations for different objects.

Most applications have some form of CRUD functionality. In fact, every programmer has had to deal with CRUD at some point. Not to mention, a CRUD application is one that utilizes forms to retrieve and return data from a database.

The first reference to CRUD operations came from Haim Kilov in 1990 in an article titled, "From semantic to object-oriented data modeling." However, the term was first made popular by James Martin's 1983 book, *Managing the Data-base Environment*. Here's a breakdown:

- CREATE procedures: Performs the INSERT statement to create a new record.

- READ procedures: Reads the table records based on the primary keynoted within the input parameter.

- UPDATE procedures: Executes an UPDATE statement on the table based on the specified primary key for a record within the WHERE clause of the statement.

- DELETE procedures: Deletes a specified row in the WHERE clause.

Working of CRUD: Executing Operations and Examples

Based on the requirements of a system, varying user may have different CRUD cycles. A customer may use CRUD to create an account and access that account when returning to a particular site. The user may then update personal data or change billing information. On the other hand, an operations manager might create product records, then call them when needed or modify line items.

During the Web 2.0 era, CRUD operations were at the foundation of most dynamic websites. However, you should differentiate CRUD from the HTTP action verbs. For example, if you want to create a new record you should use "POST." To update a record, you would use "PUT" or "PATCH." If you wanted to delete a record, you would use "DE-LETE." Through CRUD, users and administrators had the access rights to edit, delete, create or browse online records.

An application designer has many options for executing CRUD operations. One of the most efficient of choices is to create a set of stored procedures in SQL to execute operations. With regard to CRUD stored procedures, here are a few common naming conventions:

- The procedure name should end with the implemented name of the CRUD operation. The prefix should not be the same as the prefix used for other user-defined stored procedures.

- CRUD procedures for the same table will be grouped together if you use the table name after the prefix.

- After adding CRUD procedures, you can update the database schema by identifying the database entity where CRUD operations will be implemented.

Here's an example, illustrating an asp.net MVC 4 CRUD operation using ADO.NET.

```
CREATE PROCEDURE Usp_InsertUpdateDelete_Customer
@CustomerID BIGINT = 0
,@Name NVARCHAR(100) = NULL
,@Mobileno NVARCHAR(15) = NULL
,@Address NVARCHAR(300) = 0
,@Birthdate DATETIME = NULL
,@EmailID NVARCHAR(15) = NULL
,@Query INT
AS
BEGIN
IF (@Query = 1)
BEGIN
INSERT INTO Customer(
NAME
,Address
,Mobileno
,Birthdate
,EmailID
)
VALUES (
@Name
,@Address
,@Mobileno
,@Birthdate
,@EmailID
)

IF (@@ROWCOUNT > 0)
```

```
BEGIN
SELECT 'Insert'
END
END

IF (@Query = 2)
BEGIN
UPDATE Customer
SET NAME = @Name
,Address = @Address
,Mobileno = @Mobileno
,Birthdate = @Birthdate
,EmailID = @EmailID
WHERE Customer.CustomerID = @CustomerID

SELECT 'Update'
END

IF (@Query = 3)
BEGIN
DELETE
FROM Customer
WHERE Customer.CustomerID = @CustomerID

SELECT 'Deleted'
END

IF (@Query = 4)
BEGIN
SELECT *
FROM Customer
END
END

IF (@Query = 5)
BEGIN
SELECT *
FROM Customer
WHERE Customer.CustomerID = @CustomerID
END
```

- CRUD Operations Using Hibernate (Annotation and Configuration);

- Gibraltar – CRUD Examples;

- Example: CRUD Operations – Amazon DynamoDB;

- MongoDB Java CRUD Operations Example Tutorial.

Benefits of CRUD

Instead of using ad-hoc SQL statements, many programmers prefer to use CRUD because of its performance. When a stored procedure is first executed, the execution plan is stored in SQL Server's procedure cache and reused for all applications of the stored procedure.

When a SQL statement is executed in SQL Server, the relational engine searches the procedure cache to ensure an existing execution plan for that particular SQL statement is available and uses the current plan to decrease the need for optimization, parsing and recompiling steps for the SQL statement.

If an execution plan is not available, then the SQL Server will create a new execution plan for the query. Moreover, when you remove SQL statements from the application code, all the SQL can be kept in the database while only stored procedure invocations are in the client application. When you use stored procedures, it helps to decrease database coupling.

Furthermore, using CRUD operations helps to prevent SQL injection attacks. By utilizing stored procedures instead of string concatenation to build dynamic queries from user input data for all SQL Statements means that everything placed into a parameter gets quoted.

CRUD Prevents Casual Browsing and Changes

Application roles are a SQL Server technique that lets code switch identities without informing the user. To work with ad hoc SQL statements, users must have the required permissions on the database tables. Once permission is granted, users can read and manipulate data in applications such as Excel, Word, and others. Users can even bypass the application's business rules.

Yet, this is an unwanted situation that can be prevented through the Application Role. Through integrated security for database access and an Application Role, these types of loopholes can be closed. CRUD comes in since Application roles are added to the database using a stored procedure. It is also implemented by granting permission to execute the CRUD stored procedures and revoking direct access to the tables.

Once an Application Role is added, permissions are assigned, and a password is given. The password is also coded into the application, making it difficult to change. For manipulating data, CRUD is the method to use.

Relation

A relation, or table, in a relational database has certain properties. First off, its name must be unique in the database, i.e. a database cannot contain multiple tables of the same name. Next, each relation must have a set of columns or attributes, and it must have a set of rows to contain the data. As with the table names, no attributes can have the same name.

Next, no tuple (or row) can be a duplicate. In practice, a database might actually contain duplicate rows, but there should be practices in place to avoid this, such as the use of unique primary keys (next up).

Given that a tuple cannot be a duplicate, it follows that a relation must contain at least one attribute (or column) that identifies each tuple (or row) uniquely. This is usually the primary key. This primary key cannot be duplicated. This means that no tuple can have the same unique, primary key. The key cannot have a NULL value, which simply means that the value must be known.

Further, each cell, or field, must contain a single value. For example, you cannot enter something like "Tom Smith" and expect the database to understand that you have a first and last name; rather, the database will understand that the value of that cell is exactly what has been entered.

Finally, all attributes—or columns—must be of the same domain, meaning that they must have the same data type. You cannot mix a string and a number in a single cell.

All these properties, or constraints, serve to ensure data integrity, important to maintain the accuracy of data.

Types of Relationships

Before you begin to establish relationships between tables in the database, you must know what types of relationships can exist between a given pair of tables. Knowing how to identify them properly is an invaluable skill for designing a database successfully.

There are three specific types of relationships that can exist between a pair of tables: one-to-one, one-to-many, and many-to-many. The tables participate in only one type of relationship at any given time.

One-to-one Relationships

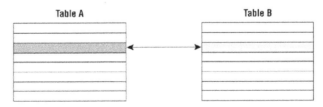

A pair of tables bears a one-to-one relationship when a single record in the first table is related to only one record in the second table, and a single record in the second table is related to only one record in the first table. Below figure shows a generic example of a one-to-one relationship.

As you can see, a single record in TABLE A is related to only one record in TABLE B, and a single record in TABLE B is related to only one record in TABLE A. A one-to-one relationship usually (but not always) involves a subset table. Below figure shows an example of a typical one-to-one relationship that you might find in a database for an organization's human resources department. This example also illustrates a situation where neither of the tables is a subset table.

Employees

EmpID	EmpFirst Name	EmpLast Name	Home Phone	<< other fields >>
100	Zachary	Erlich	553-3992	....
101	Susan	McLain	790-3992	....
102	Joe	Rosales	551-4993	....

Compensation

EmpID	Hourly Rate	Commission Rate	<< other fields >>
100	25.00	5.0%	....
101	19.75	3.5%	....
102	22.50	5.0%	....

Figure: A typical example of a one-to-one relationship

Although the fields in these tables could be combined into a single table, the database designer chose to place the fields that can be viewed by anyone in the organization in the EMPLOYEES table and the fields that can be viewed only by authorized personnel in the COMPENSATION table. Only one record is required to store the compensation data for a given employee, so there is a distinct one-to-one relationship between a record in the EMPLOYEES table and a record in the COMPENSATION table.

A one-to-one relationship usually (but not always) involves a subset table. (Indeed, neither of the tables in Figure 10.4 is a subset table.) Figure below shows a generic example of how you create a relationship diagram for a one-to-one relationship.

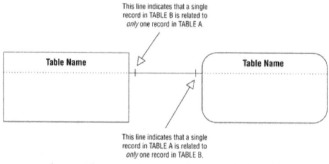

Figure: Diagramming a one-to-one relationship

The line that appears between the tables in the diagram indicates the type of relationship, and there is a particular line that you use for each type. Figure below shows the relationship diagram for the EMPLOYEES and COMPENSATION tables in Figure above (Note that a Data Table symbol represents each table.)

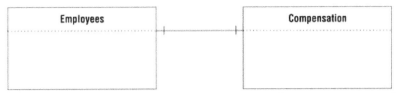

Figure: The relationship diagram for the EMPLOYEES and COMPENSATION tables.

One-to-many Relationships

A one-to-many relationship exists between a pair of tables when a single record in the first table can be related to one or more records in the second table, but a single record in the second table can be related to only one record in the first table. Let's look at a generic example of this type of relationship.

Say you're working with two tables, TABLE A and TABLE B, that have a one-to-many relationship between them. Because of the relationship, a single record in TABLE A can be related to one or more records in TABLE B. Figure below shows the relationship from the perspective of TABLE A.

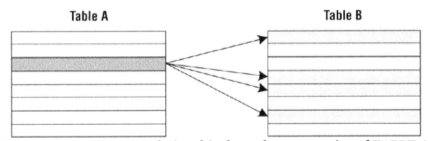

Figure: A one-to-many relationship from the perspective of TABLE A.

Conversely, a single record in the TABLE B can be related to only one record in TABLE A. Figure below shows the relationship from the perspective of TABLE B.

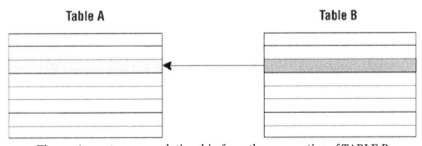

Figure: A one-to-many relationship from the perspective of TABLE B

This is by far the most common relationship that exists between a pair of tables in a database, and it is the easiest to identify. It is crucial from a data-integrity standpoint because it helps to eliminate duplicate data and to keep redundant data to an absolute minimum. Figure 10.9 shows a common example of a one-to-many relationship that you might find in a database for a video rental store.

Customers

Customer Rentals

Customer ID	CustFirst Name	CustLast Name	<< other fields >>
9001	Paul	Litwin	....
9002	Alison	Balter	....
9003	Andy	Baron	....
9004	Chris	Kunicki	....
9005	Mary	Chipman	....

Customer ID	Video ID	Checkout Date
9002	80115	09/26/01
9001	64558	09/28/01
9003	10202	09/28/01
9003	11354	09/28/01
9003	78422	10/02/01
9005	30556	09/26/01
9004	20655	10/05/01

Fig: A typical example of a one-to-many relationship

A customer can check out any number of videos, so a single record in the CUSTOMERS table can be related to one or more records in the CUSTOMER RENTALS table. A single video, however, is associated with only one customer at any given time, so a single record in the CUSTOMER RENTALS table is related to only one record in the CUSTOMERS table.

Figure below shows a generic example of how you create a relationship diagram for a one-to-many relationship.

Diagramming a one-to-many relationship.

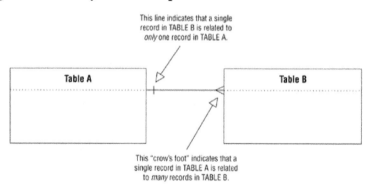

Note that the crow's foot symbol is always located next to the table on the "many" side of the relationship. Figure below shows the relationship diagram for the CUSTOMERS and CUSTOMER RENTALS tables in Figure above.

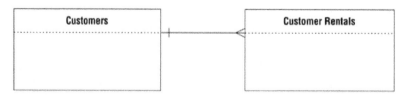

Fig: The relationship diagram for the CUSTOMERS and CUSTOMER RENTALS tables.

Many-to-many Relationships

A pair of tables bears a many-to-many relationship when a single record in the first table can be related to one or more records in the second table and a single record in the second table can be related to one or more records in the first table.

Assume once again that you're working with TABLE A and TABLE B and that there is a many-to-many relationship between them. Because of the relationship, a single record in TABLE A can be related to one or more records (but not necessarily all) in TABLE B. Conversely, a single record in the TABLE B can be related to one or more records (but not necessarily all) in TABLE A. Figure above shows the relationship from the perspective of each table.

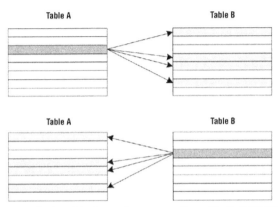

Fig: A many-to-many relationship from the perspective of both TABLE A and TABLE B.

This is the second most common relationship that exists between a pair of tables in a database. It can be a little more difficult to identify than a one-to-many relationship, so you must be sure to examine the tables carefully. Figure below shows a typical example of a many-to-many relationship that you might find in a school database, which happens to be a classic example of this type of relationship (no pun intended!).

Students

Student ID	StudFirst Name	StudLast Name	StudStreet Address	StudCity	StudState	StudZipcode	<< other fields >>
60001	Zachary	Erlich	1204 Bryant Road	Seattle	WA	98125	.....
60002	Susan	McLain	101 C Street, Apt. 32	Redmond	WA	99052	.....
60003	Joe	Rosales	201 Cherry Lane SE	Redmond	WA	98073	.....
60004	Diana	Barlet	4141 Lake City Way	Woodinville	WA	98072	.....
60005	Tom	Wickerath	2100 Mineola Avenue	Bellevue	WA	98006	.....

Classes

Class ID	Class Name	Class Category	Credits	Instructor ID	Classroom	<< other fields >>
900001	Advanced Calculus	Math	5	220087	2201	.....
900002	Advanced Music Theory	Music	3	220039	7012	.....
900003	American History	History	5	220148	3305	....
900004	Computers in Business	Computer Science	2	220387	5115	.....
900005	Computers in Society	Computer Science	2	220387	5117	.....
900006	Introduction to Biology	Biology	5	220498	3112	.....
900007	Introduction to Database Design	Computer Science	5	220516	5105	.....
900008	Introduction to Physics	Physics	4	220087	2205	.....
900009	Introduction to Political Science	Political Science	5	220337	3308	.....

Fig: A typical example of a many-to-many relationship

A student can attend one or more classes during a school year, so a single record in the STUDENTS table can be related to one or more records in the CLASSES table.

Conversely, one or more students will attend a given class, so a single record in the CLASSES table can be related to one or more records in the STUDENTS table.

Figure below shows a generic example of how you create a relationship diagram for a many-to-many relationship.

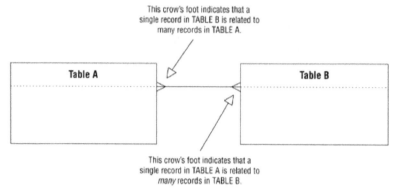

Fig: Diagramming a many-to-many relationship

In this case, there is a crow's foot symbol located next to each table. Figure below shows the relationship diagram for the STUDENTS and CLASSES tables in Figure above.

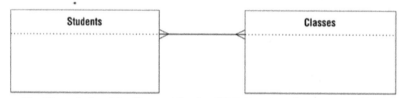

Fig: The relationship diagram for the STUDENTS and CLASSES tables

Problems with Many-to-many Relationships

A many-to-many relationship has an inherent peculiarity that you must address before you can effectively use the data from the tables involved in the relationship. The issue is this: How do you easily associate records from the first table with records in the second table in order to establish the relationship? This is an important question because you'll encounter problems such as these if you do not establish the relationship properly:

- It will be tedious and somewhat difficult to retrieve information from one of the tables.

- One of the tables will contain a large amount of redundant data.

- Duplicate data will exist within both tables.

- It will be difficult for you to insert, update, and delete data.

There are two common methods that novice and inexperienced developers use in a futile attempt to address this situation.

Table Structures

Students		Classes	
Student ID	PK	Class ID	PK
StudFirst Name		Class Name	
StudLast Name		Class Category	
StudStreet Address		Credits	
StudCity		Instructor ID	
StudState		Classroom	
StudZipcode		Class Description	
StudHome Phone		Catalog Code	
StudEmail Address			
Social Security Number			

Fig: Structures of the STUDENTS and CLASSES tables

Note: As this example unfolds, keep in mind that every many-to-many relationship you encounter will exhibit these same issues.

As you can see, there is no actual connection between the two tables, so you have no way of associating records in one table with records in the other table. The first method you might use to attempt to establish a connection involves taking a field from one table and incorporating it a given number of times within the other table. (This approach usually appeals to people who are accustomed to working with spreadsheets.) For example, you could take the STUDENT ID field from the STUDENTS table and incorporate it within the CLASSES table structure, creating as many copies of the field as you need to represent the maximum number of students that could attend any class. Figure below shows the revised version of the CLASSES table structure.

Table Structures

Classes				
Class ID	PK	Student ID 1	Student ID 9	Student ID 17
Class Name		Student ID 2	Student ID 10	Student ID 18
Class Category		Student ID 3	Student ID 11	Student ID 19
Credits		Student ID 4	Student ID 12	Student ID 20
Instructor ID		Student ID 5	Student ID 13	Student ID 21
Classroom		Student ID 6	Student ID 14	Student ID 22
Class Description		Student ID 7	Student ID 15	Student ID 23
Catalog Code		Student ID 8	Student ID 16	Student ID 24

Fig: Incorporating STUDENT ID fields within the CLASSES table structure.

This structure is likely to be problematic, so you might try taking the CLASS ID field from the CLASSES table and incorporating it within the STUDENTS table structure instead. Figure below shows the revised version of the STUDENTS table structure.

Do these structures look (vaguely) familiar? They should. All you've done using this method is introduce a "flattened" multivalued field into the table structure. In doing so, you've also introduced the problems associated with a multivalued field. Although you know how to resolve a multivalued field, this is not a good or proper way to establish the relationship.

Table Structures

Students

Student ID	PK	Class ID 1
StudFirst Name		Class ID 2
StudLast Name		Class ID 3
StudStreet Address		Class ID 4
StudCity		Class ID 5
StudState		Class ID 6
StudZipcode		Class ID 7
StudHome Phone		Class ID 8
StudEmail Address		
Social Security Number		

Fig: Incorporating CLASS ID fields within the STUDENTS table structure

The second method you might attempt to use is simply a variation of the first method. In this case, you take one or more fields from one table and incorporate a single instance of each field within the other table. For example, you could take the CLASS ID, CLASS NAME, and INSTRUCTOR ID fields from the CLASSES table and incorporate them into the STUDENTS table in order to identify the classes in which a student is currently enrolled. This may seem to be a distinct improvement over the first method, but you'll see that there are problems that arise from such modifications when you load the revised STUDENTS table with sample data.

Clearly illustrates the problems you'll encounter using this method:

- The table contains unnecessary duplicate fields. You learned all about unnecessary duplicate fields and the problems they pose back in Chapter 7, so you know that using them here is not a good idea. Besides, it is very likely that the CLASS NAME and INSTRUCTOR ID fields are not appropriate in the STUDENTS table the CLASS ID field identifies the class sufficiently, and it is really all you need to identify the classes a student is taking.

- There is a large amount of redundant data. Even if you remove the CLASS NAME and INSTRUCTOR ID fields from the STUDENTS table, the CLASS ID field will still produce a lot of redundant data.

- It is difficult to insert a new record. If you enter a record in the STUDENTS table for a new class (instead of entering it in the CLASSES table) without also entering student data, the fields pertaining to the student will be null including the primary key of the STUDENTS table (STUDENT ID). This will automatically trigger a violation of the Elements of a Primary Key because the primary key cannot be null; therefore, you cannot insert the record into the table until you can provide a proper primary key value.

- It is difficult to delete a record. This is especially true if the only data about a new class has been recorded in the particular student record you want to delete. Note the record for Diana Bar let, for example. If Diana decides not to attend any classes this year and you delete her record, you will lose the data for the "Introduction to Database Design" class. That might not create a serious problem unless someone neglected to enter the data about this class into the CLASSES table as well. Once you delete Diana's record, you'll have to re-enter all of the data for the class in the CLASSES table.

Students

Student ID	Student First Name	Student Last Name	Class ID	Class Name	Instructor ID	<< other fields >>
60001	Zachary	Erlich	900009	Introduction to Political Science	220087	......
60001	Zachary	Erlich	900002	Advanced Music Theory	220039	......
60001	Zachary	Erlich	900003	American History	220148	......
60001	Zachary	Erlich	900004	Computers in Business	220121	......
60002	Susan	McLain	900009	Introduction to Political Science	220087	......
60002	Susan	McLain	900002	Advanced Music Theory	220039	......
60002	Susan	McLain	900006	Introduction to Biology	220117	......
60003	Joe	Rosales	900004	Computers in Business	220121	......
60003	Joe	Rosales	900001	Advanced Calculus	220101	......
60003	Joe	Rosales	900008	Introduction to Physics	220075	......
60004	Diana	Barlet	900007	Introduction to Database Design	220120	......

Fig: The revised STUDENTS table with sample data

Fortunately, you will not have to worry about any of these problems because you're going to learn the proper way to establish a many-to-many relationship.

Self-referencing Relationships

It is instead a relationship that exists between the records within a table. Ironically, you'll still regard this throughout the design process as a table relationship.

A table bears a self-referencing relationship (also known as a recursive relationship) to itself when a given record in the table is related to other records within the table. Similar to its dual-table counterpart, a self-referencing relationship can be one-to-one, one-to-many, or many-to-many.

One-to-one

A self-referencing one-to-one relationship exists when a given record in the table can be related to only one other record within the table. The MEMBERS table in figure is an example of a table with this type of relationship. In this case, a given member can sponsor only one other member within the organization; the SPONSOR ID field stores the member identification number of the member acting as a sponsor. Note that Susan McLain is Tom Wickerath's sponsor.

Members

Member ID	MbrFirst Name	MbrLast Name	Sponsor ID	<< other fields >>
1001	Zachary	Erlich		......
1002	Susan	McLain	1001	......
1003	Joe	Rosales		......
1004	Diana	Barlet	1003	......
1005	Tom	Wickerath	1002	......

Fig: Example of a self-referencing one-to-one relationship

Database Keys

A Key is a data item that exclusively identifies a record. In other words, key is a set of column(s) that is used to uniquely identify the record in a table. It is used to fetch or retrieve records / data-rows from data table according to the condition/requirement. Key provides several types of constraints like column can't store duplicate values or null values. Keys are also used to generate relationship among different database tables or views.

Types of Keys

Database supports the following types of keys:

- Super Key
- Minimal Super Key
- Candidate Key
- Primary Key
- Unique Key
- Alternate Key

- Composite Key

- Foreign Key

- Natural Key

- Surrogate Key

Now we take two tables for better understanding of the key. First table is "Branch Info" and second table is "Student_Information".

Branch_Id	Branch_Name	Branch_Code
1	Computer Scie...	CSE
2	Electronics	ECE
3	Mechnical	MCE
4	Information Te...	ITE
5	Civil	CVE
NULL	*NULL*	*NULL*

Table: Branch_Info

Student_Id	College_Id	Student_Name	Rtu_Roll_No	Father_Name	Address	Branch_Id	Session
1	1210038	Pankaj	12emccs138	Suresh	Alwar	1	2012-16
2	1210039	Priya	12emccs139	Ram	Mathura	1	2012-16
3	1310048	Rahul	13emmce210	Sambhu	Alwar	3	2013-17
4	1310078	Neeraj	13emcve078	Nathu	Jaipur	5	2013-17
5	1210047	Sandeep	12emccs047	Om Parkash	Alwar	1	2012-16
6	1210048	Sanjeev	12emece048	Omi	Delhi	2	2012-16
NULL	*NULL*	*NULL*	*NULL*	*NULL*	*NULL*	*NULL*	*NULL*

Table: Student_Information

Now we read about each key.

Candidate Key

A Candidate key is an attribute or set of attributes that uniquely identifies a record. Among the set of candidate, one candidate key is chosen as Primary key. So a table can have multiple candidate key but each table can have maximum one primary key.

Example:

Possible Candidate Keys in Branch_Info table.

1. Branch_Id

2. Branch_Name

3. Branch_Code

Possible Candidate keys in Student_Information table.

1. Student_Id

2. College_Id

3. Rtu_Roll_No

Primary Key

A Primary key uniquely identifies each record in a table and must never be the same for the 2 records. Primary key is a set of one or more fields (columns) of a table that uniquely identify a record in database table. A table can have only one primary key and one candidate key can select as a primary key. The primary key should be chosen such that its attributes are never or rarely changed, for example, we can't select Student_Id field as a primary key because in some case Student_Id of student may be changed.

Example:

Primary Key in Branch_Info table:

1. Branch_Id

Primary Key in Student_Information Table:

1. College_Id

Alternate Key

Alternate keys are candidate keys that are not selected as primary key. Alternate key can also work as a primary key. Alternate key is also called "Secondary Key".

Example:

Alternate Key in Branch_Info table:

1. Branch_Name

2. Branch_Code

Alternate Key in Student_Information table:

1. Student_Id

2. Rtu_Roll_No

Unique Key

A unique key is a set of one or more attribute that can be used to uniquely identify the records in table. Unique key is similar to primary key but unique key field can contain a "Null" value but primary key doesn't allow "Null" value. Other difference is that primary key field contain a clustered index and unique field contain a non-clustered index.

Example:

Possible Unique Key in Branch_Info table.

    1.   Branch_Name

Possible Unique Key in Student_Information table:

    1.   Rtu_Roll_No

Composite Key

Composite key is a combination of more than one attributes that can be used to uniquely identity each record. It is also known as "Compound" key. A composite key may be a candidate or primary key.

Example:

Composite Key in Branch_Info table.

    1.   { Branch_Name, Branch_Code}

        Composite Key in Student_Information table:

    2.   { Student_Id, Student_Name }

Super Key

Super key is a set of on e or more than one keys that can be used to uniquely identify the record in table. A Super key for an entity is a set of one or more attributes whose combined value uniquely identifies the entity in the entity set. A super key is a combine form of Primary Key, Alternate key and Unique key and Primary Key, Unique Key and Alternate Key are subset of super key. A Super Key is simply a non-minimal Candidate Key, that is to say one with additional columns not strictly required to ensure uniqueness of the row. A super key can have a single column.

Example:

Super Keys in Branch_Info Table.

    1.   Branch_Id

    2.   Branch_Name

3. Branch_Code

4. { Branch_Id, Branch_Code }

5. { Branch_Name , Branch_Code }

Super Keys in Student_Information Table:

1. Student_Id

2. College_Id

3. Rtu_Roll_No

4. { Student_Id, Student_Name}

5. { College_Id, Branch_Id }

6. { Rtu_Roll_No, Session }

Minimal Super Key

A minimal super key is a minimum set of columns that can be used to uniquely identify a row. In other wordsm the minimum number of columns that can be combined to give a unique value for every row in the table.

Example:

Minimal Super Keys in Branch_Info Table.

1. Branch_Id

2. Branch_Name

3. Branch_Code

Minimal Super Keys in Student_Information Table:

1. Student_Id

2. College_Id

3. Rtu_Roll_No

Natural Keys

A natural key is a key composed of columns that actually have a logical relationship to other columns within a table. For example, if we use Student_Id, Student_Name and Father_Name columns to form a key then it would be "Natural Key" because there is definitely a relationship between these columns and other columns that exist in table. Natural keys are often called "Business Key " or "Domain Key".

Surrogate Key

Surrogate key is an artificial key that is used to uniquely identify the record in table. For example, in SQL Server or Sybase database system contain an artificial key that is known as "Identity". Surrogate keys are just simple sequential number. Surrogate keys are only used to act as a primary key.

Example:

Branch_Id is a Surrogate Key in Branch_Info table and Student_Id is a Surrogate key of Student_Information table.

Foreign Keys

Foreign key is used to generate the relationship between the tables. Foreign key is a field in database table that is Primary key in another table. A foreign key can accept null and duplicate value.

Example:

Branch_Id is a Foreign Key in Student_Information table that primary key exist in Branch_Info(Branch_Id) table.

In conclusion, database generally only contain primary key, foreign key, unique key and surrogate key and other remaining keys are just concept. A table must have a unique key. According to Dr. E. F. Codd 's third rule *"Every single data element (value) is guaranteed to be accessible logically with a combination of table-name, primary-key (row value), and attribute-name (column value)"*. So each table must have keys , because use of keys make data highly reliable and provide several types of content like unique data and null values.

Database Designing Languages and Optimization

A holistic study of database designing requires an understanding of database designing languages and optimization. This chapter discusses in detail the different concepts of query language, data control language, data definition language, data manipulation language, database engine, database tuning and database trigger, among others for an extensive understanding of the subject.

Query Language

A query is a question, often expressed in a formal way. A database query can be either a select query or an action query. A select query is a data retrieval query, while an action query asks for additional operations on the data, such as insertion, updating or deletion.

Query language is a computer programming language used to retrieve information from a database.

The uses of databases are manifold. They provide a means of retrieving records or parts of records and performing various calculations before displaying the results. The interface by which such manipulations are specified is called the query language. Whereas early query languages were originally so complex that interacting with electronic databases could be done only by specially trained individuals, modern interfaces are more user-friendly, allowing casual users to access database information.

The main types of popular query modes are the menu, the "fill-in-the-blank" technique, and the structured query. Particularly suited for novices, the menu requires a person to choose from several alternatives displayed on a monitor. The fill-in-the-blank technique is one in which the user is prompted to enter key words as search statements. The structured query approach is effective with relational databases. It has a formal, powerful syntax that is in fact a programming language, and it is able to accommodate logical operators. One implementation of this approach, the Structured Query Language (SQL), has the form:

select [field Fa, Fb, . . ., Fn]

from [database Da, Db, . . ., Dn]

where, [field Fa = abc] *and* [field Fb = def].

Structured query languages support database searching and other operations by using commands such as "find", "delete", "print", "sum" and so forth. The sentence like structure of a SQL query resembles natural language except that its syntax is limited and fixed. Instead of using a SQL statement, it is possible to represent queries in tabular form. The technique, referred to as query-by-example (or QBE), displays an empty tabular form and expects the searcher to enter the search specifications into appropriate columns. The program then constructs a SQL-type query from the table and executes it.

The most flexible query language is of course natural language. The use of natural-language sentences in a constrained form to search databases is allowed by some commercial database management software. These programs parse the syntax of the query; recognize its action words and their synonyms; identify the names of files, records, and fields; and perform the logical operations required. Experimental systems that accept such natural-language queries in spoken voice have been developed; however, the ability to employ unrestricted natural language to query unstructured information will require further advances in machine understanding of natural language, particularly in techniques of representing the semantic and pragmatic context of ideas.

In a relational database, which contains records or rows of information, the SQL SELECT statement query allows the user to choose data and return it from the database to an application. The resulting query is stored in a result-table, which is called the result-set. The SELECT statement can be broken down into other categories, such as FROM, WHERE and ORDER BY. The SQL SELECT query also can group and aggregate data, such as summarize or analyze.

Search a Query

The text typed into search engines, such as Bing, Google or Yahoo, is called a query. Search-engine queries provide information that is much different from SQL languages because they don't require keyword or positional parameters. A search-engine query is a request for information on a particular topic, and the request is made once a user selects 'Enter.'

Once the request is made, the search engine uses an algorithm to determine the best results, which are sorted based on significance according to the search engine details of which are not revealed publicly.

Types of search queries include navigational, informational and transactional. Navigational searches are intended to find a particular website, such as ESPN.com; informational searches are designed to cover a broad topic, such a comparison between a new iPhone and Android device; and transactional searches seek to complete a transaction.

Data Control Language

The Data Control Language (DCL) is a subset of the Structured Query Language (SQL) and allows database administrators to configure security access to relational databases. It complements the Data Definition Language (DDL), which is used to add and delete database objects, and the Data Manipulation Language (DML) used to retrieve, insert, and modify the contents of a database.

DCL is the simplest of the SQL subsets, as it consists of only three commands: GRANT, REVOKE, and DENY. Combined, these three commands provide administrators with the flexibility to set and remove database permissions in an extremely granular fashion.

Adding Permissions with the GRANT Command

The GRANT command is used by administrators to add new permissions to a database user. It has a very simple syntax, defined as follows:

```
GRANT [privilege]

ON [object]

TO [user]

[WITH GRANT OPTION]
```

Here's the rundown on each of the parameters you can supply with this command:

- Privilege: can be either the keyword ALL (to grant a wide variety of permissions) or a specific database permission or set of permissions. Examples include CREATE DATABASE, SELECT, INSERT, UPDATE, DELETE, EXECUTE and CREATE VIEW.

- Object: can be any database object. The valid privilege options vary based on the type of database object you include in this clause. Typically, the object will be either a database, function, stored procedure, table or view.

- User: can be any database user. You can also substitute a role for the user in this clause if you wish to make use of role-based database security.

- If you include the optional With Grant Option clause at the end of the GRANT command, you not only grant the specified user the permissions defined in the SQL statement but also give the user the ability to grant those same permissions to *other* database users. For this reason, use this clause with care.

For example, assume you wish to grant the user Joe the ability to retrieve information from the employees table in a database called HR. You might use the following SQL command:

```
GRANT SELECT

ON HR.employees

TO Joe
```

Joe will now have the ability to retrieve information from the employees table. He will not, however, be able to grant other users permission to retrieve information from that table because you did not include the WITH GRANT OPTION clause in the GRANT statement.

Revoking Database Access

The REVOKE command is used to remove database access from a user previously granted such access. The syntax for this command is defined as follows:

```
REVOKE [GRANT OPTION FOR] [permission]

ON [object]

FROM [user]

[CASCADE]
```

Here's the rundown on the parameters for the REVOKE command:

- Permission: specifies the database permissions to remove from the identified user. The command revokes both GRANT and DENY assertions previously made for the identified permission.

- Object: can be any database object. The valid privilege options vary based on the type of database object you include in this clause. Typically, the object will be either a database, function, stored procedure, table or view.

- User: can be any database user. You can also substitute a role for the user in this clause if you wish to make use of role-based database security.

- The GRANT OPTION FOR clause removes the specified user's ability to grant the specified permission to other users. Note: *If you include the GRANT OPTION FOR clause in a REVOKE statement, the primary permission is not revoked.* This clause revokes *only* the granting ability.

- The CASCADE option also revokes the specified permission from any users that the specified user granted the permission.

For example, the following command revokes the permission granted to Joe in the previous:

```
REVOKE SELECT

ON HR.employees

FROM Joe
```

Explicitly Denying Database Access

The DENY command is used to explicitly prevent a user from receiving a particular permission. This is helpful when a user is a member of a role or group that is granted permission and you want to prevent that individual user from inheriting the permission by creating an exception. The syntax for this command is as follows:

```
DENY [permission]

ON [object]

TO [user]
```

The parameters for the DENY command are identical to those used for the GRANT command. For example, if you wished to ensure that Matthew would never receive the ability to delete information from the employees table, issue the following command:

```
DENY DELETE

ON HR.employees

TO Matthew
```

Data Definition Language

- DDL stands for Data Definition Language.
- It is a language used for defining and modifying the data and its structure.
- It is used to build and modify the structure of your tables and other objects in the database.

DDL commands are as follows:

1. CREATE
2. DROP
3. ALTER
4. RENAME
5. TRUNCATE

- These commands can be used to add, remove or modify tables within a database.
- DDL has pre-defined syntax for describing the data.

CREATE Command

- CREATE command is used for creating objects in the database.
- It creates a new table.

Syntax:

CREATE TABLE <table_name>

(column_name1 datatype,column_name2 datatype,

. . .column_name_n datatype);

Example: CREATE command

CREATE TABLE employee

(empid INT, ename CHAR,age INT, city CHAR(25), phone_no VARCHAR(20));

DROP Command

- DROP command allows to remove entire database objects from the database.
- It removes entire data structure from the database.
- It deletes a table, index or view.

Syntax:

DROP TABLE <table_name>;

or

DROP DATABASE <database_name>;

Example: DROP Command

DROP TABLE employee;

or

DROP DATABASE employees;

- If you want to remove individual records, then use DELETE command of the DML statement.

ALTER Command

- An ALTER command allows to Alter or modify the structure of the database.
- It modifies an existing database object.

- Using this command, you can add additional column, drop existing column and even change the data type of columns.

Syntax:

ALTER TABLE <table_name>

ADD <column_name datatype>;

or

ALTER TABLE <table_name>

CHANGE <old_column_name> <new_column_name>;

or

ALTER TABLE <table_name>

DROP COLUMN <column_name>;

Example: ALTER Command

ALTER TABLE employee

ADD (address varchar2(50));

or

ALTER TABLE employee

CHANGE (phone_no) (contact_no);

or

ALTER TABLE employee

DROP COLUMN age;

To view the changed structure of table, use 'DESCRIBE' command.

For example:

DESCRIBE TABLE employee;

RENAME Command

- RENAME command is used to rename an object.

- It renames a database table.

Syntax:

RENAME TABLE <old_name> TO <new_name>;

Example:

RENAME TABLE emp TO employee;

TRUNCATE Command

- TRUNCATE command is used to delete all the rows from the table permanently.
- It removes all the records from a table, including all spaces allocated for the records.
- This command is same as DELETE command, but TRUNCATE command does not generate any rollback data.

Syntax:

TRUNCATE TABLE <table_name>;

Example:

TRUNCATE TABLE employee;

Data Manipulation Language

A data manipulation language (DML) is a family of computer languages including commands permitting users to manipulate data in a database. This manipulation involves inserting data into database tables, retrieving existing data, deleting data from existing tables and modifying existing data. DML is mostly incorporated in SQL databases.

Data manipulation language is of two types:

a) Procedural – The type of data needed and the mechanism to get it is specified by the user.

b) Non Procedural – Only the type of data needed is specified by the user.

The basic DML commands are:

1. SELECT

2. INSERT

3. UPDATE

4. DELETE

DML performs read-only queries of data.

SELECT Command

- SELECT command is used to retrieve data from the database.

- This command allows database users to retrieve the specific information they desire from an operational database.

- It returns a result set of records from one or more tables.

SELECT Command has many Optional Clauses are as Stated Below:

Clause	Description
WHERE	It specifies which rows to retrieve.
GROUP BY	It is used to arrange the data into groups.
HAVING	It selects among the groups defined by the GROUP BY clause.
ORDER BY	It specifies an order in which to return the rows.
AS	It provides an alias which can be used to temporarily rename tables or columns.

Syntax:

SELECT * FROM <table_name>;

Example:

SELECT Command

SELECT * FROM employee;

or

SELECT * FROM employee

where salary >=10,000;

INSERT Command

- INSERT command is used for inserting a data into a table.

- Using this command, you can add one or more records to any single table in a database.

- It is also used to add records to an existing code.

Syntax:

INSERT INTO <table_name> (`column_name1` <datatype>, `column_name2` <data-type>, ..., `column_name_n` <database>) VALUES (`value1`, `value2`, ..., `value n`);

Example:

INSERT INTO employee (`eid` int, `ename` varchar(20), `city` varchar(20))

VALUES (`1`, `ABC`, `PUNE`);

UPDATE Command

- UPDATE command is used to modify the records present in existing table.
- This command updates existing data within a table.
- It changes the data of one or more records in a table.

Syntax:

UPDATE <table_name>

SET <column_name = value>

WHERE condition;

Example: UPDATE Command

UPDATE EMPLOYEE

SET SALARY=20000

WHERE ENAME='ABC';

DELETE Command

- DELETE command is used to delete some or all records from the existing table.
- It deletes all the records from a table.

Syntax:

DELETE FROM <table_name> WHERE <condition>;

Example:

DELETE Command

DELETE FROM employee

WHERE emp_id = '001';

If we does not write the WHERE condition, then all rows will get deleted.

Database Administration and Automation

Databases are critical for every organization, as are DBAs and database resources. The scope of business today has surpassed all previous levels for companies to stay competitive, and now we have multi-petabytes of data to deal with on a daily basis, spread across multiple locations including private data centers and public clouds. And DBAs not only have to deal with databases and data but also make sure that compliance, security, costs, data protection, availability, DR, migrations, and upgrades (just to name a few responsibilities) are taken care of.

With this amount of disparate data, smart DBAs must "clone" themselves by automating as much as they can. But when that is not sufficient due to the fact that there are simply too many databases to manage, it's an even smarter move for database administrators to look for tools that can provide a self-service, single-window management terminal of all their database automation needs.

Pushing Changes through the Pipeline can be Complicated

It is a complex process to set up and manage databases when your application depends on multiple sources of data and needs to remain highly available to meet SLAs and deliver fast response times. When you are running multiple environments ranging from DEV and UAT to PROD, it can be quick and easy for you to make structural changes such as logical and physical database structures to DEV or UAT environments, but achieving such shifts in PROD is not the same.

Then there are the simple database administration tasks that require DBA capability, but the DBA might not be available to perform at a certain time. You may have just completed an incredible database modification and need a complete backup of the database on prod. Or, say your development team has confirmed a fix for a bug that is certified on the UAT database.

If the DBA is smart and has automated tasks such as PROD deployment scripts prior to becoming unavailable, the IT team does not have to wait for the release to be completed because the DBA has already automated database scripts for production deployments. In this way, by automating database tasks, DBAs not only lighten their burden but also help IT teams deliver on time.

Yes, databases can be complex; but they are critical. Automation allows you to standardize the process of database changes across the development, UAT, and production environments, and these changes can then be tested and certified before finally moving to production. This drastically reduces the time to launch new products so that you can stay ahead of the competition and be free to innovate.

Automation at your Fingertips

So where exactly does the art of automation stand today? With many database engines, there are certain database administration tasks that are already automated. For instance, Oracle provides maintenance windows, where automated cleanup activities and the gathering of database statistics are performed, and storage, as well as other resource utilization, is possible as well.

You can write your own shell scripts to perform certain DBA tasks, such as taking backup, moving archive logs from one storage to another dense storage etc. DBAs can also create scripts that are a useful deployment of code changes from databases to databases.

LOOK BEFORE YOU LAUNCH!
DO YOU HAVE THE NEEDED RESOURCES TO SUPPORT AUTOMATION?

But in the age of cloud data centers, keeping options for automation limited to only DBAs may result in a failure to deliver on time. Because you may have multiple databases and multiple environments, each running a different software solution with varied availability and performance requirements, you simply may not have all of your resources available when you need them.

We will be looking at two methods to automate your database administration tasks: the traditional way and another way that uses new innovative tools and leads you to the database automation methods of the future.

Database Administration Tasks - Old School Automation

Traditionally, there have been several methods and tools for automating a majority of database administration tasks. Some of these come built into a database, and others are performed by DBAs and developers either via shell scripts or database code and maintained by configuration managers using different versions for different environments.

Numerous DBA tasks are performed using scripts and should be version-maintained so that they do not create any conflict. These tasks cover everything from database activities such as the creation of logical database structures, including tables, views, index procedures, and triggers to DBA tasks such as adding or extending logical storage for table spaces and data files, creating alerts on overall database utilization, and restoring a database in case of failure.

The best practice is to create your database code as application-centric as possible so that when you move from DEV to UAT to prod, it is done with ease and you are able to reduce time to market for optimal results. Code and data are the two most critical aspects and need to be dealt with separately from database administration tasks.

For instance, a change in logical structure may be easily performed on dev, but you then may need to perform several steps on PROD before deployment, such as a simple case of adding a column with a NOT NULL constraint on the column. On the other hand, you may have a storage requirement on DEV that does not match with the PROD environment, and hence you keep different versions of script to automate them.

Traditionally, you will automate these tasks using tools or schedulers, such as UC4, shell scripts and cron jobs, Oracle Scheduler, and Enterprise Manager Console. But these can become very cumbersome to manage when you have to deal with multiple databases.

Luckily, there are several database orchestration and automation tools that can prove a boon to any DBA by providing a self-service and completely automated environment, where tasks ranging from installation, setup, and deployment to backup and monitoring are all automated and monitored through a single-window system.

Database Smarts: Automate to Innovate

When you are stuck as a developer or a DBA performing database administration activities that you could automate using script and schedulers, then you are basically wasting your and your organization's time due to redundancy and inefficiency. Bill Gates said "I always choose a lazy person to do a difficult job because he will find an easy way to do it." The assumption here is, of course, that the lazy person is smart; very smart. And that's where automation comes in.

You may or may not already have an automated creation of procedures and some sort of code to save time, but the real beauty of fully integrated automation when faced with managing multiple databases of different calibers is that you don't even need much of a DBA background to implement this feature.

How a new approach to the database can make DevOps a success:

- For database administration to fully contribute to the DevOps workflow, and avoid the pitfalls that can easily break a deployment, a new approach is needed. The key is a move to greater systematization and automation, ensuring un-interrupted consistency from defining tasks through application deployment.

- Specifically, a fully automated enforced version control for the database, much like that used for code development, can address one of the most vexing problems of database stability and security: consistent versioning. This ensures a single source of truth throughout development, creating an automatic process for preventing code overrides and conflicts, configuration drifts and other causes of instability that can break a deployment.

- An effective control mechanism includes a check-in/check-out process and database object locking, preventing employees from straying from a well-defined revision process, whether out of absentmindedness or habit. As no object (table, schema, etc.) can be checked out by more than one user at a time, all revisions are managed and sequential.

- In order to mitigate the risk of configuration drift, baseline aware analysis is used to check changed object structure (or content) against the object as it is maintained in the source control repository. That repository preserves a baseline that has been defined for every object and in accordance with every check-in, allowing for three-way comparisons. That is, when a developer wants to commit and deploy his changes, the version control solution should automatically compare the developer's copy, the object baseline (the object as it was when the developer checked it out), and the most current revision of the object in the target environment (e.g., integration or QA). If a difference between the baseline and the current revision is detected, then that would mean someone else, maybe from another team or project working on another development branch, has already modified the object. In that case, the developer would not be able to deploy his changes, until the conflict between his local copy and the newer updates to the target environments are resolved.

- By automatically analyzing code and changes produced by developers, such safe automation can be achieved. The DBA has a clear interest in assuring that bad practices, or non-policy actions, are blocked automatically or trigger a warning, rather than depending on his ability or responsibility to review every bit of code being pushed forward by developers. Practices like dropping an index, rebuilding an index in mid-day, and so on, should trigger a warning before rolling all the way to production.

- The result of all this automation is an evolutionary database development that ensures zero downtime, high availability, scalability and fail-safe continuous delivery in any environment.

Significance for Developers

For developers, a reliable and responsive database provides agility and flexibility, while increasing productivity and efficiency, as well as eliminating conflicts with the DBA down the line. For operations teams, it is a promise of security, stability, repeatability and validity in deployment configurations.

Preventing database-linked errors at the coding or integration phases, as well as raising flags of potential conflicts and non-policy changes, at early stages of SDLC, allows a faster and much more efficient response. Reducing the amount of errors and conflicts early on, long before production, is critical to a better deployment process. The DBA would become less of a bottleneck for the development teams with less downtime and faster deployment which translates to better customer experience.

Moreover, many database-linked problems could be resolved by development team leaders in early consultation with DBAs, or even on their own in many cases, thanks to detailed database version logs. The overall improved self-sufficiency among the development teams, as a result of the automated database versioning, reduces the number of errors and increases team efficiency. For added security and control in such a situation, the database management solution should be configured to granularly define personnel roles and responsibilities. Such effective separation of duties, alongside enforced version control, is critical to preventing unauthorized or accidental version overrides.

Effective monitoring and versioning should be consistently applied at all stages, with a solution that can analyze database versions and object change histories at any point in their lifecycle. This will provide the audit trail necessary for regulatory compliance and key aspects of quality control. And as technology advances and consumer protection develops accordingly, comprehensive audit trail capabilities will become more and more important for regulatory adherence.

In order to ensure the most streamlined, cost-efficient and documented compliance, the reporting solution should be directly and automatically connected to the database monitoring system. This minimizes manual documentation requirements for development teams and cuts down on the time required to reply to compliance audit requests for information.

In the event of an emergency, reliable source control, safe automation and a monitoring mechanism provide a clear, functional recovery point for the database.

Significance for DBAs

Safe automation and source control enforcement in the database reduce the number of errors developers insert into the system, by scanning code for non-policy changes and preventing code overrides. A full and comprehensive object change history provides information on each change, including the developer who made the change and comments regarding the original business requirement. Labels and a baseline for deployment scripts provide the DBA with additional and valuable information, while risky updates are immediately highlighted or blocked so they can't trickle down to production.

This includes identifying otherwise undocumented hotfixes – the configuration drift problem that is one of the great banes of developers and DBAs - implemented in the target schema at any point during development. And if teams are working in separate development environments, only coming together during a QA phase, then identifying changes made to the target environments will also prevent code overwrites.

The source control also identifies who made what change to the database, possibly providing more information on the business requirement behind the change. This is invaluable information for DBAs dealing with problematic scripts during deployment.

Minimizing the errors during development and deployment, while providing additional information about the changes and identifying those that are potentially harmful, allows the DBA to be more efficient. Reducing the amount of "noise" (in the form of developer errors they have to deal with) lowers the DBA's stress levels and makes the development teams more self-sufficient. This allows the DBA to focus more time on tasks such as tuning, maintenance, planning the deployment process, and providing expert guidance.

Significance for Management

A systematic and automated approach to database management requires fewer resources to run and monitor it- and the results will be far more consistent. By mitigating the risk of human error through automation, the company can lead employees to greater efficiency, prevent workarounds and redo's due to overrides, and track down harmful updates before they are executed.

Database changes and monitoring should also be driven by clear business requirements, such as tasks from TFS, JIRA or similar work management tools. In this way, the database is both up to date and playing its role in meeting business goals.

Safe automation, fully enforced database source control and change tracking, integrated into the development processes, provides compliance with regulatory requirements. This alleviates the need for additional third-party applications.

This end-to-end process, along with open communication and enhanced collaboration internally, optimizes the development to production cycle and reduces its cost. The result is accelerated time to market and greater customer satisfaction, as the end product becomes more stable, of better overall quality, and often more quickly reflects user feedback from previous releases.

Taking the Company Forward

Effective database administration can influence the success of DevOps initiatives, which in turn contributes to the success of the business. The key is safe automation and enforced source control for the database, which prevents many errors from reaching the deployment stage.

The result is more independent development teams, faster and earlier corrective measures, as well as more stable deployment configurations. For database administrators, relieved of the pressure of constantly having to juggle and merge various teams' database changes, automation frees up time to help their organizations take bigger steps forward in ongoing innovation.

Database Engine

A database engine is the underlying system that a database uses to function. Many different technologies rely on internal "engines," which are the fundamental building blocks on which they operate.

In general, referring to an "engine" for a technology implies that that specific module contains the core code for that technology's operations. In database design, a database engine is composed of the component of the system that actually stores and retrieves data.

In order to streamline the use of a database engine from beyond that technology's interface, a technology called application programming interfaces (API) has emerged. Many database tools can be accessed through these resources rather than going through the actual database user interface.

While the database engine is often referred to as the inherent data storage system, the use of the term "engine" in IT often points toward proprietary design and ownership. A software engine is something that a company guards from the competition and preserves as a unique offering to markets. The reuse or simulation of a software engine is a controversial kind of activity that would have to be worked out between competing technology companies.

List of Storage Engines

MySQL supported storage engines:

- InnoDB
- MyISAM
- Memory
- CSV

- Merge

- Archive

- Federated

- Blackhole

- Example

InnoDB is the most widely used storage engine with transaction support. It is an ACID compliant storage engine. It supports row-level locking, crash recovery and multi-version concurrency control. It is the only engine which provides foreign key referential integrity constraint. Oracle recommends using InnoDB for tables except for specialized use cases.

MyISAM is the original storage engine. It is a fast storage engine. It does not support transactions. MyISAM provides table-level locking. It is used mostly in Web and data warehousing.

Memory storage engine creates tables in memory. It is the fastest engine. It provides table-level locking. It does not support transactions. Memory storage engine is ideal for creating temporary tables or quick lookups. The data is lost when the database is restarted.

CSV stores data in CSV files. It provides great flexibility because data in this format is easily integrated into other applications.

Merge operates on underlying MyISAM tables. Merge tables help manage large volumes of data more easily. It logically groups a series of identical MyISAM tables, and references them as one object. Good for data warehousing environments.

Archive storage engine is optimized for high speed inserting. It compresses data as it is inserted. It does not support transactions. It is ideal for storing and retrieving large amounts of seldom referenced historical, archived data.

The *Blackhole* storage engine accepts but does not store data. Retrievals always return an empty set. The functionality can be used in distributed database design where data is automatically replicated, but not stored locally. This storage engine can be used to perform performance tests or other testing.

Federated storage engine offers the ability to separate MySQL servers to create one logical database from many physical servers. Queries on the local server are automatically executed on the remote (federated) tables. No data is stored on the local tables. It is good for distributed environments.

```
mysql> SHOW ENGINES\G
```

```
************************* 1. row *************************
```

```
    Engine: InnoDB

   Support: DEFAULT

   Comment: Supports transactions, row-level locking, and foreign keys
Transactions: YES

      XA: YES

 Savepoints: YES

*************************** 2. row ***************************

    Engine: CSV

   Support: YES

   Comment: CSV storage engine
Transactions: NO

      XA: NO

 Savepoints: NO

...
```

The SHOW ENGINES command shows all available engines that the server supports.

Choosing the Right Engine

No storage engine is ideal for all circumstances. Some perform best under certain conditions and perform worse in other situations. There are tradeoffs than must be considered. A more secure solution takes more resources; it might be slower, take more CPU time, and disk space. MySQL is very flexible in the fact that it provides several different storage engines. Some of them, like the Archive engine, are created to be used in specific situations.

In some cases the answer is clear. Whenever we are dealing with some payment systems, we are obliged to use the most secure solution. We cannot afford to lose such sensitive data. InnoDB is the way to go. If we want full-text search, then we can choose either MyISAM or InnoDB. Only InnoDB supports foreign key referential integrity constraint and if we plan to use this constraint, then the choice is clear.

Specifying and Altering Storage Engines

The storage engine is specified at the time of the table creation.

```
mysql> CREATE TABLE Cars(Id INTEGER PRIMARY KEY, Name VARCHAR(50),

   -> Cost INTEGER) ENGINE='MyISAM';
```

The ENGINE keyword specifies the storage engine used for this particular table.

If we do not specify the storage engine explicitly, then the default storage engine is used. Prior to MySQL 5.5 the default storage engine was MyISAM. For MySQL 5.5 and later, the default storage engine is InnoDB.

It is possible to migrate to a different storage engine. Note that migrating a large table might take a long time. Also we might run into some problems when migrating tables. Some features might not be supported in both tables.

```
mysql> SELECT ENGINE FROM information_schema.TABLES
    -> WHERE TABLE_SCHEMA='mydb'
    -> AND TABLE_NAME='Cars';
+--------+
| ENGINE |
+--------+
| InnoDB |
+--------+
1 row in set (0,05 sec)
```

This SQL statement finds out the storage engine used for a Cars table in mydb database. We could also use SELECT CREATE TABLE Cars SQL statement. The information_schema is a table which stores technical information about our tables.

```
mysql> ALTER TABLE Cars ENGINE='MyISAM';
```

This SQL statement changes the storage engine of the Cars table to MyISAM.

```
mysql> SELECT ENGINE FROM information_schema.TABLES
    -> WHERE TABLE_SCHEMA='mydb'
    -> AND TABLE_NAME='Cars';
+--------+
| ENGINE |
+--------+
| MyISAM |
+--------+
1 row in set (0,00 sec)
```

Now the storage engine of the table is MyISAM.

Database Trigger

Database triggers are named program units that are executed in response to events that occur in the database. Five different types of events can have trigger code attached to them:

- *Data Manipulation Language (DML) statements*

  DML triggers are available to fire whenever a record is inserted into, updated in, or deleted from a table. These triggers can be used to perform validation, set default values, audit changes, and even disallow certain DML operations.

- *Data Definition Language (DDL) statements*

  DDL triggers fire whenever DDL is executed—for example, whenever a table is created. These triggers can perform auditing and prevent certain DDL statements from occurring.

- *Database events*

  Database event triggers fire whenever the database starts up or is shut down, whenever a user logs on or off, and whenever an Oracle error occurs. For Oracle8i Database and above, these triggers provide a means of tracking activity in the database.

- *INSTEAD OF*

  INSTEAD OF triggers are essentially alternatives to DML triggers. They fire when inserts, updates, and deletes are about to occur; your code specifies what to do in place of these DML operations. INSTEAD OF triggers control operations on views not tables. They can be used to make non-updateable views updateable and to override the behavior of views that are updateable.

DML Triggers

Data Manipulation Language (DML) triggers fire when records are inserted into, updated within, or deleted from a particular table. These are the most common type of triggers, especially for developers; the other trigger types are used primarily by DBAs.

There are many options regarding DML triggers. They can fire after or before a DML statement or they can fire after or before each row is processed within a statement. They can fire for INSERT, UPDATE or DELETE statements, or combinations of the three.

Transaction Participation

By default, DML triggers participate in the transaction from which they were fired. This means that:

- If a trigger raises an exception, that part of the transaction will be rolled back.

- If the trigger performs any DML itself (such as inserting a row into a log table), then that DML becomes a part of the main transaction.

- You cannot issue a COMMIT or ROLLBACK from within a DML trigger.

Creating a DML Trigger

To create (or replace) a DML trigger, shown here:

```
1 CREATE [OR REPLACE] TRIGGER trigger name

2 {BEFORE | AFTER}

3 {INSERT | DELETE | UPDATE | UPDATE OF column list} ON table name

4 [FOR EACH ROW]

5 [WHEN (...)]

6 [DECLARE ... ]

7 BEGIN

8  ... executable statements ...

9 [EXCEPTION ... ]

10 END [trigger name];
```

The following table provides an explanation of these different elements:

Line(s)	Description
1	States that a trigger is to be created with the name supplied. Specifying OR REPLACE is optional. If the trigger exists and REPLACE is not specified, then your attempt to create the trigger anew will result in an ORA-4081 error. It is possible, by the way, for a table and a trigger (or procedure and trigger, for that matter) to have the same name. We recommend, however, that you adopt naming conventions to avoid the confusion that will result from this sharing of names.
2	Specifies if the trigger is to fire BEFORE or AFTER the statement or row is processed.
3	Specifies the type of DML to which the trigger applies: INSERT, UPDATE, or DELETE. Note that UPDATE can be specified for the whole record or just for a column list separated by commas. The columns can be combined (separated with an OR) and may be specified in any order. Line 3 also specifies the table to which the trigger is to apply. Remember that each DML trigger can apply to only one table.
4	If FOR EACH ROW is specified, then the trigger will activate for each row processed by a statement. If this clause is missing, the default behavior is to fire only once for the statement (a statement-level trigger).
5	An optional WHEN clause that allows you to specify logic to avoid unnecessary execution of the trigger.

Line(s)	Description
6	Optional declaration section for the anonymous block that constitutes the trigger code. If you do not need to declare local variables, you do not need this keyword. Note that you should never try to declare the NEW and OLD pseudo-records. This is done automatically.
7–8	The execution section of the trigger. This is required and must contain at least one statement.
9	Optional exception section. This section will trap and handle (or attempt to handle) any exceptions raised in the execution section only.
10	Required END statement for the trigger. You can include the name of the trigger after the END keyword to explicitly document which trigger you are ending.

Here are a few examples of DML trigger usage:

- We want to make sure that whenever an employee is added or changed, all necessary validation is run. Notice that necessary fields of the NEW pseudo-record to individual check routines is passed in this row-level trigger:

```
CREATE OR REPLACE TRIGGER validate_employee_changes

    AFTER INSERT OR UPDATE

    ON employee

    FOR EACH ROW

BEGIN

    check_age (:NEW.date_of_birth);

    check_resume (:NEW.resume);

END;
```

- The following BEFORE INSERT trigger captures audit information for the CEO compensation table. It also relies on the Oracle8*i* Database autonomous transaction feature to commit this new row without affecting the "outer" or main transaction:

```
CREATE OR REPLACE TRIGGER bef_ins_ceo_comp

    AFTER INSERT

    ON ceo_compensation

    FOR EACH ROW

DECLARE

    PRAGMA AUTONOMOUS_TRANSACTION;

BEGIN

    INSERT INTO ceo_comp_history

        VALUES (:NEW.name,
```

```
        :OLD.compensation, :NEW.compensation,

        'AFTER INSERT', SYSDATE);

    COMMIT;

END;
```

The WHEN Clause

Use the WHEN clause to fine-tune the situations under which the body of the trigger code will actually execute. In the following example, I use the WHEN clause to make sure that the trigger code does not execute unless the new salary is changing to a *different* value:

```
CREATE OR REPLACE TRIGGER check_raise

   AFTER UPDATE OF salary

   ON employee

   FOR EACH ROW

WHEN (OLD.salary != NEW.salary) OR

    (OLD.salary IS NULL AND NEW.salary IS NOT NULL) OR

    (OLD.salary IS NOT NULL AND NEW.salary IS NULL)

   BEGIN

    ...
```

In other words, if a user issues an UPDATE to a row and for some reason sets the salary to its current value, the trigger will and must fire, but the reality is that you really don't need any of the PL/SQL code in the body of the trigger to execute. By checking this condition in the WHEN clause, you avoid some of the overhead of starting up the PL/SQL block associated with the trigger.

In most cases, you will reference fields in the OLD and NEW pseudo-records in the WHEN clause, as in the example shown above. You may also, however, write code that invokes built-in functions, as in the following WHEN clause that uses SYSDATE to restrict the INSERT trigger to only fire between 9 A.M. and 5 P.M.:

```
CREATE OR REPLACE TRIGGER valid_when_clause

BEFORE INSERT ON frame

FOR EACH ROW

WHEN ( TO_CHAR(SYSDATE,'HH24') BETWEEN 9 AND 17 )

   ...
```

Working with NEW and OLD Pseudo Records

Whenever a row-level trigger fires, the PL/SQL runtime engine creates and populates two data structures that function much like records. They are the NEW and OLD pseudo-records ("pseudo" because they don't share all the properties of real PL/SQL records). OLD stores the original values of the record being processed by the trigger; NEW contains the new values. These records have the same structure as a record declared using %ROWTYPE on the table to which the trigger is attached.

Here are some rules to keep in mind when working with NEW and OLD:

- With triggers on INSERT operations, the OLD structure does not contain any data; there *is* no "old" set of values.

- With triggers on UPDATE operations, both the OLD and NEW structures are populated. OLD contains the values prior to the update; NEW contains the values the row will contain after the update is performed.

- With triggers on DELETE operations, the NEW structure does not contain any data; the record is about to be erased.

- You cannot change the field values of the OLD structure; attempting to do so will raise the ORA-04085 error. You *can* modify the field values of the NEW structure.

- You cannot pass a NEW or OLD structure as a record parameter to a procedure or function called within the trigger. You can pass only individual fields of the pseudo-record that *can* be passed as parameters.

- When referencing the NEW and OLD structures within the anonymous block for the trigger, you must preface those keywords with a colon, as in:

```
IF :NEW.salary > 10000 THEN...
```

- You cannot perform record-level operations with the NEW and OLD structures. For example, the following statement will cause the trigger compilation to fail:

```
BEGIN :new := NULL; END;
```

Determining the DML Action within a Trigger

Oracle offers a set of functions (also known as *operational directives*) that allow you to determine which DML action caused the firing of the current trigger. Each of these functions returns TRUE or FALSE, as described below:

- *INSERTING*

  Returns TRUE if the trigger was fired by an insert into the table to which the trigger is attached, and FALSE if not.

- *UPDATING*

    Returns TRUE if the trigger was fired by an update of the table to which the trigger is attached and FALSE if not.

- *DELETING*

    Returns TRUE if the trigger was fired by a delete from the table to which the trigger is attached, and FALSE if not.

Using these directives, it is possible to create a single trigger that consolidates the actions required for each of the different types of operations.

DDL Triggers

Oracle allows you to define triggers that will fire when Data Definition Language (DDL) statements are executed. Simply put, DDL is any SQL statement used to create or modify a database object such as a table or an index. Here are some examples of DDL statements:

- CREATE TABLE

- ALTER INDEX

- DROP TRIGGER

Each of these statements results in the creation, alteration, or removal of a database object.

The syntax for creating these triggers is remarkably similar to that of DML triggers, except that the firing events differ and they are not applied to individual tables.

Creating a DDL Trigger

To create (or replace) a DDL trigger, this is shown here:

```
1 CREATE [OR REPLACE] TRIGGER trigger name

2 {BEFORE | AFTER } {DDL event} ON {DATABASE | SCHEMA}

3 [WHEN (...)]

4 DECLARE

5 Variable declarations

6 BEGIN

7 ... some code...

8 END;
```

The following table summarizes what is happening in this code:

Line(s)	Description
1	Specifies that a trigger is to be created with the name supplied. Specifying OR REPLACE is optional. If the trigger exists and REPLACE is not specified, then good old Oracle error ORA-4081 will appear stating just that.
2	This line has a lot to say. It defines whether the trigger will fire before, after, or instead of the particular DDL event, as well as whether it will fire for all operations within the database or just within the current schema. Note that the INSTEAD OF option is available only in Oracle9i Release 1 and higher.
3	An optional WHEN clause that allows you to specify logic to avoid unnecessary execution of the trigger.
4–7	These lines simply demonstrate the PL/SQL contents of the trigger.

Here's an example of a somewhat uninformed town crier trigger that announces the creation of all objects:

```
/* File on web: uninformed_town_crier.sql */

SQL> CREATE OR REPLACE TRIGGER town_crier

  2 AFTER CREATE ON SCHEMA

  3 BEGIN

  4   DBMS_OUTPUT.PUT_LINE('I believe you have created something!');

  5 END;

  6 /

Trigger created.
```

Database Event Triggers

Database event triggers fire whenever database-wide events occur. There are five database event triggers:

- *STARTUP*

  Fires when the database is opened;

- *SHUTDOWN*

  Fires when the database is shut down normally;

- *SERVERERROR*

Fires when an Oracle error is raised;

- *LOGON*

    Fires when an Oracle session begins;

- *LOGOFF*

    Fires when an Oracle session terminates normally.

As any DBA will immediately see, these triggers offer stunning possibilities for automated administration and very granular control.

Creating a Database Event Trigger

The syntax used to create these triggers is quite similar to that used for DDL triggers:

```
1 CREATE [OR REPLACE] TRIGGER trigger name

2 {BEFORE | AFTER} {database event} ON {DATABASE | SCHEMA}

3 DECLARE

4 Variable declarations

5 BEGIN

6 ... some code...

7 END;
```

There are restrictions regarding what events can be combined with what BEFORE and AFTER attributes. Some situations just don't make sense:

- *No BEFORE STARTUP triggers*

Even if such triggers could be created, when would they fire? Attempts to create triggers of this type will be met by this straightforward error message:

```
ORA-30500: database open triggers and server error triggers ca
```

- No AFTER SHUTDOWN triggers

Again, when would they fire? Attempts to create such triggers are deflected with this message:

```
ORA-30501: instance shutdown triggers cannot have AFTER type
```

- No BEFORE LOGON triggers

It would require some amazingly perceptive code to implement these triggers: "Wait, I think someone is going to log on—do something" Being strictly reality-based, Oracle stops these triggers with this message:

```
ORA-30508: client logon triggers cannot have BEFORE type
```

- No AFTER LOGOFF triggers

"No wait, please come back! Don't sign off!" Attempts to create such triggers are stopped with this message:

```
ORA-30509: client logoff triggers cannot have AFTER type
```

- No BEFORE SERVERERROR

These triggers would be every programmer's dream. Think of the possibilities.

```
CREATE OR REPLACE TRIGGER BEFORE_SERVERERROR

BEFORE SERVERERROR ON DATABASE

BEGIN

 diagnose_impending_error;

 fix_error_condition;

 continue_as_if_nothing_happened;

END;

Unfortunately, our dreams are shattered by this error message:

ORA-30500: database open triggers and server error triggers
```

Database Tuning

Database tuning is comprised of a group of activities used to optimize and regulate the performance of a database. It refers to configuration of the database files, the database management system (DBMS) as well as the hardware and operating system on which the database is hosted. The goal of database tuning is to maximize the application of system resources in an attempt to execute transactions as efficiently and quickly as possible. The large majority of DBMS are designed with efficiency in mind; however, it is possible to enhance a database's performance via custom settings and configurations.

The tuning of a database management system centers around the configuration of memory and the processing resources of the computer running the DBMS. This can involve setting the recovery interval of the DMBS, establishing the level of concurrency control, and assigning which network protocols are used to communicate throughout the database. Memory utilized by the DBMS is allocated for data, execution procedures, procedure cache, and work space. Since it is faster to directly access data in memory than data on storage, it is possible to decrease the average access time of database transactions by maintaining a decent sized data cache. Database performance can also be improved by using the cache to store execution procedures as they would not need to be recompiled with every transaction. By assigning processing resources to specific functions and activities, it is also possible to improve the concurrency of the system. "Database concurrency controls ensure that transactions occur in an ordered fashion. The main job of these controls is to protect transactions issued by different users/applications from the effects of each other. They must preserve the four characteristics of database transactions:

- Atomicity,

- Isolation,

- Consistency,

- Durability.

Input/Output tuning is another major component of database tuning. I/O tuning mainly deals with database transaction logs. Database transaction logs are files that are associated with temporary work spaces as well as both table and index file storage. Transaction logs and temporary spaces are heavy consumers of I/O and affect performance for all users of the database. Placing them appropriately is crucial. The main goal of I/O tuning a database is to optimize and balance the read and write transactions of the system in order to achieve an increased speed in database transactions and a decreased database access time.

Another method of ensuring that a database is fast and reliable is the Use of RAID in the creation of the database. RAID stands for Redundant Array of Independent Disks. Here is an example as to why RAID is superior to a single disk. If data are stored on one disk, the entire database is completely reliant on that one disk; if it were to fail, the database would not exist anymore. Another drawback to having it on a single disk is the read/write time. One hard disk can only be so fast. If there is a lot of I/O data being processed, it can be a lengthy process. One thing that RAID does is it divides and replicates the data onto several independent disks. Instead of having all our eggs in one basket, we have diversified our risk or disk failure away. If we had a RAID 6 array with 4 drives, the tolerance for failure is 2 disks. This means that if 2 hard drives fail completely, the database will still function perfectly. On top of failure tolerance, another great upside to using RAID is tasks are performed faster. There is an increase in speed equal to this multiplication factor: $(n-2)$ X. Reading is faster, and writing is faster because instead of one disk trying to find all the data, the task is broken down into parts, and each hard disk does part of the job.

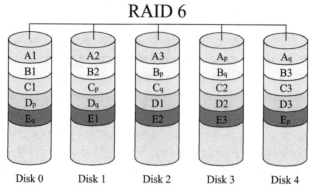

Figure: This shows the data layout for a RAID-6 array

Another common part of database tuning revolves around database maintenance. Database maintenance includes things such as backing up the database as well as the de-fragmentation of the data residing within the database. When a database is under heavy use, transaction log entries must be removed in order to create space for future entries. Since regular transaction log backups are smaller in size, they take less time to complete and, therefore, interrupt scheduled database activity for much shorter periods of time. Much like a computer system, the defragmentation of database tables and indexes greatly increase the efficiency of the database's ability in accessing data. A database's level of fragmentation depends on the data's nature, how the data is manipulated, and the amount of free space left in database pages.

Database-specific Tuning

Oracle

- Number of processes— On most operating systems, each connection to the Oracle server spawns a shadow process to service the connection. Thus, the maximum number of processes allowed for the Oracle server must account for the number of simultaneous users, as well as the number of background processes used by the Oracle server. The default number is usually not big enough for a system that needs to support a large number of concurrent operations. The current setting of this parameter can be obtained with the following query:

  ```
  SELECT name, value FROM v$parameter WHERE name = 'processes';
  ```

- Buffer pool size: The buffer pool usually is the largest part of the Oracle server system global area (SGA). This is the location where the Oracle server caches data that it has read from disk. For read-mostly applications, the single most important statistic that affects data base performance is the buffer cache hit ratio. The buffer pool should be large enough to provide upwards of a 95% cache hit ratio. Set the buffer pool size by changing the value, in data base blocks, of the db_cache_size parameter in the init.ora file.

- Shared pool size: The share pool in an important part of the Oracle server system global area (SGA). The SGA is a group of shared memory structures that contain data and control information for one Oracle database instance. If multiple users are concurrently connected to the same instance, the data in the instance's SGA is shared among the users. The shared pool portion of the SGA caches data for two major areas: the library cache and the dictionary cache. The library cache stores SQL-related information and control structures (for example, parsed SQL statement, locks). The dictionary cache stores operational metadata for SQL processing.

  For most applications, the shared pool size is critical to Oracle performance. If the shared pool is too small, the server must dedicate resources to managing the limited amount of available space. This consumes CPU resources and causes contention because Oracle imposes restrictions on the parallel management of the various caches. The more you use triggers and stored procedures, the larger the shared pool must be. The SHARED_POOL_SIZE initialization parameter specifies the size of the shared pool in bytes.

  The following query monitors the amount of free memory in the share pool:

  ```
  SELECT * FROM v$sgastat

  WHERE name = 'free memory' AND pool = 'shared pool';
  ```

- Maximum opened cursor: To prevent any single connection taking all the resources in the Oracle server, the OPEN_CURSORS initialization parameter allows administrators to limit the maximum number of opened cursors for each connection. Unfortunately, the default value for this parameter is too small for systems such as Web-Logic Server. Cursor information can be monitored using the following query:

  ```
  SELECT name, value FROM v$sysstat

  WHERE name LIKE 'opened cursor%';
  ```

- Database block size: A block is Oracle's basic unit for storing data and the smallest unit of I/O. One data block corresponds to a specific number of bytes of physical database space on disk. This concept of a block is specific to Oracle RDBMS and should not be confused with the block size of the underlying operating system. Note that since the block size affects physical storage, this value can be set only during the creation of the database; it cannot be changed once the database has been created. The current setting of this parameter can be obtained with the following query:

  ```
  SELECT name, value FROM v$parameter WHERE name = 'db_block_
  size';
  ```

- Sort area size: Increasing the sort area increases the performance of large sorts because it allows the sort to be performed in memory during query processing. This can be important, as there is only one sort area for each connection at any point in time. The default value of this init.ora parameter is usually the size of 6– 8 data blocks. This value is usually sufficient for OLTP operations but should be increased for decision support operation, large bulk operations, or large index-related operations (for example, recreating an index). When performing these types of operations, you should tune the following init.ora parameters (which are currently set for 8K data blocks):

```
sort_area_size = 65536

sort_area_retained_size = 65536
```

Microsoft SQL Server

The following guidelines pertain to performance tuning parameters for Microsoft SQL Server databases:

- Store tempdb on a fast I/O device.

- Increase the recovery interval if perfmon shows an increase in I/O.

- Use an I/O block size larger than 2 KB.

Sybase

The following guidelines pertain to performance tuning parameters for Sybase databases:

- Lower recovery interval setting results in more frequent checkpoint operations, resulting in more I/O operations.

- Use an I/O block size larger than 2 KB.

- Sybase controls the number of engines in a symmetric multiprocessor (SMP) environment. They recommend configuring this setting to equal the number of CPUs minus 1.

Database Normalization

Database normalization is process used to organize a database into tables and columns. The idea is that a table should be about a *specific* topic and that only those columns which support that topic are included. For example, a spreadsheet containing information about sales people and customers serves several purposes:

- Identify sales people in your organization;

- List all customers your company calls upon to sell product;

- Identify which sales people call on specific customers.

By limiting a table to one purpose you reduce the number of duplicate data that is contained within your database, which helps eliminate some issues stemming from database modifications. To assist in achieving these objectives, some rules for database table organization have been developed. The stages of organization are called normal forms; there are three normal forms most databases adhere to using.

As tables satisfy each successive normalization form, they become less prone to database modification anomalies and more focused toward a sole purpose or topic.

Reasons for Normalization

There are three main reasons to normalize a database:

- The first is to minimize duplicate data,

- The second is to minimize avoid data modification issues,

- The third is to simplify queries.

As we go through the various states of normalization we'll discuss how each form addresses these issues, but to start, let's look at some data which hasn't been normalized and discuss some potential pitfalls. Consider the following table:

SalesStaff						
EmployeeID	SalesPerson	SalesOffice	OfficeNumber	Customer1	Customer2	Customer3
1003	Mary Smith	Chicago	312-555-1212	Ford	GM	
1004	John Hunt	New York	212-555-1212	Dell	HP	Apple
1005	Martin Hap	Chicago	312-555-1212	Boeing		

The first thing to notice is this table serves many purposes including:

1. Identifying the organization's salespeople;

2. Listing the sales offices and phone numbers;

3. Associating a salesperson with an sales office;

4. Showing each salesperson's customers.

As a DBA this raises a red flag. Having the table serve many purposes introduces many of the challenges, namely, data duplication, data update issues, and increased effort to query data.

Data Duplication and Modification Anomalies

Notice that for each Sales Person we have listed both the Sales Office and Office Number. This information is duplicated for each Sales Person. Duplicated information presents two problems:

- It increases storage and decrease performance.

- It becomes more difficult to maintain data changes.

For example:

- Consider if we move the Chicago office to Evanston, IL. To properly reflect this in our table, we need to update the entries for all the Sales Persons currently in Chicago. Our table is a small example, but you can see if it were larger, that potentially this could involve hundreds of updates.

- Also consider what would happen if John Hunt quits. If we remove his entry, then we lose the information for New York.

These situations are modification anomalies, There are three modification anomalies that can occur:

1. Insert Anomaly

There are facts we cannot record until we know information for the entire row. In our example we cannot record a new sales office until we also know the sales person. Why? Because in order to create the record we need provide a primary key. In our case this is the EmployeeID.

EmployeeID	SalesPerson	SalesOffice	OfficeNumber	Customer1	Customer2	Customer3
1003	Mary Smith	Chicago	312-555-1212	Ford	GM	
1004	John Hunt	New York	212-555-1212	Dell	HP	Apple
1005	Martin Hap	Chicago	312-555-1212	Boeing		
???	???	Atlanta	312-555-1212			

2. Update Anomaly

The same information is recorded in multiple rows. For instance if the office number changes then, there are multiple updates that need to be made. If these updates are not successfully completed across all rows, then an inconsistency occurs.

EmployeeID	SalesPerson	SalesOffice	OfficeNumber	Customer1	Customer2	Customer3
1003	Mary Smith	Chicago	312-555-1212	Ford	GM	
1004	John Hunt	New York	212-555-1212	Dell	HP	Apple
1005	Martin Hap	Chicago	312-555-1212	Boeing		

3. Deletion Anomaly

Deletion of a row can cause more than one set of facts to be removed. For instance, if John Hunt retires, then deleting that row cause use to lose information about the New York office.

EmployeeID	SalesPerson	SalesOffice	OfficeNumber	Customer1	Customer2	Customer3
1003	Mary Smith	Chicago	312-555-1212	Ford	GM	
~~1004~~	~~John Hunt~~	~~New York~~	~~212-555-1212~~	~~Dell~~	~~HP~~	~~Apple~~
1005	Martin Hap	Chicago	312-555-1212	Boeing		

Search and Sort Issues

The last reason we'll consider is making it easier to search and sort your data. In the Sales-staff table if you want to search for a specific customer such as Ford, you would have to write a query like:

```
SELECT SalesOffice

FROM SalesStaff

WHERE Customer1 = 'Ford' OR

    Customer2 = 'Ford' OR

    Customer3 = 'Ford'
```

Clearly if the customer were somehow in one column our query would be simpler. Also, consider if you want to run a query and sort by customer. The way the table is currently defined this isn't possible, unless you use three separate queries with a UNION. These anomalies can be eliminated or reduced by properly separating the data into different tables, to house the data in tables which serve a single purpose. The process to do this is called normalization, and the various stages you can achieve are called the normal forms.

Here are the most commonly used normal forms:

- First normal form(1NF);

- Second normal form(2NF);

- Third normal form(3NF);

- Boyce and Codd normal form (BCNF).

First Normal Form (1NF)

As per the rule of first normal form, an attribute (column) of a table cannot hold multiple values. It should hold only atomic values.

Example: Suppose a company wants to store the names and contact details of its employees. It creates a table that looks like this:

Search and Sort Issues	emp_name	emp_address	emp_mobile
101	Herschel	New Delhi	8912312390
102	Jon	Kanpur	8812121212 9900012222
103	Ron	Chennai	7778881212
104	Lester	Bangalore	9990000123 8123450987

Two employees (Jon & Lester) are having two mobile numbers so the company stored them in the same field as you can see in the table above.

This table is not in 1NF as the rule says "each attribute of a table must have atomic (single) values", the emp_mobile values for employees Jon & Lester violates that rule.

To make the table complies with 1NF we should have the data like this:

emp_id	emp_name	emp_address	emp_mobile
101	Herschel	New Delhi	8912312390
102	Jon	Kanpur	8812121212
102	Jon	Kanpur	9900012222
103	Ron	Chennai	7778881212
104	Lester	Bangalore	9990000123
104	Lester	Bangalore	8123450987

Second Normal Form (2NF)

A table is said to be in 2NF if both the following conditions hold:

- Table is in 1NF (First normal form);

- No non-prime attribute is dependent on the proper subset of any candidate key of table.

An attribute that is not part of any candidate key is known as non-prime attribute.

Example: Suppose a school wants to store the data of teachers and the subjects they teach. They create a table that looks like this: Since a teacher can teach more than one subjects, the table can have multiple rows for a same teacher.

teacher_id	subject	teacher_age
111	Maths	38
111	Physics	38
222	Biology	38
333	Physics	40
333	Chemistry	40

Candidate Keys: {teacher_id, subject};

Non-prime attribute: teacher_age.

The table is in 1 NF because each attribute has atomic values. However, it is not in 2NF because non-prime attribute teacher_age is dependent on teacher_id alone which is a proper subset of candidate key. This violates the rule for 2NF as the rule says "no non-prime attribute is dependent on the proper subset of any candidate key of the table".

To make the table complies with 2NF we can break it in two tables like this: teacher_details table:

teacher_id	teacher_age
111	38
222	38
333	40

teacher_subject table:

teacher_id	subject
111	Maths
111	Physics
222	Biology
333	Physics
333	Chemistry

Now the tables comply with Second normal form (2NF).

Third Normal Form (3NF)

A table design is said to be in 3NF if both the following conditions hold:

- Table must be in 2NF

- Transitive functional dependency of non-prime attribute on any super key should be removed.

An attribute that is not part of any candidate key is known as non-prime attribute.

In other words 3NF can be explained like this: A table is in 3NF if it is in 2NF and for each functional dependency X-> Y at least one of the following conditions hold:

- X is a super key of table;

- Y is a prime attribute of table.

An attribute that is a part of one of the candidate keys is known as prime attribute.

Example: Suppose a company wants to store the complete address of each employee, they create a table named employee_details that looks like this:

emp_id	emp_name	emp_zip	emp_state	emp_city	emp_district
1001	John	282005	UP	Agra	Dayal Bagh
1002	Ajeet	222008	TN	Chennai	M-City
1006	Lora	282007	TN	Chennai	Urrapakkam
1101	Lilly	292008	UK	Pauri	Bhagwan
1201	Steve	222999	MP	Gwalior	Ratan

Super keys: {emp_id}, {emp_id, emp_name}, {emp_id, emp_name, emp_zip}...so on;

Candidate Keys: {emp_id};

Non-prime attributes: all attributes except emp_id are non-prime as they are not part of any candidate keys.

Here, emp_state, emp_city & emp_district dependent on emp_zip. And, emp_zip is dependent on emp_id that makes non-prime attributes (emp_state, emp_city & emp_district) transitively dependent on super key (emp_id). This violates the rule of 3NF.

To make this table complies with 3NF we have to break the table into two tables to remove the transitive dependency:

employee table:

emp_id	emp_name	emp_zip
1001	John	282005
1002	Ajeet	222008
1006	Lora	282007
1101	Lilly	292008
1201	Steve	222999

employee_zip table:

emp_zip	emp_state	emp_city	emp_district
282005	UP	Agra	Dayal Bagh
222008	TN	Chennai	M-City
282007	TN	Chennai	Urrapakkam
292008	UK	Pauri	Bhagwan
222999	MP	Gwalior	Ratan

Boyce Codd Normal Form (BCNF)

It is an advance version of 3NF that's why it is also referred as 3.5NF. BCNF is stricter than 3NF. A table complies with BCNF if it is in 3NF and for every functional dependency X->Y, X should be the super key of the table.

Example: Suppose there is company wherein employees work in more than one department. They store the data like this:

emp_id	emp_nationality	emp_dept	dept_type	dept_no_of_emp
1001	Austrian	Production and planning	D001	200
1001	Austrian	stores	D001	250
1002	American	design and technical support	D134	100
1002	American	Purchasing department	D134	600

Functional dependencies in the table above:

emp_id -> emp_nationality;

emp_dept -> {dept_type, dept_no_of_emp}.

Candidate key: {emp_id, emp_dept}

The table is not in BCNF as neither emp_id nor emp_dept alone are keys.

To make the table comply with BCNF we can break the table in three tables like this:

emp_nationality table:

emp_id	emp_nationality
1001	Austrian
1002	American

emp_dept table:

emp_dept	dept_type	dept_no_of_emp
Production and planning	D001	200
stores	D001	250
design and technical support	D134	100
Purchasing department	D134	600

emp_dept_mapping table:

emp_id	emp_dept
1001	Production and planning
1001	stores
1002	design and technical support
1002	Purchasing department

Functional dependencies:

emp_id -> emp_nationality

emp_dept -> {dept_type, dept_no_of_emp}

Candidate keys:

For first table: emp_id

For second table: emp_dept

For third table: {emp_id, emp_dept}

This is now in BCNF as in both the functional dependencies left side part is a key.

References

- Query-language, technology: britannica.com, Retrieved 21 April 2018
- Data-control-language-dcl-1019477: lifewire.com, Retrieved 18 June 2018
- Data-manipulation-language-1179: techopedia.com, Retrieved 27 May 2018
- Automate-database-administration-tasks: dbmaestro.com, Retrieved 11 May 2018
- Get-ready-to-learn-sql-database-normalization-explained-in-simple-english: essentialsql.com, Retrieved 29 May 2018

5

Database Management Systems

A database management system is the software that enables the interaction with end users, applications and with the database for capturing and analyzing the data. The topics elaborated in this chapter, such as object oriented database management system, column store database management system, federated database system, in-memory database, etc. will help in providing a better perspective about database management systems.

Object Oriented Database Management System

An object-oriented database management system (OODBMS) is a database management system that supports the creation and modeling of data as objects. OODBMS also includes support for classes of objects and the inheritance of class properties, and incorporates methods, subclasses and their objects. Most of the object databases also offer some kind of query language, permitting objects to be found through a declarative programming approach, also called an object database management system (ODMS).

An object-oriented database management system represents information in the form of objects as used in object-oriented programming. OODBMS allows object-oriented programmers to develop products, store them as objects and replicate or modify existing objects to produce new ones within OODBMS. OODBMS allows programmers to enjoy the consistency that comes with one programming environment because the database is integrated with the programming language and uses the same representation model. Certain object-oriented databases are designed to work with object-oriented programming languages such as Delphi, Python, Java, Perl, C and Visual Basic .NET.

Comparison to Relational Databases

Relational databases store data in tables that are two dimensional. The tables have rows and columns. Relational database tables are "normalized" so data is not repeated more often than necessary. All table columns depend on a primary key (a unique value in the column) to identify the column. Once the specific column is identified, data from one or more rows associated with that column may be obtained or changed.

To put objects into relational databases, they must be described in terms of simple string, integer, or real number data. For instance in the case of an airplane. The wing may be placed in one table with rows and columns describing its dimensions and characteristics. The fuselage may be in another table, the propeller in another table, tires, and so on.

Breaking complex information out into simple data takes time and is labor intensive. Code must be written to accomplish this task.

Object Persistence

With traditional databases, data manipulated by the application is transient and data in the database is persisted (Stored on a permanent storage device). In object databases, the application can manipulate both transient and persisted data.

When to use Object Databases

Object databases should be used when there is complex data and/or complex data relationships. This includes a many to many object relationship. Object databases should not be used when there would be few join tables and there are large volumes of simple transactional data.

Object databases work well with:

- CAS Applications (CASE-computer aided software engineering, CAD-computer aided design, CAM-computer aided manufacture).

- Multimedia Applications.

- Object projects that change over time.

- Commerce.

Object Database Advantages over RDBMS

- Objects don't require assembly and disassembly saving coding time and execution time to assemble or disassemble objects.

- Reduced paging.

- Easier navigation.

- Better concurrency control - A hierarchy of objects may be locked.

- Data model is based on the real world.

- Works well for distributed architectures.

- Less code required when applications are object oriented.

Object Database Disadvantages Compared to RDBMS

- Lower efficiency when data is simple and relationships are simple.

- Relational tables are simpler.

- Late binding may slow access speed.

- More user tools exist for RDBMS.

- Standards for RDBMS are more stable.

- Support for RDBMS is more certain and change is less likely to be required.

ODBMS Standards

- Object Data Management Group

- Object Database Standard ODM6.2.0

- Object Query Language

- OQL support of SQL92

Storing Data

Two basic methods are used to store objects by different database vendors.

- Each object has a unique ID and is defined as a subclass of a base class, using inheritance to determine attributes.

- Virtual memory mapping is used for object storage and management.

Data transfers are either done on a per object basis or on a per page (normally 4K) basis.

Object Exchange Model

OEM Model

An OEM object contains an object identifier, a descriptive textual label, a type and a value. In most cases, the object identifier is used only within a system implementation and remains hidden from an end user. A value may be atomic or complex. Atomic OEM values can be integers, reals, strings, images, video clips, sound clips, queries, programs, or any other data value that should be considered indivisible by the database. Types are always associated with atomic values, but the different types are not specific to OEM. A complex OEM value, on the other hand, is a collection of 0 or more OEM objects. The complex OEM object can be thought of as the parent of any number of OEM children objects. Note that a single OEM object may have multiple parent objects. With this simple recursive definition, we can build arbitrarily complex OEM networks to model relationships among data.

The basic idea is very simple: each value we wish to exchange is given a label (or tag) that describes its meaning. For example, if we wish to exchange the temperature value 80 degrees Fahrenheit, we may describe it as:

(temperature-in-Fahrenheit, integer, 80)

where the string "temperature-in-Fahrenheit" is a human-readable label, "integer" indicates the type of the value, and "80" is the value itself. If we wish to exchange a complex object, then each component of the object has its own label. For example, an object representing a set of two temperatures may look like:

$$\left(\text{set-of-temperatures}, \text{set}, \{cmpnt_1, cmpnt_2\} \right)$$

$$cmpnt_1 \text{ is } \{\text{temperature-in-Fahrenheit}, \text{integer}, 80\}$$

$$cmpnt_2 \text{ is } \{\text{temperature-in-Celsius}, \text{integer}, 20\}$$

A main feature of OEM is that it is self-describing. We need not define in advance the structure of an object, and there is no notion of a fixed schema or object class. In a sense, each object contains its own schema. For example, "temperature-in-fahrenheit" above plays the role of a column name, were this object to be stored in a relation, and "integer" would be the domain for that column.

Note that unlike in a database schema a label here can play two roles identifying an object component and identifying the meaning of an object component To illustrate consider the following object:

$$\left(\text{person-record}, \text{set}, \{cmpnt_1, cmpnt_2, cmpnt_3\} \right)$$

$$cmpnt_1 \text{ is} \langle \text{person-name}, \text{string}, \text{"Fred"} \rangle$$

$$cmpnt_2 \text{ is} \langle \text{office-number-in-building-5}, \text{integer}, 333 \rangle$$

$$cmpnt_3 \text{ is} \langle \text{department}, \text{string}, \text{"toy"} \rangle$$

Like a column name in a relation the label person name identifies which component in the persons record contains the person s name In addition the label person name identifies the meaning of the component **it** is the name of a person, We would not expect to find a dog's name "Fido" or spot in this component

Thus we suggest that labels should be as descriptive as possible For instance in our example above replacing person name by name would not be advisable In addition if an information source exports objects with a particular label then we assume that the source can answer the question What does this label mean The answer should be a human readable description a type of man page similar in flavor to Unix Manual pages For example if we ask the source that exports the above object about person name it might reply with a text note explaining that this label refers to names of employees of a certain corporation the names do not exceed characters and upper vs. lower case is not relevant.

It is particularly important to note that labels are relative to the source that exports them That is we do not expect labels to be drawn from an ontology shared by all information sources For example a client might see the label person name originating from two different sources that provide personnel data for two different companies and the label may mean something different for each source the client is responsible for understanding the differences If the client happens to be a mediator that exports combined personnel data for the two companies then the mediator may choose to de ne a new label generic person name along with a man page to indicate that the information is not with respect to a particular company.

We believe that a self-describing object exchange model provides the flexibility needed in a heterogeneous, dynamic environment. For example, personnel records could have fewer or more components than the ones suggested above; in our temperatures set, we could dynamically add temperatures in Kelvin, say. In spite of this flexibility, the model remains very simple.

The idea of self-describing models is not new-such models have been used in a variety of systems. Consequently, the reader may at this point wonder why we are writing a paper about a self-describing model, if such models have been used for many years. A first reason is that we believe it is useful to formally cast a self-describing model in the context of information exchange in heterogeneous systems (something that has not been done before, to the best of our knowledge), and to extend the model to include object nesting as illustrated above. To do this, a number of issues had to be addressed. A second reason is to provide an appropriate object request language based on the model. Our language is similar to nested-SQL languages; however, we believe that the use of labels within objects leads to a language that is more intuitive than nested-SQL.

Specification

Each object in OEM has the following structure

Label	Type	Value	Object ID

Where, the four fields are:

- Label: A variable-length character string describing what the object represents.

- Type: The data type of the object's value. Each type is either an atom (or basic) type (such as integer, string, real number, etc.), or the type set or list. The possible atom types are not fixed and may vary from information source to information source.

- Value: A variable-length value for the object.

- Object-ID: A unique variable-length identifier for the object or (for null). The use of this field is described below.

In denoting an object on paper we often drop the Object-ID field i.e. we write (label type value) as in the examples above.

Object identifiers henceforth referred to as OID s may appear in set and list values as well as in the Object-ID field We provide a simple example to show how sets and similarly lists are represented without OID s and to motivate the kind of OID s that are used in OEM Then we discuss OID's in set and list values.

Suppose an object representing an employee has label "employee" and a set value. The set consists of three sub objects, a "name," an "office," and a "photo." All four objects are exported by an information source IS through a translator, and they are being examined by a client C. The only way C can retrieve the employee object is by posing a query that returns the object as an answer.

Assume for the moment that the employee object is fetched into C's memory along with its three sub objects. The value field of the employee object will be a set of object references, say fo$_1$; o$_2$; o3g. Reference o$_1$ will be the memory location for the name sub object, o2 for the office, and o3 for the photo. Thus, on the client side, the retrieved object will look like:

$$\langle employee, set, \{o_1, o_2, o_3,\} \rangle$$

o_1 is location of $\langle name, string, "some name" \rangle$

o_2 is location of $\langle office, string, "some office" \rangle$

o_3 is location of $\langle photo, bitmap, "some bits" \rangle$

On the information source side, the employee object may map to a real object of the same structure, or it may be an "illusion" created by the translator from other information. Suppose *IS* is an object database, and the employee object is stored as four objects with OID's id_0 (employee), id_1 (name), id_2 (office), and id_3 (photo). In this case, the retrieved object on the client side would have id_0 in the Object-ID field for the employee object, id_1 in the Object-ID field for the name object, and so on. The non-null Object-ID fields tell client C that the objects it has correspond to identifiable objects at *IS*.

Now suppose instead that *IS* is a relational database, and that the employee "object" is actually a tuple. Hence, the name, office, and photo objects (attributes of the tuple) do not have OID's, so their Object-ID field at the client side will be (null). The employee object may have an immutable tuple identifier, which can be used in the Object-ID field at the client. Alternatively, the employee's Object-ID field at the client might contain or it might contain an SQL statement that retrieves the employee record based on its key attribute.

So far we have assumed that the client retrieves the employee object and all of its sub objects. However, for performance reasons, the translator may prefer not to copy all sub objects. For example, if the photo sub-objects is a large bitmap, it may be preferable to retrieve the name and office sub objects in their entirety, but retrieve only a "place-holder" for the photo object. In this case, the value field for the employee object at the client will contain $\{o_1, o_2, id_3\}$. This indicates that the name and office sub objects can be found at memory locations o_1 and o_2, but the photo sub object must be explicitly retrieved using OID id_3.

Thus, at the client, sets and lists contain elements that may be of two forms, as follows. We assume there is an internal tag that indicates the form of each element.

Local Object Reference: This identifies an object stored at the client. It will typically be a memory location, but if local objects are cached in an object database, then object references could be Local OID's in this database.

Remote OID: This identifies an object at the information source. Each Remote OID is either lexical or non-lexical. Lexical OID's are printable strings, and they may be specified directly in our query language. Non-lexical OID's are "black boxes," such as the tuple identifiers or SQL queries described above. Clients may pass non-lexical OID's to translators using special interfaces, but since the OID's are not printable, they cannot be used in queries. Remote OID's could be classified further by other properties, such as whether they are permanent or temporary. (Or, OID's could include a "valid time-stamp" specifying when they expire.) We do not consider these further classifications here, although we may incorporate these concepts in a future extension of our model.

Note: the regardless of the representation used in set and list values, the translator always gives the client the illusion of an object repository. Thus, we can think of our employee object as:

$$\langle employee, set, \{cmpnt_1, cmpnt_2, cmpnt_3\}\rangle$$

$$cmpnt_1 \text{ is } \langle name, string, "some name"\rangle$$
$$cmpnt_2 \text{ is } \langle office, string, "some office"\rangle$$
$$cmpnt_3 \text{ is } \langle photo, bits, "some bits"\rangle$$

Where, each $cmpnt_1$ is some mnemonic identifier for the sub object.

A final issue regarding OEM is that of duplicate objects at the client. Suppose, for example, that set object A at the information source has B and C as sub objects. Both B and C are of set type, and both have as sub objects the same object D. A query at a client retrieves A and its entire sub objects. Will the client have a single copy of object

D, or will objects B and C point to different copies of D? Our model does not require a single copy of D at the client, since this would place a heavy burden on translators that are not dealing with real objects at the information source. However, if both copies of D have the same (non-null) Object-ID field, then the client can discern that the two objects correspond to the same object at the source. Also note that we do not require translators to discover cyclic objects at the source. Suppose, for example, that A has B as a sub object and B has A as a sub object. If the client fetches A from a "smart" translator, the translator would return only two objects, a copy of A and a copy of B. Each object's set value would be a reference for the other object. However, a "dumb" translator is free to return, say, four objects, A_1, B_1, A_2, B_2, where A_1 references B_1, B_1 references A_2, A_2 references B_2, and B_2 contains the empty set to indicate that for performance reasons the chain was not followed.

Related Models and Systems

Labeled fields are used as the basis of several data models or data formatting conventions. For example, a tagged le system uses labels instead of positions to identify fields; this is useful when records may have a large number of possible fields, but most fields are empty. Electronic mail messages consist of label-value, pairs. More recently, Lotus Notes has used a label-value model to represent office documents and Teknekron Software Systems has used a self-describing object model for exchange of information in their stock trading systems. In and self-describing databases are proposed as a solution to obtaining the increased flexibility required by heterogeneous systems.

Recent projects on heterogeneous database systems (e.g.,) have applied object-oriented (OO) data models to the problem of database integration. OEM differs from these and other OO data models in several ways. First, OEM is an information exchange model. OEM does not specify how objects are stored at the source. OEM does specify how objects are received at a client, but after objects are received they can be stored in any way the client likes. OEM explicitly handles cross-system OID's.

In a conventional OO system there may also be client copies of server objects, but there the client copy is logically identical to the server copy and an application program at the client is not aware of the difference.

A very important difference between OEM and conventional OO models is that OEM is much simpler. OEM supports only object nesting and object identity; other features such as classes, methods, and inheritance are omitted. (Incidentally, claims that the only two essential features of an OO data model are nesting and object identity.) Our primary reason for choosing a very simple model is to facilitate integration. Simple data models have an advantage over complex models when used for integration, since the operations to transform and merge data will be correspondingly simpler. Meanwhile, a simple model can still be very powerful: advanced features can be "emulated" when they are necessary. For example, if we wish to model an employee class with subclasses "active" and "retired," we can add a sub object to each employee object with label "subclass" and value "active" or "retired." Of course this is not identical to having classes and subclasses, since OEM does not force objects to conform to the rules for a class. While some may view this as a weakness of OEM, we view it as an advantage, since it lets us cope with the heterogeneity we expect to find in real-world information sources.

The flexible nature of OEM can allow us to model complex features of a source in a simple way. For example, consider a deductive database that contains a parent relation and supports the recursive ancestor relation through derivation rules. If we wish to provide an OEM model of this data in which it is easy to locate a person's ancestors, we can make the object that corresponds to each person contain as sub objects the objects that correspond to his/her parents. It is then simple to pose a query in our OEM query language that retrieves all of a person's ancestors. In addition, a user can browse through a person's "family tree" using the browsing facility.

A final distinct difference between OEM and conventional OO models is the use of labels in place of a schema. Clearly, it would be trivial to add labels to a conventional OO model (e.g., all objects could have an attribute called "label"). The only difference then is that in OEM labels are first-class citizens. We believe this small change makes interpretation and manipulation of objects more straightforward. Note that the schema-less nature of OEM is particularly useful when a client does not know in advance the labels or structure of OEM objects. In traditional data models, a client must be aware of the schema in order to pose a query. In our model, a client can discover the structure of the information as queries are posed.

Query Language

To request OEM objects from information source, a client issues queries in a language we refer to as OEM-QL. OEM-QL adapts existing SQL-like languages for object-oriented models to OEM.

The basic construct in OEM-QL is an SQL-like SELECT-FROM-WHERE expression. The syntax is:

> SELECT *Fetch – Expression*
> FROM *Object*
> WHERE *Condition*

The result of this query is itself an object, with the special label answer:

$$\langle answer, set, \{obj_1, obj_2, \dots, obj_n\}\rangle$$

Each returned sub object obj_i is a component of the object specified in the FROM clause of the query, where the component is located by the Fetch-Expression and satisfies the condition. We assume that the Object in the FROM clause is specified using a lexical object-identifier, and that for every information source there is a distinguished object with lexical identifier "root." (Sources may or may not support additional lexical identifiers.) Certainly the query language may be extended with a call interface that allows non-lexical object identifiers in FROM clauses.

The Fetch-Expression in the SELECT clause and the Condition in the WHERE clause both use the notion of a path, which describes a traversal through an object using sub object structure and labels. For example, the path "bibliography document author" describes components that have label "author," and that are sub objects of an object with label "document" that is in turn a sub object of an object with label "bibliography." Paths are used in the Fetch-Expression to specify which components are returned in the answer object; paths are used in the Condition to qualify the fetched objects or other (related) components in the same object structure. A path specified in a Fetch-Expression may be terminated by the special symbol "OID," in which case only object identifiers are returned in the answer object, rather than the objects themselves.

For the examples, suppose that we are accessing a bibliographic information source with the object structure shown in Figure above. Let the entire object (i.e., the top-level object with label "bibliography") be the distinguished object with lexical object identifier "root". Note that although much of this object structure is regular-|components have the same labels and types-there are some irregularities. For example, the call number format is different for each document shown, and the third document uses a different structure for author information.

Example: This example retrieves the topic of each document for which "Ullman" is one of the authors:

    SELECT bibliography.document.topic
    FROM root
    WHERE bibliography.document.author-set.author-last-name = "Ullman"

$\langle bibliography, set, \{doc_1, doc_2, \dots, doc_n\}\rangle$

doc_1 is $\langle document, set, \{authors_1, topic_1, cal\,l-number_1\}\rangle$

$authors_1$ is $\langle author-set, set, \{author_1\}\rangle$

$author_1^1$ is $\langle author-last-name, string, \backslash Ullman"\rangle$

$topic_1$ is $\langle topic, string, \backslash Databases"\rangle$

$cal\,l-number_1$ is $\langle internal-call-no, integer, 25\rangle$

doc_2 is $\langle document, set, \{authors_2, topicl, cal\,l-number_2\}\rangle$

$authors_2$ is $\langle author-set, set, \{author_2^1, author_2^2, author_2^3\}\rangle$

$author_2^1$ is $\langle author-last-name,\ string,\ "Aho"\rangle$

$author_2^2$ is $\langle author-last-name,\ string,\ "Hopcroft"\rangle$

$author_2^3$ is $\langle author-last-name,\ string,\ "Ullman"\rangle$

$topic_2$ is $\langle topic,\ string,\ "Algorithms"\rangle$

$cal\ l-number_2$ is $\langle dewey-decimal,\ string,\ "BR273"\rangle$

doc_n is $\langle document,\ set, \{authors_n,\ topic_n,\ cal\ l-number_n\}\rangle$

$authors_n$ is $\langle single-author-full-name,\ string,\ \backslash\ Michael\ Crichton\rangle$

$topic_n$ is $\langle topic,\ string,\ "Dinosaurs"\rangle$

$cal\ l-number_n$ is $\langle fiction-call-no,\ integer,\ 95\rangle$

Above are the first Object structure for example queries

Intuitively, the query's WHERE clause finds all paths through the sub object structure with the sequence of labels [bibliography, document, author-set, author last-name] such that the object at the end of the path has value "Ullman." For each such path, the FROM clause species that one component of the answer object is the object obtained by traversing the same path, except ending with label topic instead of labels [author-set, author-last-name]. Hence, for the portion of the object structure shown in figure above the query returns:

$\langle answer,\ set, \{obj_1,\ obj_2\}\ \rangle$

obj_1 is $\langle topic,\ string,\ "Databases"\rangle$

obj_2 is $\langle topic,\ string,\ "Algorithms"\rangle$ □

Example: This second example illustrates the use of "wild-cards" and an existential WHERE clause. This query retrieves the topics of all documents with internal call numbers.

```
SELECT bibliography.?.topic
FROM root
WHERE bibliography.?.internal-call-no
```

The "?" label matches any label. Therefore, for this query, the document labels could be replaced by any other strings and the query would produce the same result. By convention, two occurrences of ? in the same query must match the same label unless variables are used. Note that there is no comparison operator in the WHERE clause of this query, just a path. This means we only check that the object with the specified path exists; its value is irrelevant. Hence, for the portion of the object structure the query returns:

$\langle answer,\ set\{obj_1\}\rangle,$

$obj_1\ is\ \langle topic,\ string,\ "Databases"\rangle\ \square$

In examples the wild-card symbol was used to match any label. We also allow "wild-paths," specified by the symbol "$*$". Symbol matches any path of length one or more Using $*$, the query in the previous example would be expressed as:

SELECT $*$.topic
FROM root
WHERE $*$.internal-call-no

The use of $*$ followed by a single label is a convenient and common way to locate objects with a certain label in a complex structure. Similar to, two occurrences of $*$ in the same query must match the same sequence of labels, unless variables are used.

Example: This example illustrates how variables are used to specify different paths with the same label sequence. This query retrieves each document for which both "Aho" and "Hopcroft" are authors:

SELECT bibliography.document
FROM root
WHERE bibliography.document.author-set.author-last-name(a_1)="Aho"
    AND bibliography.document.author-set.author-last-name(a_2)="Hopcroft"

Here, the query's WHERE clause finds all paths through the subobject structure with the sequence of labels [bibliography, document, author-set], and with two distinct path completions with label author and with values "Aho" and "Hopcroft" respectively. The answer object contains one \document component for each such path. Hence, for the portion of the object structure the query returns:

$\langle answer,\ set,\{obj\}\rangle\ fgi$

    $obj\ is\ \langle document,\ set,\{authors_2,\ topic_2,\ cal\ l-number_2\}\rangle$

        $authors_2\ is\ \langle author-set,\ set,\{author_2^1,\ author_2^2, author_2^3\}\rangle$

            $author_2^1\ is\ \langle author-last-name,\ string,\ "Aho"\rangle$

            $author_2^2\ is\ \langle author-last-name,\ string,\ "Hopcroft"\rangle$

            $author_2^3\ is\ \langle author-last-name,\ string,\ "Ullman"\rangle$

        $topic_2\ is\ \langle topic,\ string,\ "Algorithms"\rangle$

        $cal\ l-no_2\ is\ \langle dewey-decimal,\ string,\ \backslash BR273"\rangle\ \square$

Example: This example illustrates how object identifiers may be retrieved instead of objects. This query retrieves the OID's for all documents with a Dewey Decimal call number:

SELECT *.OID

FROM root

WHERE *.dewey-decimal

In this query, since the path in the FROM clause ends with \OID," only object identifiers are returned. Hence, for the portion of the object structure shown in Figure above the query returns:

$\langle answer, set, \{id_1\} \rangle$

where id_1 is the OID for the object

Example: Although we have used only equality predicates so far, OEM-QL permits any predicate to be used in the condition of a WHERE clause. The predicates that can be evaluated for a given information source depend on the translator and the source. Suppose, for example, that a bibliographic information source supports a predicate called author that takes as parameters a document and the last name of an author; the predicate returns true if the document has at least one author with the given last name.

Then the query in example might be written as:

SELECT bibliography.document

FROM root'

WHERE author(bibliography.document,"Aho")

and author(bibliography.document,"Hopcroft")

One of the translators we have built is for a bibliographic information source called Folio that does in fact support a rich set of predicates. All of the predicates supported by Folio are available to the client through OEM-QL.

The basic OEM-QL described in this paper is certainly amenable to extensions. For example, here we have allowed only one object in the FROM clause, so "joins" between objects cannot be described at the top level of a query. The language can easily be extended to allow multiple objects in the FROM clause. Similarly, the SELECT clause allows only one path to be specified; "constructors" can be added so that new object structures can be created as the result of a query. While these extensions are clearly useful, and we plan to incorporate them in the near future, we also expect that many translators (especially translators for unstructured and semi-structured information sources) will support only the basic OEM-QL (some may even support just a subset), since supporting the full extended language may result in unreasonable increase of the translator's complexity. One useful extension we plan for OEM-QL, and we expect will be supported by most translators, is the ability to express queries about labels and object structure: we expect that clients will frequently need to "learn" about the objects exported by an information source before meaningful queries can be posed.

Column Store Database Management System

A column store database is a type of database that stores data using a column oriented model.

A column store database can also be referred to as:

- Column database;
- Column family database;
- Column oriented database;
- Wide column store database;
- Wide column store;
- Columnar database;
- Columnar store.

Column store databases are considered No-SQL databases, as they use a different data model to relational databases.

Structure of a Column Store Database

Columns store databases use a concept called a *key space*. A key space is kind of like a schema in the relational model. The key space contains all the column families (kind of like tables in the relational model), which contain rows, which contain columns.

Like this:

A keys pace containing column families

Here's a closer look at a column family:

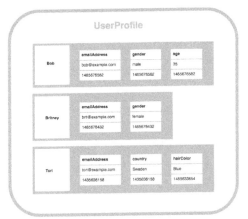

A column family containing 3 rows, each row contains its own set of columns

As the above diagram shows:

- A column family consists of multiple rows.

- Each row can contain a different number of columns to the other rows. And the columns don't have to match the columns in the other rows (i.e. they can have different column names, data types etc).

- Each column is contained to its row. It doesn't span all rows like in a relational database. Each column contains a name/value pair, along with a timestamp. Note that this example uses Unix/Epoch time for the timestamp.

Here's how each row is constructed:

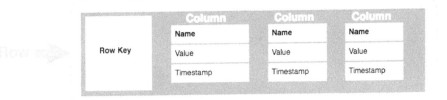

Here's a breakdown of each element in the row:

- Row Key: Each row has a unique key, which is a unique identifier for that row.

- Column: Each column contains a name, a value, and timestamp.

- Name: This is the name of the name/value pair.

- Value: This is the value of the name/value pair.

- Timestamp: This provides the date and time that the data was inserted. This can be used to determine the most recent version of data.

Some DBMSs expand on the column family concept to provide extra functionality/storage ability. For example, Cassandra has the concept of *composite columns*, which allow you to nest objects inside a column.

Data Representation in Memory

```
address 00 |   A  l  e  x  \0  m  a  l  e  \0  26

address 11 |   B  e  t  i  n  a  \0  f  e  m  a  l  e  \0  22

address 26 |   C  l  a  r  a  \0  f  e  m  a  l  e  \0  23

address 40 |   D  i  e  t  e  r  \0  m  a  l  e  \0  28

address 53 |   E  m  i  l  \0  m  a  l  e  \0  29

address 64 |   F  r  e  d  e  r  i  k  e  \0  f  e  m  a  l  e  \0  27
```

\0 is the Null character and terminates a string.

Let's focus on two aspects. Predictability and Locality.

Predictability

Can we predict the address for each tuple? Can we predict the address within a tuple for each attribute? In our example we can't predict the address where we will find Dieter without looking at all the data. Tuples with a variable length prevent such predictions.

Locality

Are the attributes of two tuples next to each other? Computing the average age of our persons we need to look at address 10, 25, 39, 52 and 63. That's a problem because we reduce the probability to read the data from memory cache or the same block on disk. We further complicate any forecasts of the CPU what memory area we need next.

On-disk Representation

File data.txt

```
Alex;male;26

Betina;female;22

Clara;female;23

Dieter;male;28

Emil;male;29

Frederike;female;27
```

To calculate the average age we need to read the complete file data.txt. Although we are only interested in the age attribute.

Column Oriented Approach

A different approach is column-oriented. You can compare the approach with an array holding the data for each attribute (column).

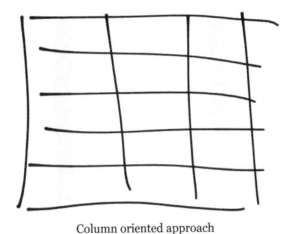

Column oriented approach

Representation of Data in Memory

```
address 00 | A l e x \0 B e t i n a \0 C l a r a \0 D i e t e r \0 E m
i l \0 F r e d e r i k e \0

address 40 |   m a l e \0 f e m a l e \0 f e m a l e \0 m a l e \0 m a
l e \0 f e m a l e \0

address 77 |   26 22 23 28 29 27
```

Predictability

We still can't guess the address where we find Dieter. But if we have found Dieter we can easily calculate where we can find his age by adding 77 + 3= 80 => 28. If we deal with fixed length types (integer, float, boolean) we can predict exactly where we find our data.

Locality

To calculate the average age we only need to look at the memory block 77–82. The probability to hit the cache (or block) is very high during iteration.

On-disk Representation

The data set can be persisted to disk like this:

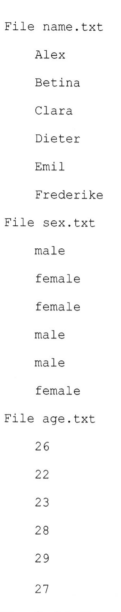

File name.txt

 Alex

 Betina

 Clara

 Dieter

 Emil

 Frederike

File sex.txt

 male

 female

 female

 male

 male

 female

File age.txt

 26

 22

 23

 28

 29

 27

To calculate the average age we only need to read file age.txt. We only read data that we need to calculate our result.

Benefits of Column Store Databases

Some key benefits of columnar databases include:

- Compression: Column stores are very efficient at data compression and/or partitioning.

- Aggregation queries: Due to their structure, columnar databases perform particularly well with aggregation queries (such as SUM, COUNT, AVG).

- Scalability: Columnar databases are very scalable. They are well suited to massively parallel processing (MPP), which involves having data spread across a large cluster of machines – often thousands of machines.

- Fast to load and query: Columnar stores can be loaded extremely fast. A billion row table could be loaded within a few seconds. You can start querying and analyzing almost immediately.

These are just some of the benefits that make columnar databases a popular choice for organizations dealing with big data.

Examples of Column Store DBMSs

- Bigtable

- Cassandra

- HBase

- Vertica

- Druid

- Accumulo

- Hypertable

Federated Database System

A federated database is a system in which several databases appear to function as a single entity. Each component database in the system is completely self-sustained and functional. When an application queries federated database the system figures out which of its component databases contains the data being requested and passes the request to it. Federated databases can be thought of as database virtualization in much the same way that storage virtualization makes several drives appear as one.

A federated database may be composed of a heterogeneous collection of databases, in which case it lets applications look at data in a more unified way without having to duplicate it across databases or make multiple queries and manually combine the results. If your customers are looking for this type of configuration, IBM Information Integration may be a good place to start.

In a homogeneous environment, federated databases can help distribute the load of very large databases (VLDBs). In this configuration, each component database has an identical schema but only a subset of the total rows. The federated database system distributes queries to the appropriate component database; the goal of the system is to ensure that a typical query will need to use only one component, thus drastically reducing the number of rows that need to be searched. When a federated database is used for load distribution, rows are distributed to its components based on a primary key. Picking this key isn't trivial -- it can make the difference between a successful configuration and an unsuccessful one. Ideally, most or all queries should end up hitting only one component database.

For instance, a bank may use a federated database in which transactions are split by year. Users will often only look at transactions in the past year and the system will only need to touch one or two component databases. On the other hand, splitting the databases by customer ID isn't likely to work well; a given set of transactions will involve a random distribution of customer IDs, meaning that the query will be sent out to many, or potentially all, of the component databases. This eliminates the benefit of the federated database nearly all of the rows end up being searched and will only increase the query's overall latency because of the query redirects.

Notion of Federated Databases and Systems

In a federation of heterogeneous databases, there is the need for data sharing among the diverse databases, and for resource consolidation of all supporting software, hardware, and personnel, although each database has its own autonomy in terms of, for example, its integrity constraint, application specificity and security requirements. Thus, federated databases and systems deal with heterogeneous databases. They must provide data sharing and resource consolidation without violating the autonomies of individual databases.

Factors Prompting the Arrival of Federated Databases and Systems

- The replacement of traditional data processing practices with modem homogeneous database systems.

In traditional data processing, data are stored on tapes. A data processing task requires the manual handling of tapes and transactions. To process data on tapes for a new query, data processing professionals must first write the necessary transactions offline and then run the new transactions against necessary tapes manually. For routine data processing involving regular and standard transactions, there is already considerable manual work which is not only error-prone, but also labor-intensive. For ad hoc queries, their routines and practices are greatly affected. There are more errors in developing the new transactions and in running them against existing tapes. There are also more labor-intensive efforts on the part of data processing professionals in developing new transactions and in handling tapes. The introduction of modern database systems as replacements for traditional data processing practices has greatly reduced labor-intensive and error prone pitfalls. Since data are stored on disks and managed by the database system automatically, there is no manual handling of storage media. Regular and standard transactions are cataloged in and executed by the database system routinely. There is also no need for any manual handling of regular and standard transactions. For ad hoc queries, the modern database system provides an ad hoe query capability. Thus, database professionals may develop new transactions for queries on-line and query the existing database directly. Finally, each modern database system is highly specialized to deliver the most effective and efficient on-line processing of a class of data processing tasks. For example, the relational database system is particularly suitable for keeping records. Thus, data processing tasks on payroll records, on employee records, and on other record collections may be taken over by the relational database system. Despite the diversity of the record-keeping tasks and differences in the record type, the same relational database system can handle them effectively and efficiently. Thus, the relational database system is said to handle homogeneous databases of records, since all the records are stored on the disks with the same format (i.e., the relational form), and are accessible and manipulatable by transactions written in the same relational data language (e.g., SQL). The sameness (i.e., homogeneity) in the data model and data language is introduced, of course, for the effective and efficient handling and processing of the intended databases. For these reasons, the relational database system is termed a homogeneous database system for record keeping.

There are other homogeneous database systems which are specialized in other distinct and major tasks beyond data processing of records. For example, the hierarchical database system supports the hierarchical databases; the network database system the network databases; the functional database system the functional databases; the object-oriented database system the object-oriented databases; and so on. The great proliferation of many homogeneous databases and database systems indicates that traditional data processing (using tapes and relying on manual handling of tapes and transactions) is disappearing. It also indicates that the homogeneous database systems not only replace traditional data processing tasks, but also open up new database applications. Thus, database systems become an indispensable means in an organization for handling information needs.

- The proliferation of heterogeneous databases in an organization

Typically, each department in an organization has its own information needs and focuses on a specific database application. For example, the personnel department may use a record-keeping database system to keep track of employee records. The use of a relational database system such as ORACLE to support the database, and writing transactions in SQL to access and manipulate employee records, has been in vogue.

The engineering department may focus on design specifications in terms of product assemblies. Each assembly consists of many subassemblies, each subassembly many components, each component many parts, each part many design specs, each spec many figures and numbers. These design specs can best be organized as a hierarchical database of facts and figures supported by a hierarchical database system. Thus, we may use, for example, an IBM IMS to support the hierarchical database and a data language, DIHI, to write transactions for accessing and manipulating the database.

The inventory department, on the other hand, may wish to use a network database to represent the many-to-many relationships among their inventory records. For example, a part (therefore, a part record) may be supplied by (related to) several suppliers (several supplier records); a supplier (a supplier record) on the other hand may be supplying (related to) several parts (part records). Thus, in this example, there is a many-to-many relationship between the part records and the supplier records. There are many such many-to-many relationships in a real inventory collection (i.e., a network database). Such databases can be supported by a network database system such as Unisys DBMS 1100 and by transactions written in a network data language such as CODASYL-DML

The research-and-development department may want to experiment with a functional database to support expert-system applications using a functional database system such as CCA Local Database Manager and a data language such as CCA Duplex. It may also desire to try an object-oriented database system and its object oriented data language on new applications in manufacture engineering. Many new and experimental object-oriented database systems and data languages (e.g., HP IRIS) have been proposed and prototyped recently.

Databases, data languages, and database systems in different departments, although homogeneous with respect to their own departments, are heterogeneous in the organization; this is because they are based on different data models, data languages, and database systems. If departments of an organization attempt to computerize all their useful information into databases, using suitable database systems and employing stylized data languages to write transactions for their highly specialized applications, then it is inevitable that a proliferation of heterogeneous databases and systems will result. As we enter the Information Age, the race towards computerized information and the proliferation of heterogeneous databases, data languages, and database systems in an organization will be intensified. This proliferation is not reversible; nor can the proliferation be restricted to one data model, to one data language, and to one database system. In other words, the proliferation is on the heterogeneity of databases and systems in all the departments, not just on a collection of homogeneous databases and systems in a single department.

- Data sharing of various databases in the organization

The effective use of information scattered in different departments requires data sharing among the departments for corporate planning and decision-making, marketing strategies, regulatory compliances, inter-departmental communications and coordination and other multi-departmental activities. In fact, the effectiveness of sharing data within an organization may well be the most important surviving factor of the organization in the Information Age. What would be the most expeditious way to share data among heterogeneous databases? There are three requirements in federated databases and systems:

1. The first requirement is that the user must be able to access a heterogeneous database as if it were the user's homogeneous database. In other words, the user should not be required to learn the data model of the heterogeneous database. Nor should the user be required to write transactions in the data language supported by the other database system of the heterogeneous database. Instead, the user continues to view the heterogeneous database. by way of the user's familiar data model and writes transactions against the database in the user's familiar data language. For example, a relational database user in the personnel department may access a hierarchical database in the engineering department as if it were a relational database by writing SQL transactions for such accesses and manipulations of the database. We term this requirement the transparent access to heterogeneous databases.

2. The second requirement allows the owner of a database to share the database with others without compromising the owner's integrity constraint, application specificity, and security requirement In other words, the autonomy of the owner's database is upheld, despite the fact that multiple accesses and manipulations are being made by users of other departments. We term this requirement the local autonomy of each heterogeneous database.

3. The third requirement is that federated databases and systems are multi model and multilingual. By multi model we mean that a database system in the federation supports various databases in many different data models. For example, a multi model database system may support relational databases, hierarchical databases, network databases, functional databases, object-oriented databases, and other model-based databases. By multilingual we mean that the database system executes transactions, each of which may be written in a distinct data language, for its corresponding model-oriented databases. For example, a multilingual database system may execute SQL transactions against relational databases, DL/I transactions against hierarchical databases, CODASYL-DML transactions against network databases, Duplex transactions against functional databases, and transactions written in an object-oriented or new data language against object-oriented or new databases, respectively. Without being multi model and multilingual, federated databases and systems will not be able to support heterogeneous databases and systems which are the necessary condition of the federation.

Unless the aforementioned three requirements are met, data sharing among heterogeneous databases scattered in different parts of an organization (i.e., federation) will not become effective. Here, the emphasis of requirements is on the effectiveness of federated databases and systems.

- Resource consolidation of supporting software, hardware, and personnel heterogeneous

Databases scattered in different departments in an organization are likely to be supported respectively by different sets of computer hardware, database systems, and database professionals. Such supports are both inefficient and unaccountable. They are inefficient due to the duplication of hardware, software, and personnel in supporting several, separate, and complete database systems and their databases. They are unaccountable because if there is any difficulty in data sharing it is hard to hold a particular department and its database system responsible for the difficulty. Consequently, communications and cooperation among the departments in terms of data sharing will be hindered.

The architecture of federated databases and systems must be special-purpose and parallel. This requirement may overcome inefficiency and unaccountability issues. By special-purpose we mean that the computer and its secondary storage are dedicated to and specialized in the support of the databases and database-system software. Due to the recent advances in computer technology, it is entirely cost-effective to construct special-purpose computers for better database management performance than mainframes and super minis. These special-purpose database computers are termed database back ends for short, back ends. The backend architecture must also be parallel. Parallel backend architecture is termed the multi backend architecture. Specialization and parallelism are the two most important architectural principles for the improvement of the computer performance and efficiency.

By multi backend we mean that federated database systems, whether centralized or distributed, have been off-loaded from the mainframe computers into specialized backend computers. They can be supported by a single backend and its database store. However, they are likely run on multiple back ends and their respective database stores where the back ends, not database stores, are interconnected by way of a communication net. With identical back ends, this architecture requires that the database-system software be replicatable over the identical back ends. However, the federated databases are not replicated. They are required, nevertheless, to be clustered or partitioned. The distribution of data aggregates in a cluster must induce parallel accesses to all the aggregates in the cluster. Thus, the distribution and redistribution of federated databases on existing and new database stores are required to be automatic. When the number of the back ends at a site is two or greater, the back ends and their stores are configured parallel to sustain the multiple-transactions-and-multiple-database-streams (MTMD) operation. These requirements allow federated databases and systems to be run more efficiently with built-in, processing-and-accessing parallelism, to be maintained by fewer personnel, to be supported with identical hardware, replica table software, and reconfigurable databases, and to be charged with the sole responsibility for the support of federated databases and the database-system software.

It is important to note that, unlike the previous requirements for data sharing which emphasize the effectiveness of federated databases and systems, these architectural requirements emphasize efficiency of the federated databases and systems.

The architecture of the multi backend database system allows the user to scale the system in terms of the number of back ends and their stores, i.e., the degree of its parallelism, for the performance gain and capacity growth of federated databases and systems.

For accountability, we require federated database systems to provide deadlock free accesses to their databases, although these accesses may have already met integrity constraints, application specificities, and security requirements. Otherwise, concurrent accesses for authorized and necessary data will be indefinitely delayed or deferred. Thus, the search for effective and efficient access and concurrency controls in federated databases and systems is aimed to address the accountability issue. We also can discuss in the following section the need for effective and efficient access and concurrency controls in terms of their necessary role in upholding the local autonomy of a federated database system and its databases.

- Access and concurrency controls for local autonomies of federated databases.

To uphold the local autonomy of departmental databases in terms of integrity constraint, application specificity, and security requirement, accesses to departmental databases must be controlled. Thus, federated databases and systems are required to provide access and concurrency control mechanisms for triggering the particular integrity constraint, for interfacing with the specific model/language software, for enforcing the necessary security requirement, and for controlling concurrent accesses to heterogeneous databases of separate departments.

Here, we simply point out that effective and efficient access and concurrency controls are necessary for upholding autonomies of local databases and thus a requirement for federated databases and systems to be truly effective in data sharing and highly efficient in resource consolidation. Consequently, this requirement underscores all previous requirements.

Five Requirements for Federated Databases and Systems

All solutions for and approaches to federated databases and systems will be examined in terms of five requirements. Data sharing requires:

1. Transparent accesses to heterogeneous databases in the federation;

2. The local autonomy of each heterogeneous database;

3. Multi model and multilingual capabilities of federated database systems. Resource consolidation requires;

4. Multi backend capability. Upholding local autonomies of federated databases requires;

5. Effective and efficient access and concurrency control mechanisms.

In-memory Database

In-memory databases put the working set of data into system memory, either completely, or partially, based on the identification of tables that will benefit most from DRAM speed.

There is an obvious performance benefit in the reduced latency in-memory database solutions bring, even over heavily cached systems, which can only optimize database read requests.

But in-memory databases are subtler than that. This is because they provide an opportunity to optimize the way data is managed compared to traditional databases on disk-based media.

When all data is kept in memory, the need to deal with issues arising from the use of traditional spinning disks disappears. This means, for example, there is no need to maintain additional cache copies of data and manage synchronization between them.

Data can also be compressed and decompressed in memory more easily, resulting in the opportunity to make space savings over the equivalent disk copy.

So, why not simply create a RAM disk in memory and move the database to this virtual volume to achieve similar results?

This could be done, but the internal algorithms of the database would still manage data as if it were on disk and so perform tasks such as pre-fetching, caching and lazy writes. And that would be less than optimal in terms of performance and use more processor time.

Instead, in-memory database solutions have logic specifically adapted to work with data in DRAM.

However, system memory is volatile, which means in-memory databases only conform to three out of four of the Acid model of database characteristics - atomic, consistent, isolated and durable. Of these, durability cannot directly be served by in-memory database solutions, because data is lost when power is removed from the server.

Overcoming the Shortcomings of Volatile Memory

But there are solutions to the problem. These include keeping additional copies of data in clustered and scale-out databases that allow systems to keep running by replicating updates to one or more standby systems.

Some database systems also perform periodic commits-to-disk to maintain state to a point from which recovery can be performed in the case of a server crash. Here there is a trade-off between the time between commits (and subsequent recovery) and the overhead of the commit process on performance.

Because of the perceived risk of in-memory databases over traditional OLTP databases, a degree of caution has been evident with regard to the types of applications it is used for. The result is that in-memory database technology has largely been avoided for general OLTP applications, and instead targeted at specific data types or analytics requirements (including batch reporting) where re-running transactions can easily be achieved.

This also makes sense from a budget perspective as DRAM is still more expensive than disk or even flash, which can provide the I/O performance required without compromising data durability.

Having said that, in-memory databases are set to move into the OLTP world as the acceptance and adoption of the technology continues, and businesses have started to use SAP Hana for OLTP workloads.

In addition, the release of Microsoft SQL Server 2014 promises to offer in-memory capability with the use of "memory optimized tables" that allow portions of a database to be placed into system memory.

Meanwhile, database giant Oracle has announced an in-memory option for its main database platform, which promises high levels of performance without application changes.

Storage for In-memory Databases

Although the operation of in-memory databases occurs in system memory, there is a need for permanent storage media.

There are two main in-memory database storage requirements: Permanent media to store committed transactions, thereby maintaining durability and for recovery purposes if a database does need to be reloaded into memory, and; permanent storage to hold a copy or backup of the database in its entirety.

When processing commits, disk I/O performance is the biggest bottleneck to performance and minimizing I/O overhead is critical. This suggests the best possible storage media to use is flash. Moving flash closer to the processor reduces latency and so PCIe SSD or the recently released range of NVDIMM memory channel storage devices provides the lowest latency possible.

Memory channel storage puts flash on hardware that uses the DIMM form factor and plugs directly into the motherboard of the server, providing solid-state storage on the DRAM bus. This results in extremely low latency I/O but does require Bios changes and operating system (OS) drivers to allow the OS to identify the memory as non-volatile. Bios amendments are required to prevent the server failing the memory on POST boot-time checks.

IBM is the first server vendor to release NVDIMM technology in its new X6 products, using the brand name eXflash. Both X6 server and eXflash technology have been combined with IBM's DB2 database to create an in-memory option called BLU Acceleration. IBM claims speed improvements of almost 100 times over previous deployments of DB2.

In-memory database performance can be improved by having only a small amount of non-volatile local storage, so we can expect to see increased adoption of memory channel storage for databases as vendors adapt and optimize their products.

With regard to the requirement to reload databases more quickly, then clearly flash is a benefit here too. Reading an entire database into memory from flash will always be much faster than from spinning disk.

The issue here, of course, is one of cost, with flash being significantly more expensive than disk and, in the case of in-memory database use, being accessed very infrequently. However, in clustered environments the investment in a shared flash-based solution may be a wise one.

In-memory databases promise great leaps in performance, but as we have seen, these solutions still need some traditional storage to operate, irrespective of where the main processing occurs.

In-memory Databases and Shared Cache

In-memory databases are allowed to use shared cache if they are opened using a URI filename. If the unadorned ":memory:" name is used to specify the in-memory database, then that database always has a private cache and is this only visible to the database connection that originally opened it. However, the same in-memory database can be opened by two or more database connections as follows:

```
rc = sqlite3_open ("file::memory:?cache=shared", &db);
```

or,

```
ATTACH DATABASE 'file::memory:?cache=shared' AS aux1;
```

This allows separate database connections to share the same in-memory database. Of course, all database connections sharing the in-memory database need to be in the same process. The database is automatically deleted and memory is reclaimed when the last connection to the database closes.

If two or more distinct but shareable in-memory databases are needed in a single process, then the mode=memory query parameter can be used with a URI filename to create a named in-memory database:

```
rc = sqlite3_open ("file:memdb1?mode=memory&cache=shared", &db);
```

or,

```
ATTACH DATABASE 'file:memdb1?mode=memory&cache=shared' AS aux1;
```

When, an in-memory database is named in this way, it will only share its cache with another connection that uses exactly the same name.

Temporary Databases

When the name of the database file handed to sqlite3_open() or to ATTACH is an empty string, then a new temporary file is created to hold the database:

```
rc = sqlite3_open("", &db);

ATTACH DATABASE '' AS aux2;
```

A different temporary file is created each time, so that just like as with the special ":memory:" string, two database connections to temporary databases each have their own private database. Temporary databases are automatically deleted when the connection that created them closes.

Even though a disk file is allocated for each temporary database, in practice the temporary database usually resides in the in-memory pager cache and hence is very little difference between a pure in-memory database created by ":memory:" and a temporary database created by an empty filename. The sole difference is that a ":memory:" database must remain in memory at all times whereas parts of a temporary database might be flushed to disk if database becomes large or if SQLite comes under memory pressure.

The previous paragraphs describe the behavior of temporary databases under the default SQLite configuration. An application can use the Temp store pragma and the SQLITE_TEMP_STORE compile-time parameter to force temporary databases to behave as pure in-memory databases, if desired.

Applications of In-memory Database

In-memory databases are most commonly used in applications that demand very fast data access, storage and manipulation, and in systems that don't typically have a disk but nevertheless must manage appreciable quantities of data.

An important use for in-memory database systems is in real-time embedded systems. IMDSs running on real-time operating systems (RTOSs) provide the responsiveness needed in applications including IP network routing, telecom switching, and industrial control. IMDSs manage music databases in MP3 players and handle programming data in set-top boxes. In-memory databases' typically small memory and CPU footprint make them ideal because most embedded systems are highly resource-constrained.

Non-embedded applications requiring exceptional performance are an important growth area for in-memory database systems. For example, algorithmic trading and other applications for financial markets use IMDSs to provide instant manipulation of data, in order to identify and leverage market opportunities. Some multi-user Web applications such as e-commerce and social networking sites use in-memory databases to cache portions of their back-end on-disk database systems. These enterprise-scale applications sometimes require very large in-memory data stores, and this need is met by 64-bit IMDS editions.

Object-relational Database Management System

An object relational database management system (ORDBMS) is a database management system with that is similar to a relational database, except that it has an object-oriented database model. This system supports objects, classes and inheritance in database schemas and query language.

Object relational database management systems provide a middle ground between relational and object-oriented databases. In an ORDBMS, data is manipulated using queries in a query language. These systems bridge the gap between conceptual data modeling techniques such as entity relationship diagrams and object relational mapping using classes and inheritance. ORDBMSs also support data model extensions with custom data types and methods. This allows developers to raise the abstraction levels at which problem domains are viewed.

Data Model

A data model is a way of thinking about data, and the object-relational data model amounts to objects in a relational framework. An ORDBMS's chief task is to provide a flexible framework for organizing and manipulating software objects corresponding to real-world phenomenon.

The object-relational data model can be broken into three areas:

- Structural Features: This aspect of the data model deals with how a database's data can be structured or organized.

- Manipulation: Because a single data set often needs to support multiple user views, and because data values need to be continually updated to reflect the state of the world, the data model provides a means to manipulate data.

- Integrity and Security: A DBMS's data model allows the developers to declare rules that ensure the correctness of the data values in the database.

Enhanced Table Structures

An OR database consists of group of tables made up of rows. All rows in a table are structurally identical in that they all consist of a fixed number of values of specific *data types* stored in columns that are named as part of the table's definition. The most important distinction between SQL-92 tables and object-relational database tables is the way that ORDBMS columns are not limited to a standardized set of data types.

The first thing to note about this table is the way that its column headings consist of both a name and a data type. Second, note how several columns have internal structure. In a SQL-92 DBMS, such structure would be broken up into several separate columns, and operations over a data value such as Employee's Name would need to list every component column. Third, this table contains several instances of unconventional data types. Lives At is a geographic point, which is a latitude/longitude pair that describes a position on the globe. Resume contains documents, which is a kind of Binary Large Object (BLOB).

People and Employees

Name::PersonName	DOB::date
(Grossmann , Marcel)	
(Millikan , Robert)	
(Mach , Ernst)	
(Ishiwara , Jun)	

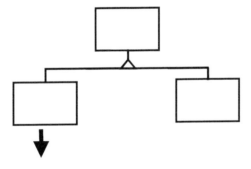

Employees					
Name::PersonName	DOB::date	Salary::Currency	Address::MailAddress	LivesAt::-GeoPoint	Resume::Document
(Einstein , Albert)	03-14-1879	DM125,000	(12 Gehrenstrasse. .)	()	Physics, theoretical . . .
(Curie , Marie)		F125,000	(19a Rue de Seine . .)	()	Physics, experimental . . .
(Planck , Max)		DM115,000	(153 Volkenstrasse .)	()	Physics, experimental . .
(Hilbert , David)		SF210,000	(10 Geneva Avenue .)	()	Mathematics, politics. . .

Inheritance in an Object-Relational Database

Employees				
Name::PersonName	**DOB::date**	**Address::MailAddress**	**LivesAt::Point**	**Resume::Document**
('Einstein','Albert')	03-14-1879	('12 Gehrenstrasse ..)	'(-127.4, 45.1)'	'Physics, theoretical
('Curie','Marie')	11-07-1867	('19a Rue de Seine ..)	'(-115.3, 27.5)'	'Physics, experimental
('Planck','Max')	04-23-1858	('153 Volkenstrasse .)	'(-121.8, 31.1)'	'Physics, experimental
('Hilbert','David')	01-23-1862	('10 Geneva Avenue .)	'(-119.2,37.81)'	'Mathematics, politics

Structure and Data for an Object-Relational Table

In addition to defining the structure of a table, you can include integrity constraints in its definition. Tables should all have a *key*, which is a subset of attributes whose data values can never be repeated in the table. Keys are not absolutely required as part of the table's definition, but they are a very good idea. A table can have several keys, but only one of these is granted the title of *primary key*. In our example table, the combination of the Name and DOB columns contains data values that are unique within the table. On balance, it is far more likely that an end user made a data entry mistake than two employees share names and dates of birth.

Object-oriented Schema Features

Another difference between relational DBMSs and ORDBMSs is the way in which object-relational database schema supports features co-opted from object-oriented approaches to software engineering. We have already seen that an object-relational table can contain:

Temporary_Employees		
Name::PersonName	**DOB::date**	**Booked::SET(Period NOT NULL)**
('Szilard','Leo') ('Fermi','Enrico')	'2/11/1898' '9/29/1901'	{ '[6/15/1943 – 6/21/1943]','[8/21/1943 – 9/22/1943]'} { '[6/10/1938 – 10/10/1939]','[6/15/1943 – 12/1/1945]',

Non-First Normal Form (nested Relational) Table Structure

Exotic data type, in addition, object-relational tables can be organized into new kinds of relationships, and a table's columns can contain sets of data objects.

In an ORDBMS, tables can be *typed*; that is, developers can create a table with a record structure that corresponds to the definition of a data type. The type system includes a notion of *inheritance* in which data types can be organized into hierarchies. This naturally supplies a mechanism whereby tables can be arranged into hierarchies too. illustrates how the Employees table in might look as part of such a hierarchy.

In most object-oriented development environments, the concept of inheritance is limited to the structure and behavior of object classes. However, in an object-relational database, queries can address data values through the hierarchy. When you write an OR-SQL statement that addresses a table, all the records in its sub tables become involved in the query too.

Another difference between ORDBMSs and traditional relational DBMSs can be seen in the Booked column of the Temporary_Employees table. The table in illustrates how this might look.

SQL-92 DBMS columns can contain at most one data value. This is called the *first normal form* constraint. In a traditional RDBMS, situations in which a group of values are combined into a single data object, are handled by creating an entirely separate table to store the group. In an ORDBMS this group of values can be carried in rows using a *COLLECTION*, which can contain multiple data values.

Table: Data type extensibility: Partial list of functions for geographic quadrilateral data type

Data Type: GeoQuad

Expression:	Explanation:	Example Query:
GeoQuad(GeoPoint,w	Constructor function. Takes two corner points and produces a new	INSERT INTO QuadTable VALUES
GeoPoint)	Quadrilateral data type instance.	(GeoQuad ('(0,0)', '(10,10)'));

Table 1-2. Data Type Extensibility: Partial List of Functions for Geographic Quadrilateral Data Type (continued)

Data Type: GeoQuad

Expression:	Explanation:	Example Query:
GeoQuad (double, double, double, double)	Constructor function. Takes four doubles that correspond to the X and Y values of the lower left and upper right corner.	SELECT GeoQuad (MIN(X), MIN(Y), MAX(X), MAX(Y)) FROM Locations;
Contains (GeoPoint, GeoQuad)	Operator function. Returns true if the first point falls within the geographic extent of the quadrilateral.	SELECT COUNT(*) FROM QuadTable T WHERE Contains('(5,5)', T.Quad);
Union (GeoQuad, GeoQuad)	Support function that computes a new quadrilateral based on the furthest corners of the two quadrilaterals inputs.	Used internally by the ORDBMS as part of R-Tree indexing.
GeoQuad (String)	Constructor function. Creates new GeoQuad using the string. A symmetric function implements the reverse.	Used to convert literal strings in queries into the internal format for the type.
GeoQuad (String)	Constructor function. Creates new GeoQuad using the string. A symmetric function implements the reverse.	Used to convert literal strings in queries into the internal format for the type.

The ORDBMS data model is considerably richer than the RDBMS data model. Unfortunately, this new richness complicates database design. There are more alternative designs that can be used to represent a particular situation, and it is not always obvious which to pick. Unthinkingly applying some of these features, such as the COLLEC- TION columns creates problems. However there are data modeling problems for which a COLLECTION is an elegant solution. An important objective of this book is to provide some guidance on the subject of object-relational database design.

Extensibility: User-defined Types and Functions

The concept of extensibility is a principal innovation of ORDBMS technology. One of the problems you encounter developing information systems using SQL-92 is that modeling complex data structures and implementing complex functions can be difficult. One way to deal with this problem is for the DBMS vendor to build more data types and functions into their products. Because the number of interesting new data types is very large, however, this is not a reasonable solution. A better approach is to build the DBMS engine so that it can accept the addition of new, application specific functionality.

Developers can specialize or extend many of the features of an ORDBMS: the data types, OR-SQL expressions, the aggregates, and so on. In fact, it is useful to think of the core ORDBMS as being a kind of software backplane, which is a framework into which specialized software modules are embedded.

Data Types

SQL-92 specifies the syntax and behavior for about ten data types. SQL-3, the next revision of the language, standardizes perhaps a hundred more, including geographic, temporal, text types, and so on. Support for these common extensions is provided in the form of commercial Data Blade products.

However, relying on the DBMS vendor to supply all of the innovation does not address the fundamental problem. Reality is indifferent to programming language standards. With an object-relational DBMS developers can implement their own application specific data types and the behavior that goes with them. Table above lists some of the expressions added to the OR-SQL language to handle a geographic quadrilateral data type (an object with four corner points and parallel opposite edges).

To extend the ORDBMS with the GeoQuad type introduced in, a programmer would:

1. Implement each function in one of the supported procedural languages: C, Java, or SPL.

2. Compile those programs into runnable modules (shared executable libraries or Java JAR files) and place the files somewhere that the ORDBMS can read them.

3. Declare them to the database using the kind of syntax shown in below.

```
CREATE OPAQUE TYPE GeoQuad (

internallength = 32
```

```
);
--
CREATE FUNCTION GeoQuad ( lvarchar ) RETURNING GeoQuad
WITH ( NOT VARIANT,
       PARALLELIZABLE ) EXTERNAL NAME
"$INFORMIXDIR/extend/2DSpat/2DSpat.bld(GeoQuadInput)"
LANGUAGE C;
--
CREATE CAST ( lvarchar AS GeoQuad WITH GeoQuad );
--
CREATE FUNCTION GeoQuad ( double precision, double pre-
       cision,
       double precision, double precision )
RETURNING GeoQuad WITH ( NOT VARIANT,
       PARALLELIZABLE ) EXTERNAL NAME
"$INFORMIXDIR/extend/2DSpat/2DSpat.bld(GeoQuadFromDou-
bles
)"
LANGUAGE C;
```

Data type extensibility: Partial SQL declaration of user-defined data type with external implementation in C

SQL-92 includes some general-purpose analytic features through its aggregates (MIN, MAX, COUNT, AVG, and so on). Aggregate functions can be used in conjunction with other aspects of SQL-92 to answer questions about groups of data. For example, the query in Listing below uses the SQL-92 table to find out what is the mean salary of each group of Employees in different cities.

"What is the average salary of Employees for each of the cities where they live?"

```
SELECT E.City,
       AVG(E.Salary)
       FROM Employees E
       GROUP BY E.City;
```

The range of aggregates in SQL-92 is limited. In data mining and in the larger field of statistical analysis, researchers have described a tremendous number of useful analytic algorithms. For example, it might make more sense to calculate the median salary, rather than the mean salary, in the query above. Or it might be more useful to create a histogram showing how many employees fall into certain ranges of salaries. SQL-92 does not provide the means to answer such analytic questions directly. With the ORDBMS, however, these algorithms can be integrated into the server and used in the same way as built-in aggregates.

"What is the correlation coefficient between Employee salaries and the number of words in their resumes?"

```
SELECT Correlation ( E.Salary,      W o r d C o u n t (
E.Resume) )

FROM Employees E;
```

Analysis query with a user-defined aggregate (correlation)

Database Stored Procedures

Almost all RDBMSs allow you to create database procedures that implement business processes. This allows developers to move considerable portions of an information system's total functionality into the DBMS. Although centralizing CPU and memory requirements on a single machine can limit scalability, in many situations it can improve the system's overall throughput and simplify its management.

By implementing application objects within the server, using Java, for examples, it becomes possible, though not always desirable, to push code implementing one of an application-level object's behaviors into the ORDBMS. The interface in the external program simply passes the work back into the IDS engine. Above listing represents the contrasting approaches. An important point to remember is that with Java, the same logic can be deployed either within the ORDBMS or within an external program without changing the code in any way, or even recompiling it.

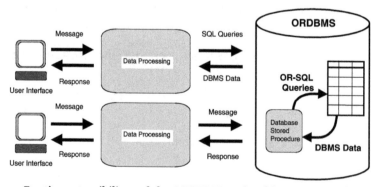

Figure: Routine extensibility and the ORDBMS as the object-server architecture

Active Database Management System

Conventional database systems are passive: they only execute queries or transactions explicitly submitted by a user or an application program. For many applications, however, it is important to monitor situations of interest, and to trigger a timely response when the situations occur. For example, an inventory control system needs to monitor the quantity in stock of items in the inventory database, so that when the quantity in stock of some item falls below a threshold, a reordering activity may be initiated. This behavior could be implemented over a passive database system in one of two ways, neither of which is satisfactory. First, the semantics of condition checking could be embedded in every program that updates the inventory database, but this is a poor approach from the software engineering perspective. Alternatively, an application program can be written to poll the database periodically to check for relevant conditions. However, if the polling frequency is too high, this can be inefficient, and if the polling frequency is too low, conditions may not be detected in a timely manner.

An active database system, in contrast, is a database system that monitors situations of interest, and when they occur, triggers an appropriate response in a timely manner. The desired behavior is expressed in production rules (also called event-condition-action rules), which are depend and stored in the database. This has the benefit that the rules can be shared by many application programs, and the database system can optimize their implementation.

The production rule paradigm originated in the field of Artificial Intelligence (AI) with expert systems rule languages such as OPS5 [Brow nstonet et al. 1985]. Typically, in AI systems, a production rule is of the form:

condition → action

An inference engine cycles through all the rules in the system, matching the condition parts of the rules with data in working memory. Of all the rules that match (the candidate set), one is selected using some conflict resolution policy, and this selected rule is red, that is, its action part is executed. The action part may modify the working memory, possibly according to the matched data, and the cycle continues until no more rules match.

This paradigm has been generalized to event-condition-action rules for active database systems. These are of the form:

on *event*

if *condition*

then *action*

This allows rules to be triggered by events such as database operations, by occurrences of database states, and by transitions between states (among other things), instead of being evaluated by an inference engine that cycles periodically through the rules. When the triggering event occurs, the condition is evaluated against the database; if the condition is satisfied, the action is executed. Rules are depend and stored in the database, and evaluated by the database system, subject to authorization, concurrency control, and recovery.

Such event-condition-action rules are a powerful and uniform mechanism for a number of useful database tasks: they can enforce integrity constraints, implement triggers and alters maintain derived data, enforce access constraints, implement version control policies, gather statistics for query optimization or database reorganization and more [Eswaran 1976, Morgenstern 1983, M. Stonebraker 1982]. Previous support for these features, when present, provided little generality and used special-purpose mechanisms for each. In addition, the inference power of production rules makes active database systems a suitable platform for building large and efficient knowledge-base and expert systems.

Characteristics of ADBMSs

1. An ADBMS is a DBMS: All the concepts required for a passive system are required for an ADBMS as well ("passive" modeling facilities, query language, multi-user access, recovery, etc). That means, if a user ignores all the active functionalities, an ADBMS can be worked with in exactly the same way as a passive DBMS.

2. An ADBMS supports definition and management of ECA-rules: An ADBMS extends a passive DBMS in that it supports reactive behavior. Reactive behavior must be specifiable/definable by the user. The means to define rules together with the data definition facilities are sometimes also called the knowledge model. The other way round, the DBMS-interface (e.g., the data definition language) is ex- tended or complemented by operations for defining rules.

- An ADBMS has to provide means for defining events, conditions and actions: We require that situations are described by (event/condition)-pairs. We also demand that the ADBMS supports the explicit definition of events. In some cases it may be useful to let a compiler or the ADBMS itself generate the event definition. In this case, we say that the event is defined implicitly. The user then specifies conditions and actions, and the ADBMS determines the event automatically (e.g., consider a consistency enforcement mechanism where only constraints and repairs are specified, but the system internally uses events signaled upon modification of data items to determine when the consistency constraint has to be checked). Nevertheless, the ADBMS also has to offer the possibility for the user to define events explicitly at the ADBMS-interface. If explicitly definable events are not provided, ECA-rules are solely an internal implementation mechanism for tasks that could also be implemented "passively", and there is no general support for reactive behavior. Thus, an ADBMS should support the notion of "event" to determine when reactions have to be performed (i.e., full-fledged ECA-rules). This is one major distinction of ADBMSs from other rule-based DBMSs, such as knowledge-based management systems (expert database systems, deductive DBMSs).

In general, we require that wherever meaningful before and after events can be defined. In case of database operations, for instance, a before event is signaled directly before the operation is actually executed. An after event is signaled directly after the operation has been performed.

If the event part is mandatory, the condition part might be omitted. We then refer to event-action rules. In this case, however, it should be possible to specify conditions as parts of actions.

All parts should be fully integrated with the (passive) data model. The event types supported should at least subsume the DML-operations and transaction statements. This means that, for example, the update of a specific relation can be defined as an event of interest. Conditions should be expressible as queries against the data- base, whereby the retrieval facilities supported by the DBMS should be applicable. Actions are principally any executable code fragment. It should at least be possible to use DML commands in actions, including transaction commands (e.g., such that the triggering transaction can be aborted).

Ultimately, it has been mentioned before that the ADBMS distinguishes event types and event occurrences.

- An ADBMS must support rule management and rule base evolution: The set of rules defined at a given point in time forms the rule base. The rule base should be managed by the ADBMS, regardless of whether the rules are stored in the database proper or separately. In other words, definitions of ECA-rules are a part of the DBMS meta information and the database. The ADBMS should store in- formation about which rules currently exist and how they are defined. This stored information on ECA-rules should be visible for users and applications.

Furthermore, the rule base must be changeable over time: it is neither sufficient to support a fixed set of ECA-rules, nor is it appropriate to support reactive behavior as ECA-rules that are hard-wired into the DBMS-code. An ADBMS must there- fore allow new ECA-rules to be defined and old ones to be deleted. It should also be possible to modify event, condition, or action definitions of existing rules.

Rules can be disabled and enabled. Disabling a rule means that the rule definition re- mains in the rule base, but that it will not trigger upon subsequent occurrences of its event. Enable is the inverse operation to disable: enabling a disabled rule means that the rule afterwards will trigger again upon occurrences of its event.

3. An ADBMS has an execution model

- An ADBMS must detect event occurrences (situations). Ideally, an ADBMS detects event occurrences of all sorts automatically, i.e., event occurrences do not have to be signaled by the user/application. Otherwise, if application programmers or users are responsible for the correct signaling of all sorts of events, this system is just a syntactic variant of a passive DBMS (although users may in addition to other things also have the right to signal events).

- An ADBMS must be able to evaluate conditions: An ADBMS must be able to evaluate conditions subsequent to event detection. It should also be possible to pass information from events to conditions. If an event has occurred for a specific object or a set of tuples in a relation, it must be possible to refer to this information in the condition. In addition, queries over the database state should be possible in conditions.

- An ADBMS must be able to execute actions: An ADBMS must be able to execute actions upon event detection and after the condition is known to hold. It must be possible to pass information from the condition to the action (e.g., information on the object for which the condition held). It should be possible to execute actions as part of the triggering transaction, and as such the action execution should be subject to concurrency control and recovery.

- An ADBMS has well-defined execution semantics: In order to have "well-defined" execution semantics, the following properties with respect to events have to hold:

  o Event consumption must be well-defined,

  o Event detection and signaling must be well-defined.

If composite events are supported by the ADBMS, event consumption must be well-defined. Event consumption determines which component events are considered for a composite event, and how event parameters of the composite event are computed from its components. Different application classes may require different consumption modes, such as "recent", "chronicle", "continuous", and "cumulative". Either an ADBMS follows a fixed strategy for event consumption, or it offers the choice out of a collection of consumption modes

In addition, rule execution must have a clear semantics, i.e., must define when, how, and on what database state conditions are evaluated and actions executed. The execution model hereby has to obey the restrictions imposed by the transaction model, e.g., transaction structures etc.

First, the relationship of condition evaluation and action execution with the trig gearing transaction must be defined. Coupling modes define when a condition is evaluated (an action is executed) with respect to the triggering event occurrence, and what the relationship to the triggering transaction is (e.g., the triggered transaction is a sub transaction of the triggering one). As mentioned above, it should at least be possible to execute actions as part of the triggering transaction. Thus, at least the coupling modes immediate and/or deferred must be provided.

Second, it must be defined whether events are instance-oriented or set-oriented. Instance-oriented events relate an event to a single instance. Set-oriented events re- late one event to a collection of instances for which the event has occurred (recall the elaboration on binding modes in section 2)

Finally, it must be defined which database state is visible for condition evaluation and action execution. One possibility is the state upon event signaling; in this case the condition evaluation "sees" the database state as it was when the event had been detected. Another possibility is the actual database state, i.e., the current state at condition evaluation or action execution time. It may also be possible (or necessary) to see multiple states in conditions and actions. In this way, it is possible to refer to the state before, say, a modification and the state after a sequence of modifications. In this case, the binding mode prior is supported; the part of the database that actually represents the change is referred to as a delta.

It is desirable but not mandatory for an ADBMS to offer multiple alternatives for each (or some) of these features. Where such flexibility is supported, rule definitions also specify a selection for each feature where choices are possible. The rule specifies can then to some extent determine the desired semantics of rule execution. Otherwise, one specific strategy is selected by the ADBMS-designer and applied for all rules. This information is then hard-wired into the ADBMS and thus cannot be determined by the user. However, note that sometimes even for simple application classes, different possibilities (e.g., for coupling modes) are required.

- Conflict resolution must either be pre-defined or user-definable: In an ADBS it can happen that multiple rules have to be triggered at the same point in time (e.g., because multiple rules have been associated with the same event, or a transaction triggers several rules which all have the coupling mode deferred). The ADBMS must then be capable of performing conflict resolution, i.e., to deter- mine in which order the rules must be executed. Since conflict resolution typically depends on the semantics of the rules (which in general is only known by the user), the rule specifies must have the opportunity to define how conflicts are resolved, e.g., by means of priorities. If the user, however, does not want to define conflict resolution, he/she is not obliged to do so, and the ADBMS will either determine some order or execute rules non-deterministically.

Optional Features

1. An ADBMS should represent information on ECA-rules in terms of its data mode:

If an ADBMS represents rules with the constructs of its data model, the possibility to inspect the rule base with the retrieval facilities comes for free. Users can then query the rule base like any other database, without being forced to learn new representation formalism.

2. An ADBMS should support a programming environment: It goes without saying that an ADBMS must be usable. The bottom line for usability is the availability of a rule definition language course, may be In order to assist the user in beneficially using the ADBMS, a number of tools should be provided:

- A Rule Browser,

- A Rule Designer,

- A Rule base Analyzer,

- A Debugger,

- A Maintenance Tool,

- A Trace Facility,

- Performance tuning tools.

These tools may be separate tools dedicated for an ADBMS-programming environment, or may be extensions of already existing DBMS- or CASE-tools. Note further that it is not intended to require that all tools are separate system we are simply interested in their functionality.

A rule browser allows inspection of the set of currently existing rules. The rule base is the extension of the catalogue (or data dictionary) in passive DBMSs, since it contains meta-information on defined ECA-rules. Clearly, when defining ECA-rules the possibility to conceive which rules have already been defined is essential.

The ADBMS should offer a design tool that assists users in defining new rules. Such a tool support is crucial when the reactive behavior as required by the universe of discourse has to be systematically mapped into ECA-rules. This support is possible in two not necessarily mutually exclusive ways: either a general design tool also covers ECA-rule design, or the reactive behavior is specified using dedicated high-level languages, such as a constraint definition language.

A rule base analyzer is a tool that allows certain properties of the currently existing rule base to be checked. Examples of such desired properties of rule sets are termination, confluence, and observably deterministic behavior. If the ADBMS supports cascaded rule execution, it is important to ensure that rule execution terminates under all circumstances. Together with the other properties, termination ensures that the current rule base is safe and correct with respect to the intended reactive behavior. In general, these properties cannot be proven automatically, but an analyzer might assist a DBA in proving them or at least in detecting inconsistencies.

A debugger is a tool that allows the controlled execution of rules (and applications) and helps to check whether the rule base implements the required reactive behavior adequately. Thus, in contrast to proving properties with an analyzer, a debugger supports test-modify cycles.

A maintenance tool for an ADBMS supports the user in performing rule base evolution. In addition to the rule definition facility, it supports deletion and modification of existing rules.

Finally, a trace tool is a facility that records event occurrences and rule executions, such that a DBA2 is enabled to realize which actions the ADBMS has triggered automatically. If such a tool is not supported, the ADBMS might perform actions that users never become aware of.

3. An ADBMS should be tunable: An ADBMS must be useful in its application domain. Especially, the ADBMS solution must not show significantly worse runtime performance than equivalent solutions on top of a passive system. There is little experience with current ADBMSs how to mea- sure their performance systematically. However, it is apparent that a practically useful ADBMS should offer the possibility to tune its rule base (whereby of course the semantics of the rules should not change due to tuning!). A problem with tuning in current ADBMSs is that the specification of rules (their conditions and actions) is essentially given by their implementation, i.e., as queries and code fragments. A feasible approach might be the equivalent to the three-schema-architecture, at the external level, user- or application-specific rules are specified (e.g., for consistency constraints), the conceptual level contains all rules relevant for the community of all users/applications, and the internal level specifies the implementation details. The internal level should then provide for the means for performance improvements, and all details concerning efficient rule execution are captured on this level.

Classification of ADBMS

In order to classify ADBMSs according to the application classes they are useful for, we consider two dimensions:

- The role of the ADBMS in an application system (supervision or control);

- The degree of integration of the application system (homogeneous or heterogeneous);

- Data Base Administrator In other words, in analogy to passive DBMSs we require physical database design for ADBMSs.

Supervision means that the ADBMS verifies requests for database operations against the database (or vice versa), and eventually performs simple actions (e.g., notification, transaction abort, update propagation). An ADBMS that controls the application system is in addition, able to trigger external functions, e.g., application programs. In this case, the ADBMS is able to control the behavior of the entire application environment (and not only the state of the database), and can do so possibly over a period of time spanning many sessions.

We call an application system "homogeneous" if all of its components are applications of the ADBMS in question, i.e., they share a common schema and common data- bases. Otherwise, we say that the application is "heterogeneous". Particularly, the ADBMS may have to control systems that are implemented on top of other platforms. Combining these dimensions leads to three classes of ADBMSs, since the combination supervision/heterogeneity is not regarded as meaningful.

ADBMSs for Supervision in Homogeneous Application Systems

The simplest case is ADBMSs for supervision in homogeneous application systems. Such an ADBMS recognizes certain user/application requests and verifies them against the database state (or verifies the database state against the most recent application requests). In this case, the (meta) rules on how to operate the entire application system are still with the user/operator of the application system, but are not necessarily expressible with ECA-rules of the ADBMS. Despite its ability to notify the user (e.g., printing messages on the console) and to abort transactions, the ADBMS has no control over the application system, i.e., it will not cause complex application programs to execute.

The kinds of events it can detect are given by the data model, it specifically does not need composite events. Thus, maintaining the event history is not necessary. For conditions, it is sufficient to query the database state and the data dictionary, and actions are DML-commands (including transaction abort).

Such a system is useful for implementing the "usual" DBMS tasks, such as (simple) consistency constraints, authorization, updates of materialized views, etc.). Furthermore, note that some of these DBMS-tasks might use the active functionality only internally as an implementation mechanism that might also be provided in a "passive" way. The benefit of active functionality is then not the support of functionality that would not be possible otherwise, but the uniformity and minimal of implementation concepts.

In general, composite events etc. are not necessarily required, but may be beneficial in some situations. Depending on the concrete application in mind, different kinds of execution semantics may be necessary (the coupling mode deferred for consistency maintenance, immediate for authorization). For (advanced) consistency maintenance, deltas ("before values") are required.

Not all the functionality required for a given application class might be implementable in this way. However, we would claim that in most cases the aforementioned ADBMS characteristics are sufficient. Table for a summary of the ADBMS features required by this application class.

Feature	Instantiation
Events (2.a)	DML-operations, not necesarily composite
Conditions (2.a)	predicates on database state / queries
Actions (2.a)	DML-action, user notification
Rule evolution (2.b)	create/delete, enable/disable
Consumption modes (3.d)	chronicle
Coupling modes (3.d)	at least immediate, deferred
Execution (3.d)	under local control

Table: ADBMSs for Supervision in Homogeneous Application Systems

ADBMSs for Control in Homogeneous Application Systems

The second class is formed by ADBMSs that are capable of controlling not only the database, but also its environment (i.e., the applications). The ADBMS is able to en- code (at least a substantial part of) the information about the application environment in the form of ECA-rules. The ADBMS is able to detect states or sequences thereof of the application system and to perform automatic reactions, including the automatic spawning of application programs. Applications are tightly integrated, and the active mechanisms are part of the homogeneous DBMS underlying the application system.

Everything that is provided by the first class of ADBMSs must be available in this kind of system, too. Additionally, in order to control the DBS-environment, including the applications, more event types are necessary (e.g., time events). The ADBMS has to keep track of the relevant part of the event history, and must also be able to evaluate restrictions on this event history. Technically speaking, composite events, event re-restrictions, and monitoring intervals (or equivalents thereof) must be provided. Composite events are necessary in order to control and monitor complex sequences of situations in the DBS-environment. Composite event restrictions (such as referring to the triggering transaction —"same transaction"—) must also be provided. Likewise, a broad variety of rule execution semantics must be supported (i.e., when the rule is executed, and how its execution relates to the triggering transaction). In other words, the coupling modes immediate, deferred, and decoupled are the bottom line.

This class of ADBMSs is characterized through feasibility for control in "tightly integrated applications". All the application programs use the same schema, transaction model, DML, etc. Particularly, it is possible to run all triggered activities under the control of the local (ADBMS-) transaction manager.

An example application domain for this type of ADBMS are stock trading application systems. Table for a summary of the ADBMS features required by this application class.

Feature	Instantiation
Events (2.a)	DML-operations, external events, composite
Conditions (2.a)	boolean function, including predicates on database state / queries
Actions (2.a)	DML-action, user notification, external programs
Rule evolution (2.b)	create/delete + modification and event history adaption, enable/disable
Consumption modes (3.d)	choice, including chronicle
Coupling modes (3.d)	at least immediate, deferred, decoupled
Execution (3.d)	under local control

ADBMSs for Control in Heterogeneous Application Systems

The third class is formed by ADBMSs that are capable of integrating possibly heterogeneous and autonomous systems. The active mechanism enables the ADBMS to perform control of such heterogeneous, loosely integrated component systems.

In addition to the capabilities of the second class described above, such an ADBMS has to be able to detect situations in other application systems (which them- selves may be based on other DBMSs), thus affecting the event definition and detection facilities. It might also be necessary to detect events from external devices.

Most important, powerful rule execution mechanisms are necessary, since it might be the case that triggered actions cannot be executed under the control of the local transaction manager. The rule execution model must support complex relationships among application steps (e.g., compensation, ordering of application steps, decencies).

Furthermore, if such an ADBMS is intended for real-time applications, it should support the specification of timing constraints for rule executions. The rule definition should also comprise contingency actions, which are executed whenever the timing constraint of a rule cannot be met. Clearly, an ADBMS for real-time applications should also possess the properties required for a "passive" real-time system.

Summarizing, in this type of ADBMS parts of the "middleware" can be moved into the DBMS, i.e., the active mechanism contributes to implementing the middleware in the ADBMS. Since the ADBMSs of this class are intended for loosely-coupled, possibly heterogeneous systems, their integration into software architectures that aim at mediation in such environments should be possible. Especially, it should be possible to integrate ADBMS-functionality into OMG's CORBA architecture. Relevant services provided by the ADBMS would then refer to event definition, registration, notification, etc.

Example application domains are advanced workflow management systems, reactive behavior in heterogeneous DBSs, real-time plant control systems, and process-centered software development environments. Table for a summary of the ADBMS features required by this application class.

Feature	Instantiation
Events (2.a)	DML-operations, external events, composite
Conditions (2.a)	boolean function, predicates on database state
Actions (2.a)	DML-action, user notification, external programs, contingency actions
Rule evolution (2.b)	create/delete + modification and event history adaption, enable/disable
Consumption modes (3.d)	choice, including chronicle
Coupling modes (3.d)	immediate, deferred, decoupled + causal dependencies
Execution (3.d)	not completely under local control

Table: ADBMSs for Control in Heterogeneous Application Systems

References

- Object-oriented-database-management-system-oodbms-12027: techopedia.com, Retrieved 31 March 2018

- What-is-a-column-store-database: database.guide, Retrieved 12 April 2018

- What-are-federated-databases, feature: searchitchannel.techtarget.com, Retrieved 12 May 2018

- In-memory-databases-What-they-do-and-the-storage-they-need: computerweekly.com, Retrieved 30 April 2018

- Object-relational-database-management-system-ordbms-8715: techopedia.com, Retrieved 31 March 2018

Permissions

Index

A
Acid, 98, 100, 141, 190
Adbms, 202-211
Alternate Key, 118, 120-121
Amazon Dynamo, 25
Associative Data Model, 94-96
Associative Model, 57, 62, 94-97
Attribute Metadata, 83-84, 86

B
Back-end Database, 8, 10, 94
Bcnf, 159, 163-164

C
Candidate Key, 118-121, 160-161, 163
Centralized Database, 1, 11-13
Cloud Computing, 13-14, 93
Cloud Database, 1, 3, 13-17, 19
Columnar Database, 178
Composite Key, 25, 119, 121
Crud, 104-108

D
Data Definition Language, 78, 124, 126, 128, 144, 149, 202
Data Duplication, 10, 157-158
Data Manipulation Language, 78, 124, 126, 131, 144
Data Types, 23, 46, 83, 93, 179, 191, 194-196, 198
Database Administration Tasks, 134-136
Database Engine, 18, 81-83, 85, 124, 140
Database Event Trigger, 151
Database Tuning, 124, 152-154
Dbaas, 13-17, 46
Ddl Trigger, 149
Deductive Database, 47, 49, 173
Deterministic Database, 34
Distributed Database, 3, 19-20, 141
Dml Trigger, 145-146

E
E-r Diagram, 65-68, 70-71
Eav Data, 79, 81, 83, 87, 89-91
Eav Modeling, 81-82, 87-88, 90, 92
Eav System, 85-86, 88
Eav/cr, 83-84, 86, 89
Eca-rules, 202-203, 205-206, 208-209
Electronic Database, 2
Entity-attribute-value Model, 57, 78-79
Extensibility, 197-200

F
Federated Database System, 165, 183, 189
Foreign Key, 58, 81, 83-84, 88, 119, 123, 141-142
Functional Dependencies, 34, 101-102, 163-164

G
Graph Database, 3-4, 46, 62, 93

H
Hierarchical Model, 26, 59, 66, 73, 75, 77

I
In-memory Database, 165, 190-194
Innodb, 140-143

K
Key-value Database, 1, 21-24

M
Many-to-many Relationship, 112-115, 117, 186
Microsoft Azure, 17-18, 46
Microsoft Sql Server, 15, 46, 91, 156, 191
Myisam, 140-143

N
Network Model, 26-27, 57, 59-60, 62-64, 73-78
No-sql Database, 3, 17, 21, 46, 62
Normalization, 29, 58, 91, 156-157, 159, 164

O

Object Database, 62, 165-167, 170-171

Object-oriented Database Model, 57, 60, 194

Oltp, 18, 21, 36, 61, 156, 191

One-to-many Relationship, 65, 111-113

One-to-one Relationship, 65, 109-110, 118

Oracle Database, 18, 46, 155

Ordbms, 194-198, 200, 211

P

Parallel Processing, 40-42, 183

Possible Worlds, 28-29, 32

Primary Key, 21, 58, 79, 101, 105, 109, 117-121, 123, 142, 158, 165, 184, 196

Probabilistic Database, 1, 28-32, 34

Q

Query Language, 2, 4, 11, 15, 44, 58, 124-126, 165, 167, 171, 173-174, 194, 202

R

Redundancy, 12, 72-73, 104, 136

Relational Database, 1-3, 15, 25, 31, 35, 44-47, 60, 78, 81, 88, 94, 96, 102, 104, 108, 125, 165, 170, 179, 185, 187, 194-198

Relational Model, 57-58, 60-62, 94-97, 178

Row Modeling, 81-82

S

Semantic, 27, 62, 90, 105, 125

Sql Database, 3, 16-17, 21, 46, 62

Stock Trading, 22, 172, 210

Structured Query Language, 2, 4, 11, 15, 44, 58, 124, 126

Surrogate Key, 79, 119, 123

T

Tree-structure Diagram, 64-69, 71

U

Unique Key, 118, 120-121, 123, 179

V

Vldb, 34-37, 39-44

X

Xml, 5-6, 8, 10, 32-33, 62, 72, 89, 94

CPSIA information can be obtained
at www.ICGtesting.com
Printed in the USA
BVHW010843310519
549715BV00013B/17/P

9 781682 857250